AF557798

A Life Well Spent

'These elegantly written memoirs reflect the many lessons which could be learnt from the author's long, intense and memorable experiences in the arena of bilateral and multilateral diplomacy. His masterly analysis and reflections on Indo-Pak relations, the politics behind the functioning of UN Commissions and the evolution of India's national security management structures shall delight future historians. A must-read for policymakers and students of international relations.'

—N.N. Vohra,
Former Governor of J&K State

'Covering a 40-year-long diplomatic journey, which started in the mid-sixties, Ambassador Satish Chandra's memoirs provide rare insights into the trials and tribulations of an Indian diplomat and a peep into knotty problems, such as India–Pakistan relations, human rights and disarmament. The author was also involved in the setting up of India's National Security Council and its institutions in 1999. The reader gets a unique view of what goes on inside the Indian Foreign Service, long regarded as an "ivory tower". An easy but fascinating read.'

—Arvind Gupta,
Director, Vivekananda International Foundation

'This book offers a very absorbing account of life in the foreign service, with engrossing insights into the functioning of the Ministry of External Affairs and the nature of interaction between diplomats in the field and at Headquarters.

The book mixes the light with the serious, the personal with the professional. The narration of how Satish Chandra contributed to thwarting Pakistan's bid to target India on human rights violations in Kashmir at the UN Human Rights Council in 1993 and 1994 makes for a gripping read. His stellar contribution to national security as Secretary of the then newly constituted National Security Council Secretariat is brought out persuasively. As one who has dealt with Pakistan for a considerable period of his diplomatic career, his robust views on the country have great merit.

The Indian Foreign Service fraternity will of course immediately relate to this captivating book, as it will find their own experience in the service reflected authentically in its pages. But for the general reader, too, the insights into the workings of our diplomacy will be rewarding.'

—**Kanwal Sibal,**
Former Foreign Secretary

'This book contains interesting and gripping accounts of global events covering a span of 40 years (1965–2005) penned by a seasoned diplomat who not only has a deep understanding of geopolitics and developments in the world at large, particularly of South Asia and our neighbourhood but is also a raconteur par excellence. His portrayals of various major personalities of that time make for an interesting read. What is a constant running thread in the book are his honest and forthright views and courage of conviction. A must-read.'

—**Gen. N.C. Vij,**
Former COAS and
Founder Vice Chairman, NDMA

A Life Well Spent

Four Decades in the Indian Foreign Service

SATISH CHANDRA

RUPA

Published by
Rupa Publications India Pvt. Ltd 2023
7/16, Ansari Road, Daryaganj
New Delhi 110002

Sales Centres:
Prayagraj Bengaluru Chennai
Hyderabad Jaipur Kathmandu
Kolkata Mumbai

P-ISBN: 978-93-5702-093-0
E-ISBN: 978-93-5702-091-6

First impression 2023

10 9 8 7 6 5 4 2 3 1

Printed in India

Dedicated to
My parents, C.N. Chandra and Vidyavati Chandra
and
My wife, Beneeta Chandra

CONTENTS

PREFACE

I was impelled to pen this tome due to many factors, notably acquainting my family and friends of the texture of my work in the Indian Foreign Service (IFS), putting to rest the mistaken notion that life in it is all glitz and glamour with little meaningful content, and providing fresh insights into developments that occurred on my watch. In the process, I have not shied away from dwelling upon the role of many dramatis personae both within and outside the Service, including some with whom I interacted, which would, hopefully, lend more colour and granularity to the issues involved and, perhaps, on occasion, even amuse. It would be remiss on my part if I were not to acknowledge that this book was unlikely to have seen the light of day but for the encouragement of my children and of Mr K.N. Bakshi and Dr Arvind Gupta—two colleagues I was privileged to work with and on whose judgement I could always rely.

My Foreign Service career from 1965 to 2005, spanning four decades, was not particularly extraordinary and was, in fact, close to the prescribed norms. Accordingly, if I had three so-called very comfortable (or 'A') postings, by way of Vienna, Washington DC and Geneva, I also had three so-called very difficult (or 'C') postings, notably Karachi, Dhaka and Islamabad. The word 'so-called' has been deliberately used, as Geneva happened to be my toughest assignment, and my 'difficult' postings had many upsides. Similarly, the duration of my postings in Delhi and abroad was not too far from the ideal of 1:2, as I served in Delhi for 14 years, exclusive of my two-year training period, as against 24 years abroad. Moreover, the duration of all my postings abroad, barring one, were between two to three years, which is close to the three-year norm. Finally, like many other colleagues in the Service, I too had the privilege of three 'Heads of Mission' or Ambassadorial postings, notably in the Philippines, the Permanent Mission of India in Geneva and Pakistan. The only somewhat unusual feature of my career pattern was that out of the 40 years of my service life, as many as 10 were spent on deputation away from the Foreign Service—five with the Department of Economic Affairs (DEA) and five with the National Security Council Secretariat (NSCS), which came under the Prime Minister's Office (PMO).

I would be less than honest if I did not mention that I had no special inclination to join the IFS. My entry into it was largely accidental as, indeed, were many of my postings. With hindsight, I have no hesitation in stating that the IFS turned out to be the perfect career option for me, from which I derived great satisfaction. It provided a work environment with minimal political interference, allowed much elbow room in determining one's pace and style of work, afforded the opportunity of interacting with the highest, abroad and at home, and insulated one from the pulls and pressures of daily life, which is the lot of most others, on account of the diplomatic privileges associated with it.

I would be remiss if I were not to thank Yamini Chowdhury for reaching out and encouraging me to write this book. I would also like to avail of this opportunity to thank Aurodeep Mukherjee and Upama Biswas for the unfailing courtesy and professionalism displayed by them through the process of editing, as well as the entire team at Rupa Publications for their help in bringing out this book.

INTRODUCTION

I had all my schooling from 1947 to 1958 at St. Columba's School, New Delhi. Like all Roman Catholic Christian Brothers' Irish schools spread through the length and breadth of India, it prioritized studies over sports, was high on discipline and instilled a strong work ethic and sense of values amongst all who passed through its portals. In order to achieve these very laudable objectives, resort to corporal punishment was, regrettably, more the norm than the exception, which, unfortunately, left some psychologically scarred for life.

Studying at St. Columba's helped me to not only form some lifelong friendships, which are a source of solace to this day, but also to do fairly well in the Senior Cambridge examinations, which I cleared with grades good enough to enable me to secure admission to the prestigious St. Stephen's College, New Delhi. Looking back, I feel I was overly cocky, as I only sought admission to St. Stephen's, confident that I would be selected. If fate had willed otherwise, I may have been rejected and I was thus remiss in not having a backup plan. Indeed, a classmate with better grades than mine was unable to secure admission to St. Stephen's! One cannot also but be thankful that one was born in a gentler and less competitive era when the cut-off grades for college admissions had not reached the current astronomical levels, enabling those like me to secure admission relatively easily.

From my very first year in college in 1959, I started preparing for the Indian Administrative Service (IAS)/IFS competitive examinations, as at that time, apart from a handful of professions like engineering, medicine, the armed forces, accountancy and law, there was not too much else on offer other than joining the private sector as an executive. I did not feel cut out for the aforesaid professions or for the private sector, where progression was popularly believed to be mired in sycophancy. Accordingly, for want of a suitable alternative, I opted for government service, which, I felt, would also give me the liberty of being my own man who could freely voice his opinion without any serious adverse consequences, even if it ran contrary to the view of superiors. Though future developments, by and large, bore out this presumption in my case, many were not so fortunate, and their career progression suffered for voicing contrarian views.

The paucity of career options induced hundreds from all over the country to sit for the civil service competitive examinations, so much so that this exercise was popularly known as the 'national hobby'. The bulk of those who qualified for the civil services were in the main liberal arts students. The culture of science students and professionals, like engineers and doctors, joining the civil services, as is the vogue today, had not caught on.

St. Stephen's College was a fertile recruiting ground for the IAS and the IFS, and many of its alumni were avid participants in the national hobby. Furthermore, a vast majority of those appearing for the competitive examinations from St. Stephen's prepared for the same on their own and did not join coaching schools, like the famous Rau's Study Circle, which had started proliferating. Most of them did not, however, regard these examinations as the be all and end all but as a challenge to be taken simply as it was there. Moreover, given the droves of Stephanians being selected for the civil services, anyone from the College who appeared for the entrance examinations had a fairly good chance of being selected. For instance, in the 1965 batch of the IFS, to which I belonged, over 30 per cent of those selected were Stephanians.

Whilst studying for my master's degree, I appeared for the IAS/IFS entrance test in 1963. I passed the written examination and was called for the interview, which, in my perception, went off rather well, leaving me confident that I would be selected for either one of these two Services. However, as I was soon to learn, perceptions sometimes do not match with reality, and thus, overconfidence is best avoided. Though not making the grade for either the IAS or the IFS, I was selected for the Internal Revenue Service (IRS).

My disappointment at failing to qualify for the IAS or the IFS in my first attempt in 1963 was aggravated by the fact that while I missed the cut by just a few marks, many Scheduled Caste and Scheduled

Tribe candidates who had obtained even 100 marks less than me were selected on account of the 22.5 per cent reservation quota provided for them by our Constitution. This, naturally, generated some bitterness and even anger. It brought home to me the inherent inequity and unfairness in the selection process, which was not genuinely merit-based and which worked against general candidates. While recognizing that backward classes needed to be compensated by the State for the centuries of neglect and prejudice faced by them, I equally felt that this should not be at the cost of merit-based selection. Quota-based selection not only led to much heartburn amongst those who lost out on account of it but was also not in the best national interest, as it compromised on efficiency.

Regrettably, quota-based selection, which was originally to have been a temporary phenomenon, not only continues to persist but has become even more pronounced with an additional reservation of 27 per cent being accorded to other backward classes in 1990. Rather than opting for such a skewed selection process, India would be much better served if it enables candidates from disadvantaged sections of society to compete in such examinations on an equal footing with general candidates by ensuring that they receive free education, healthcare, subsidised housing, etc. A quota-based selection system is also prone to misuse. In fact, a colleague from St. Stephen's, who was also a very good friend, managed to obtain a certificate to the effect that he belonged to a Scheduled Tribe and, on that basis, walked into the IFS without having to work half as much as the general-category candidates!

♦

Though disappointed at not having made the grade for either the IAS or the IFS, I decided to join the IRS and proceeded to the National Academy of Administration (renamed Lal Bahadur Shastri National Academy of Administration in 1972) in Mussoorie for the Foundation Course in July 1964. Since my father was against my joining the IRS, I was compelled to promise him that I would reappear for the IAS/IFS examination whilst undergoing the Foundation Course. Left to myself I would have been quite content to remain in the IRS and not go through the hard grind of once again taking the IAS/IFS competitive examination. My plan was to work in the Income Tax Department for a few years, and, thereafter, set up my own practice as a tax consultant.

My father's aversion to my joining the IRS arose from his conviction that the only government services worth joining were the IFS or the IAS, and that if one could not make the cut for either of them, one would be better off joining the private sector. He, moreover, rightly felt that by joining the IRS and proceeding to Mussoorie for the Foundation Course, I would jeopardize my chances of success when I reappeared for the IAS/IFS examination, as I would not be able to devote all my attention to the latter.

My father's approach was, perhaps, coloured by his own experience. In an amazing coincidence, he, too, had not succeeded in his ICS entrance examination in his first attempt and had instead been selected for the Indian Railway Service. He was himself inclined to join it but did not do so in deference to his father's wishes, who gave him the option of either returning home to tend to the considerable familial agricultural properties in Sikandrabad tehsil, Multan district, or reappearing for the ICS examination in England, where he had been sent for his higher education. Being a more obedient son than me, he did not join the Indian Railway Service and reappeared for the ICS. On so doing, he was one of the six selected to the ICS in 1920. In this backdrop, he had good reason to feel that, like him, I, too, should focus resolutely on my main objective and not do anything that may jeopardize my chances of achieving it.

◆

Whilst attending the Foundation Course at Mussoorie I discovered that several probationers like me from various central services were reappearing for the IAS/IFS examination. Indeed, as many as nine from my batch of 55 in the IRS alone were finally selected for the IAS, and I was selected for the IFS.

Reappearing for the IAS/IFS examination whilst attending the Foundation Course at the National Academy was not easy. One had not only to overcome the temptation of enjoying oneself in the salubrious climes of Mussoorie but also to devise methodologies of circumventing the Foundation Course regimen so that it did not impede my preparations for the IAS/IFS examination. The situation was aggravated by the fact that my lodgings were at Chaman Estate, a 40-minute walk from Charleville—the Academy's main campus and the locus of academic activities as well as lunch. Since visits to Charleville ate into my study time, I was compelled to keep them to a minimum. This required playing hooky from the innumerable lectures and rustling up make-do meals in my room. The former was not an entirely risk-free proposition, as every now and then, there were inspections to ensure that probationers were not dodging classes. I successfully countered detection by observing complete silence, installing thick curtains to obviate the possibility of being seen from outside and locking my room from the outside. The latter having been done, re-entry into the room was effected through a window.

I was fortunate in having B.B. Tandon, who later went on to become our Chief Election Commissioner, as my roommate. Since he, too, was reappearing for the IAS/IFS examination, the atmosphere around me was conducive to studies. The downside, of course, was that I could not enjoy the once-in-a-lifetime 'paid holiday' in Mussoorie, as the Foundation Course was popularly termed.

The room shared by me with Tandon was spartan, furnished with a couple of tables, two beds and two cupboards. The attached bathroom had no geyser or shower. Bucket baths were the norm, with a ₹15 locally procured immersion rod being used to heat the water. But what put us both off was that our room was something of a chamber of horrors infested with all manner of creepy crawlies, including centipedes, spiders and lizards. Being young and resilient, we, somehow, coped with this as also all other impediments, like differing work schedules: Tandon worked mostly at night, while I preferred to do so during the day.

On conclusion of one's written examinations for the IAS/IFS in November 1964, Tandon, R.C. Handa, another IRS batchmate who occupied a room next to ours, and I went off to Hardwar to pay obeisance to the Almighty. We stayed at one of the local ashrams for virtually free and had the customary early morning dip in the

Ganges. The water was freezing cold and the resulting discomfort was alleviated to an extent by imbibing piping hot milk and jalebis. Whilst at Hardwar, we visited Gurukul Kangri Vidyalaya, established in 1902 by Swami Shraddhanand, which impressed us both with its excellent herbal products and educational curriculum based on traditional Indian practices.

◆

The Foundation Course got over in early December 1964, and towards the end of the month, I joined duty at the Income Tax Training College in Nagpur (now called the National Academy of Direct Taxes). The College had had a chequered history. It was originally located in Bombay, then in Calcutta and finally in Nagpur in 1957. In 1964–65, when I joined the IRS, it was working out of MLA's Rest House No. 2 on Temple Road in the Civil Lines. It had about 20–30 rooms, of which one served as a lecture room, one as a staffroom, one as a common room and a couple of rooms as a dining facility. The remainder housed the probationers, with two or three to a room. I shared a room with Tandon and Handa. As with the physical infrastructure so too with the faculty—it was skimpy. The Commissioner of Income Tax, Madhya Pradesh, C.C. Ganapathy doubled up as the Principal, and the day-to-day activities were looked after by the Inspecting Assistant Commissioner of Income Tax, V.V. Badami. A couple of others instructed us on Income Tax Law and Accounts. It is heartening to note that the aforesaid shoestring facilities have been replaced by a state-of-the-art 67-acre campus that, if not superior to that of the National Academy of Administration, is certainly not inferior to it.

Though classroom interaction with Mr Ganapathy was limited, as he was only marginally involved in teaching, we did get to meet him fairly often at social events organized by the College. He was reputed to be a brilliant officer and a crack bridge player. Witty and humorous, he was quite unorthodox in his views, which made him an idol for many of us. One of his witticisms was that he never trusted officers who worked late, as this meant that they were either incompetent or corrupt. Another was that he was suspicious of those who had all outstanding reports, as this raised the strong presumption that they were darbaris!

Despite the somewhat basic surroundings in Nagpur, I greatly enjoyed my six-month stay at the Income Tax Training College, particularly after the results of the IAS examinations were known in April 1965 following my interview earlier in February. This was due to the congenial company, the absence of any work pressure and excellent food—far better and much cheaper than at Mussoorie. While the monthly mess bill at Mussoorie was around ₹220—a substantial amount, since our salary was only ₹400—at Nagpur, it was no more than ₹180!

But apart from being enjoyable, my stint at the Income Tax Training College was also extremely valuable in more ways than one. Academically, it enabled me to acquire a fairly good understanding of the basics of accountancy and income tax law, which stood me in good stead both in personal life and in administration-related work in missions abroad. Even more importantly, it enabled me to forge lifelong friendships with many colleagues who were from backgrounds very different from mine. Above all, it greatly broadened my horizons by bringing me down from the cloistered and somewhat westernized environs of Lutyens' Delhi, in which I had grown up, to the middle-class India, which largely peopled the central services like the IRS. This impacted me in many ways, such as inculcating an understanding of, and empathy for, the not-so privileged, an ability to derive pleasure from the simpler things in life, and a taste for Indian films and music that I had hitherto tended to shun. Indeed, to this day, Indian film music of the 1950s and 1960s brings back pleasant memories of my time at the Income Tax Training College, as the same was constantly on tap in our common room, which had a rich collection of gramophone records generously donated by successive batches of probationers.

◆

With God's grace, I secured sufficiently high marks to make the cut for the IFS in my second attempt. My opting for the IFS instead of the IAS was in large measure influenced by my father, who rightly felt that the IFS, being less prone to political interference, offered a smoother career than the IAS.

In retrospect, the quota-based system of selection for the civil services, of which I was so critical, was, in a sense, partly responsible for my joining the IFS. Had there been no such system, I would, in my first attempt, have made the cut for the IAS but not for the IFS. In this eventuality, I would not have appeared again in an attempt to join the IFS. It was my having to reappear for the IAS/IFS entrance test that paved the way for my entry into the IFS, as, on this occasion, I secured much higher marks than at my first attempt and was selected to it. This was the first of the many 'accidents' that characterized my service career.

It would not be out of place to mention that today, not many securing a high rank opt for the IFS. Services like the IAS, IRS, Indian Police Service (IPS) and Indian Audit and Accounts Service (IA&AS) are more popular. It is ironical that the IRS, which I gave up to join the IFS, is today preferred by many as compared to the latter. This is not a commentary on the comparative intellectual pull of these two services but, perhaps, of the possibilities of making quick money in the former! The declining popularity of the IFS may be attributed to the fact that it is no longer one of the few gateways to seeing the world as in the past, that it is intrinsically disruptive to family life, and that its members do not enjoy the vastly greater powers enjoyed by those from several other government services.

1

PROBATIONER DAYS IN INDIA

In early July 1965, I joined duty at the Ministry of External Affairs (MEA) as an IFS probationer. Normally, all new recruits to the Service reported at the National Academy of Administration in Mussoorie for undergoing a four–five-month Foundation Course common to all the Class I civil services. However, the MEA reasoned that those like me who had already undergone the Foundation Course, albeit as members of another Service, should be put to work at Headquarters immediately rather than be allowed the luxury of repeating the Course. Apart from myself, there were another five or six colleagues from other services like the IA&AS, the Railways, the IPS, etc., who had been selected for the IFS in 1965 and joined duty at Headquarters without having to repeat the Foundation Course. These, inter alia, included K.V. Rajan, C.P. Ravindranathan, R.K. Rai, G.S. Bedi and K.B. Bala.

As compared to today, when the MEA has its own building at Janpath, in the mid-1960s, much of it was accommodated in South Block, sandwiched between the PMO and the Ministry of Defence. The atmosphere was relaxed and marked by an element of informality. One often entered the Ministry through Gate No. 1, which, some years later, came to be reserved exclusively for the Prime Minister and senior officials in his office. Indeed, every now and then, one even saw the Prime Minister ambling by as one went about one's business. Over the decades, all this has drastically changed with the preponderance of security. In the mid-1960s and 1970s, there was, however, little security, and one could quite easily park one's car right outside one's office room in South Block. Enhanced security over the years has made this impossible.

◆

R.K. Rai, my batchmate, and I were fortunate to be assigned to work for the Pillai Committee, which had been set up in June 1965 to review the organization and working of the IFS and to make recommendations so as to make it better able to meet the present and future needs of Indian foreign policy. It was named after its Chairman, Sir Narayanan Raghavan Pillai, ICS, KCIE, CBE, who had been the second and last Secretary General in the MEA, and also the first Cabinet Secretary in independent India. The Committee's Secretary was Mr N. Krishnan, a 1951 batch officer who was at the time in the rank of Director.

R.K. Rai and I worked out of Mr Krishnan's spacious first-floor office in South Block for around four months, from July 1965, and thus, had the privilege of interacting with him on a daily basis. The topper of his batch, Mr Krishnan was an outstanding officer and a warm and personable human being. With a razor-sharp intellect and sound common sense, he was devoid of any arrogance. Our exchanges with him were extensive and covered not only the work at hand but a variety of other issues in a free, frank and friendly atmosphere in which the huge seniority difference was no impediment. With time, our respect and admiration for Mr Krishnan blossomed into friendship, and we were often invited to his home for lunch or dinner.

While R.K. Rai was involved in the actual drafting of elements of the Pillai Committee report, in particular those relating to the history of the Service, I was required to study and analyse the personal files of all IFS officers with a view to developing a pen portrayal of the overall characteristics of the Service. Some of the issues one looked at were the numbers selected annually, the background of those selected, the region to which they belonged, the language allocations effected, duration spent in the language area and in each posting, promotion patterns, including the time taken to reach head of mission rank, specialization patterns, etc. Indeed, most of the annexures in the Pillai Committee report pertaining to the aforesaid issues were developed by me following study of data available and discussion with Mr Krishnan and R.K. Rai.

From the vantage point of the Pillai Committee, I acquired invaluable insights not only into the origins and organization of the MEA but also the state of play in the IFS. In the process, I realized that both were works in progress and in flux. It was, however, clear that the IFS was a specialized service created for the conduct of the totality of India's foreign policy. This was done through a decision of its interim government in 1946 and the relevant Cabinet summary approved in this regard was categorical that the IFS would man all 'India's posts abroad, whether diplomatic, consular, or commercial... and in the Foreign Office at home.'[1]

◆

The MEA as we know it came into being in August 1947 under the name of the Ministry of External Affairs and Commonwealth Relations through an amalgamation of the Departments of External Affairs and of Commonwealth Relations in British India. The former controlled the Agencies General in the United States (US) and China as well as Indian representation in some British Missions such as in Persia, Afghanistan and Tibet. It was also intimately concerned with developments in India's Frontier Areas. The Department of Commonwealth Relations, which descended from the Indian Overseas Department, controlled the High Commissioners in South Africa and Australia, and the Representatives in Malaya, Ceylon and Burma. The High Commission in London, handling India's trade with the United Kingdom (UK), was under the Commerce Department, whose reluctance to cede control of the same led to a year's delay in the setting up of the MEA which, with the appointment of the Interim Government, was to have been set up in 1946.[2]

Since Prime Minister Nehru was his own Foreign Minister, the Ministry of External Affairs and Commonwealth Relations came under his direct control. The work of both these Departments under the Ministry was coordinated and supervised by a Secretary General who

---

[1]*Report of the Committee on the Indian Foreign Service,* Ministry of External Affairs, New Delhi, 1966, p. 4, https://bit.ly/3US5bBO. Accessed on 15 November 2022.

[2]Ibid. 1.

also served as the principal advisor to the Prime Minister on all foreign policy-related matters. The post of Secretary General, continued till 1964, with Sir G.S. Bajpai as the first incumbent till 1952, and Sir N.R. Pillai as the second incumbent till 1964.

Though the term 'Commonwealth Relations' was dropped from the nomenclature of the MEA in 1949, the latter continued to function essentially as two departments, with the Foreign Secretary in charge of external relations in general and an Additional Secretary, who, in course of time, was re-designated as the Commonwealth Secretary, being entrusted with relations with Commonwealth countries. In the mid-1950s, a post of Special Secretary was also created to deal with administrative matters, and over time, he was additionally entrusted with handling our relations with Africa and West Asia.

With the abolition of the post of Secretary General in 1964, the Ministry was restructured. The designations of Commonwealth Secretary and Special Secretary were also done away with, and by 1965, the Ministry had three Secretaries, notably the Foreign Secretary who headed it, and Secretary EA-I and Secretary EA-II. The Ministry had as many as 18 Divisions, headed by a Joint Secretary or Director, of which eight were territorial and 10 were functional, general service or specialized. The latter included administration, protocol, external publicity, United Nations (UN) and conferences, passports and visas, economic affairs and technical assistance, historical research, legal and treaties, policy planning, and communications and security. All Divisions were skeletally manned, and their evolution over the years had been patchy and uneven. For instance, the Economic Affairs Division set up in 1947 had, after a couple of years, fallen into disuse for over a decade and was only revived in 1961. Similarly, the Legal and Treaties Division, though envisaged in 1947 and incorporated initially under a Legal Advisor, had soon been disbanded and was only revived in 1957. Till then, all legal advice required by the Ministry was secured from the Ministry of Law and Justice.[3]

The grave manpower shortage faced by the Ministry was an inevitable consequence of the miniscule size of the Service. This,

[3]Ibid. 2–3.

naturally, impinged adversely on specialization and was also the cause of the relatively short time spent by officers in their postings and language areas. Regrettably, despite innumerable recommendations on the need to rapidly expand the Service, this has not occurred to date. The problem was compounded by the heterogeneous nature of the Service. While selection to the Service through the competitive examinations conducted by the Union Public Service Commission (UPSC) had commenced in 1947, the intake in the earlier years was pitifully small—often in single digits—and the bulk of the recruits were lateral entrants from a variety of professions who were much older than those who came in through the UPSC competitive examinations. This, inevitably, hampered the evolution of an esprit de corps so necessary in a top-notch civil service. Some idea of the mongrel character of the Service would be evident from the data given below that detail the source of recruitment of the 271 officers in the Service as on 1 January 1966[4]:

- 20 officers permanently seconded from ICS, IPS or IA&AS
- 33 officers selected by the Federal Public Service Commission
- 33 officers selected by the Special Selection Board
- 5 officers selected from the Information Service of India
- 18 officers promoted from IFS B
- 162 officers selected through UPSC competitive examinations.

While R.K. Rai and I were not present at any of the meetings of the Pillai Committee, we were privileged to occasionally meet Sir N.R. Pillai, the Chairman, who would often drop by Mr Krishnan's room for an exchange of views on the shape of the Committee report. Short-statured, cigar-smoking and soft-spoken, it was an education to listen to the Chairman on the issues under consideration, as what he said was based on decades of administrative experience and high-level interaction. In one such meeting, during which he agreed to many of the ideas put to him relating to the betterment of service conditions, emoluments, allowances, etc., he underlined that while these suggestions were, in themselves, unexceptionable, they would

[4]Ibid. 4.

not have the desired results until and unless the IFS evolved a code of conduct that demanded excellence. He argued that the sine qua non of a good civil service was that even if per chance a mediocrity somehow found his way into it, he should, by virtue of being in the Service, be transformed into a good officer, and if this did not happen, he should be removed. His short point was that the prerequisite for a really high-class Service was an esprit de corps and that improvement in service conditions, while helpful, was not critical to this.

The Pillai Committee Report is a must-read for those interested in the IFS. It, inter alia, contains a comprehensive analysis of the Service as it existed at the time as also the systems and structures in place in the MEA. It also delves in some detail into the nature of Indian Foreign Policy as well as the qualities and the role of a diplomat, underlining that in no Service does the personality of an individual count for so much as in the IFS. The Committee, while making several recommendations relating to training, including the creation of a Directorate for Training under the Ministry, felt that the creation of a separate Foreign Service Training Institute was too ambitious a project, given the very small annual intake of officers. Interestingly, many of the recommendations contained in the Report were not implemented—like the need to more than double the IFS cadre to 550 within 10 years, the need to have a powerful and effective Policy Planning set-up, and the need to revive the post of Secretary General for overall coordination and supervision of the Ministry's work, unfettered by any other work, apart from that related to the UN, external publicity and administration. The other three Secretaries, being coequals, would look after the other work involving territorial as well as line divisions.

◆

About three months into my association with the Pillai Committee, the Administration showed me a file detailing the rather bizarre drama pertaining to my recruitment to the IFS. Apparently, following my appointment to the IFS, a lady officer petitioned the UPSC that she should have been allotted the IFS rather than the IAS, as she had higher marks than me and had opted for the former. The UPSC retorted that her father had sent a letter indicating that she be allotted the IAS rather than the IFS. She, however, countered with impeccable logic that since she, and not her father, had taken the examination, her choice of Service was what mattered, and her father's choice should not have been taken into account. Consequent upon this exchange, the UPSC requested the MEA to accommodate the lady officer in the IFS. The matter was considered right up to the level of Secretary Azim Hussain, ICS, who recorded that the lady should be accommodated in the IFS and that I, as the last general candidate recruit, should be released and assigned to the IAS. At this stage, Mr Madhavan, Director Administration, resubmitted the papers to the Secretary recommending that while the Ministry would, as directed, absorb the lady in the IFS, it should consider retaining me. His argument was that my being asked to leave the IFS would be unfair to me, as having worked in the Ministry, I had developed a commitment to it and was adjudged as having the potential of being an asset to it. Fortunately, Mr Madhavan's advice was accepted, and I continued to remain in the Service. I have, since, always held Mr Madhavan in high esteem, not merely for his role in this matter but also because he never once drew my attention to the good turn he had done to me.

The aforesaid incident further brought home to me that my joining the IFS was purely an accident and nothing short of an act of Providence. Had the lady officer's father not written to the UPSC that she be allotted the IAS, or had the Ministry allowed one to revisit Mussoorie for the Foundation Course rather than making me work at Headquarters, I would have ended up in the IAS and would not have had the opportunity to be in the IFS.

◆

On completion of the Foundation Course by my batchmates and their return to Delhi in December 1965, my assignment with the Pillai Committee came to an end, and I joined them for the remainder of my training in India. This included a three–four-month attachment to the Indian School of International Studies for a series of lectures and discussions on foreign policy-related issues, interaction with the various wings of the MEA, including technical units like ciphers and accounts, for basic training, one month's attachment to a military formation on our borders, six months' district training to acquaint one with local administration, a one-week Bharat Darshan and a three-month attachment with a senior officer in the Ministry.

Though useful, our training package was somewhat ad hoc and could have been better designed. Happily, with the establishment of a Foreign Service Training Institute (renamed Sushma Swaraj Institute of Foreign Service in 2020) with its own building, things have improved and the training programmes for our probationers are now better thought out and more useful.

Having had no exposure to the military and spent all my life in an urban environment in New Delhi, both the military attachment and the district training were most useful and provided invaluable insights.

Half a dozen of my colleagues and I were attached to an army unit in the RS Pura sector overlooking Sialkot in Pakistan just 4 kilometres away. Since we were located in a battle area, there was no brick-and-mortar lodging available for us and so we had to make do with tented accommodation and open-air loos. The only individual privileged to have his personal commode was the commanding officer, and there was hell to pay when one of my batchmates had the temerity to use it!

The commanding officer, at the very outset, made it clear that it was up to us to decide whether we wished to do as we pleased or live as per the Army regimen. We, naturally, opted for the latter so as to get a better perspective on the functioning of an Army unit. The daily routine involved getting up at 4.30 a.m., and after a hot cup of tea, having an hour's run followed by some physical training exercises. After this, one had an hour off for freshening up and breakfast. This was succeeded by weapons training, with a variety of small arms, and a few lectures. Thereafter, we had a sumptuous lunch and, following a short siesta, engaged in some sporting activity, usually football or hockey. Dinner was taken early. Both at lunch and dinner, drinks were freely served. By 9.30 p.m., we were exhausted, and sleep was instantaneous. Indeed, during my Army attachment, I reached the acme of physical fitness, no doubt due to a regular regime, a high level of physical activity and wholesome food.

Whilst on military attachment, I was deeply impressed by the high morale, particularly of the junior officers. This was significant, as we were in a war zone and that too just one year after the 1965 war. The officers and men were fully geared up for military action. War games and exercises were the order of the day. Indeed, during our Army attachment, we witnessed a company-level military competition within the Brigade involving the use of live ammunition in simulated battle conditions. The competition was stiff and emotions ran high. The participating company from our battalion did not fare too well, and the commanding officer was livid. The seriousness with which the competition was undertaken was impressive and left one with great confidence in our Armed Forces.

◆

District training proved equally absorbing and was a great learning experience. In our batch, the probationers were sent to districts within their own states as assistant commissioners on training. Five months were spent at the district headquarters and one month at the state secretariat.

Being originally from Punjab, I was sent to Ludhiana, which was terra incognita for me, as I had only been there once for a couple of days as a teenager. It, however, took me only a few days to find my feet as the Deputy Commissioner, Mr Isa Das, was most helpful, and as I was quickly able to develop a small circle of friends in diverse areas, ranging from the business world to the agricultural sector, including also a few former IRS batchmates on their first posting in Ludhiana.

During my stay in Ludhiana, I was lodged in a dark cavernous room in the local dak bungalow, with its chowkidar doubling as my cook and bearer till I found an alternative. Though the dak bungalow was somewhat dilapidated, its location was ideal, as it was within walking distance from my office and the local club, which one frequented on a daily basis for tennis and bridge.

Mr Das, a Punjab Civil Service officer, was also a Stephanian, and took a keen interest in my training and ensured that I acquired a reasonable knowledge of the main aspects of district administration. He interacted with me on a regular basis and made it a point to frequently invite me home for lunch, accompany him on local tours and participate in the meetings taken by him.

My stint in Ludhiana left me enormously impressed with the energy and vigour of the locals. The district was a vibrant industrial and agricultural hub. Its manufactures were in use not only throughout India but were also widely exported to countries like the Soviet Union and Iran. It was particularly well known for its hosiery products, sports goods and bicycles. The local technicians had a strong work ethic and often worked through the night to ensure on-time fulfilment of orders. Their skill levels were high and they could, in a day or so, duplicate any metal component—whether imported or of local manufacture.

Equally impressive was the confidence level of the farmers at a time when the Green Revolution was on the verge of taking off. Many amongst them told me that if assured on-time provision of seeds, water and fertilizer, the rest of India need do nothing, as Punjab alone could feed the whole nation. This was not idle talk, as there were some farmers who had excelled even in the Ludhiana Agricultural University in terms of per acre yields of the crops grown by them.

But apart from Punjab's vibrancy, both in agriculture and in light engineering, it was passing through considerable communal tension on account of the Punjabi Suba agitation. Ludhiana was in the eye of the storm, and I witnessed first-hand two major law and order disturbances. In the first incident, Hindu–Sikh clashes occurred, allegedly as a result of cigarettes having been thrown on the Guru Granth Sahib, which was being carried in a procession. There was, fortunately, no loss of life, as the Deputy Commissioner was able to persuade all concerned to desist from taking the law into their own hands. This was possible because he was well acquainted with all the major players, including the main mischief mongers.

The second incident was much more serious, and the Deputy Commissioner, as a last resort, had to order firing after a lathicharge and tear gas shelling failed to disperse the rioters. Only about 17 rounds were fired, and three people died. As compared to this, in Jalandhar, over a hundred rounds were fired, and the casualty toll was much higher. This was a scary episode, as we came under an intense brickbat attack, and the Deputy Commissioner alongside whom I was standing, received a head injury. It is an irony that in both incidents, the Superintendent of Police was transferred, in the first incident, for not having taken firmer action, and in the second incident, for having resorted to firing! This was blatantly unfair, as whether or not to open fire is not a police decision and can only be resorted to on the orders of the civil authority.

◆

My district training exposed me to the complexities of local administration and the considerable responsibilities vested with one's IAS colleagues. I also became aware of the vastly greater powers enjoyed by them as compared to those in the IFS. The fact that the IFS counted for little as compared to the IAS in the eyes of the common Indian was vividly brought home to us in a rather funny incident whilst we were on our Bharat Darshan. Contrary to the information given to us, we discovered on arrival in Jaipur that no accommodation had been reserved for us at the circuit house. On learning of this, one of my colleagues tried to impress upon the reservation manager that we belonged to the elite IFS and as such he should use his discretion and provide us with the requisite accommodation. To this, he responded that if by IFS we meant Indian Forest Service, he could not help and that he would gladly have done so if we belonged to either the IAS or the IPS! On hearing this, we gave up and resorted to the time-honoured practice of giving the manager a generous tip, which enabled us to get the desired accommodation.

The senior officer I was attached to for training at the Ministry happened to be a Joint Secretary who had considerable clout in the Ministry and went on to become Foreign Secretary. The extent of his influence was evident from the fact that, much to the envy of my colleagues, he secured for me a spacious room at Patiala House as well as a full-time personal assistant. My assigned task was to prepare a policy paper on whether or not India should go nuclear. Before setting out on this exercise, the Joint Secretary spent a good half hour briefing me on the subject from which it was clear that he felt that India should not go nuclear. In response to my queries on whether I should prepare a paper flatly ruling out the nuclear option or one based on an objective assessment, he responded that my paper should, of course, reflect my own assessment. In these circumstances, I diligently read up all I could and six weeks later submitted a paper recommending that India should go nuclear. The Joint Secretary was deeply upset and gave me a tongue-lashing. I was a little taken aback, since he had clearly indicated that I could make recommendations on the basis of my own assessment, which may not necessarily be in tune with his thinking. What pained me was that my paper was rubbished not on the basis of facts or logic but because its core recommendation was at variance with his thinking. I could not but contrast this approach with that of Mr Krishnan, who addressed differences through reasoned dialogue, based upon cold logic and facts. However, to give the Joint Secretary credit, he did not hold this run-in against me as he went up the professional ladder. In fact, our interaction a decade and a half later in Algiers, which he was visiting as Foreign Secretary, was distinctly amicable, though here, too, we differed in our discussion on how India should deal with neighbours like Bangladesh and Pakistan. Indeed, the clash of opinions was such that he was driven to remark that Punjabis should not be allowed to deal with relations with these two countries!

On completion of my training in India, I was apprised in early 1967 of my posting to Vienna as third secretary for purposes of learning French—the compulsory foreign language allotted to me. On learning this, I requested for a change of assignment to a French-speaking station such as Paris, Brussels or Geneva, and if this was not possible, requested for a change of the compulsory foreign language allotted to me to German to facilitate my learning it in Vienna. My request was brusquely turned down, and I was told that if I persisted, I would be posted to Ouagadougou. It is needless to mention that I shut up, telling myself that a Vienna posting was acceptable even if one were called upon to learn Chinese there!

2

LEARNING THE TRADE: VIENNA

The approved route for travel to Austria from India in 1967 was by air from New Delhi to Geneva and thence by train to Vienna via Zurich. When I set out from New Delhi on the morning of 20 April 1967, the temperature was a sweltering 40 degrees centigrade, and on reaching Vienna, a couple of days later, it was snowing and around 0 degrees centigrade!

On arrival in Geneva, I was received at the airport by Ms Kamlesh Kumar, a colleague from the 1964 batch, ensconced in a hotel and invited to a dinner hosted by my first boss in the Service, Mr N. Krishnan, who had just taken over as India's Permanent Representative to the UN Offices.

As in Geneva so too in Vienna, I was received by a colleague a year senior to me, Mr C.R. Balachandran, and lodged on a temporary basis at the house occupied by the former first secretary, Mr N.N. Jha, who had just moved out on transfer. While incoming officers at various missions are entitled to lodging for the first few days in a hotel, often, as an economy drive, they are put up in premises recently vacated by outgoing officers and still on lease. This is unobjectionable provided the said premises are in good shape. Regrettably, the heating system in the house in which I was lodged was defective and consequently my first night in Vienna was eminently forgettable. I, however, got by due to some Scotch whisky, which I had the foresight to carry with me!

One's first foreign posting in the IFS always has a special place in one's heart, as it is where one not only acquires hands-on experience in the art and craft of diplomacy but also in the countless other skills so essential while working in an Embassy. This is all the more so if the posting is in as beautiful and culturally rich a city as Vienna, with centuries-old traditions, and if the environment in the Embassy is as caring and friendly, as I was fortunate to have during my tenure there from April 1967 to June 1969.

Given the excellent India–Austria relations and a miniscule Indian community in the country numbering no more than a few score, there were no work-related tensions, and the weekends were entirely one's own. One made full use of this opportunity to wallow in the country's rich cultural heritage comprising architectural delights like the Schonbrunn and Belvedere palaces, with their excellent art collections; outstanding musical performances, both classical and modern, on offer not only at the pricy Opera House but also for a pittance at the Stadtpark and the Volksgarten; and culinary treats like Sachertorte and pastries from Demel. Apart from this, there were any number of other options such as driving through the countryside and soaking in its exquisite scenic beauty or savouring a steaming cup of coffee and chocolate cake topped with whipped cream, alone with one's thoughts, in the picturesque Vienna woods, or spending an evening sipping young inexpensive wine and snacking on cold cuts and cheese at a *heuriger* in conversation with friends and acquaintances. The heuriger is a distinctive Austrian institution where the normally staid and conservative locals let their hair down and indulge in unabashed merrymaking in which even outsiders are welcome to join in. Since the wine served at heurigers is young, its alcoholic impact is somewhat delayed, and many do not realize till too late that they have imbibed a little too much! I was fortunate in the latter part of my stay in Vienna to have a studio apartment in Grinzing, which was renowned for its heurigers and a must-see for all tourists.

On the cultural front, one of the highlights of my stay in Vienna was the opportunity of meeting Zubin Mehta and hearing a live performance conducted by him. Zubin Mehta had studied in Vienna for three years in the late 1950s and had then moved on to the US. It was my good fortune that he visited Vienna whilst I was there and gave a typically electrifying performance, leading the audience to call for nearly a dozen encores.

Another important persona connected with India and living in the environs of Vienna was Netaji Subhas Chandra Bose's wife

Emilie Schenkl. She was believed to be somewhat reclusive and had little interaction with the Embassy and, in fact, I never met her. In the early 1950s, she worked with the local telephone department, and over the years, it is my understanding that some modest assistance was provided to her by the Government of India, though not from Embassy funds. Additionally, it is believed that a modest trust had been set up for her daughter Anita Schenkl (now known as Anita Bose Pfaff).

Located in the heart of Europe, Austria is ideally placed for forays into neighbouring countries like Germany, Switzerland, Italy, Czechoslovakia, Yugoslavia and Hungary. Accordingly, I visited some of these countries, but since there was so much to see in Austria itself, like the Mauthausen concentration camp, famed cities like Innsbruck and Salzburg, and so many lesser-known but nevertheless quaint and picturesque towns like Melk and Krems an der Donau, that I did not travel as much outside the country as some may imagine. One such quaint town was Kienberg bei Gaming, located about 150 kilometres west of Vienna. It was situated astride a river that boasted a small run of river hydroelectric power plant with wooden turbines generating around 200 kW of power, built, perhaps, around the beginning of the twentieth century.

◆

Austria in the mid-1960s had not quite gotten over the multiplicity of traumas that had beset it in the first half of the century. It had yet to come to terms with the fact that from being the driving force of the great Austro-Hungarian Empire, it had been reduced to a tiny country with a population of around 7 million and no political heft. Modern-day Austria emerged from the ashes of the Austro-Hungarian Empire which, once a great power, was dismembered in 1918. Its existence as an independent country was, however, short-lived, as in March 1938, it was absorbed into Germany. With the collapse of Hitler's Third Reich in 1945, Austria re-emerged as an independent country. This did not, however, mark the end of Austria's trials and tribulations, as from 1945 to 1955, it was under Four Power occupation. Genuine independence was, therefore, still something of a novelty for Austria in the 1960s, to be savoured and cherished. It must be remembered that the Second World War and the occupation had imposed much economic hardship on the country, and it was only in the 1960s that the first green shoots of economic well-being were beginning to make themselves felt. The upside of the absence of any considerable economic prosperity in the country was that the student uprisings that engulfed much of Western Europe more or less totally bypassed Austria.

In retrospect, one cannot but marvel at the manner in which Austria not only came out of the many traumas it faced but also adopted a path that has made it a centre of well-being, as testified by the fact that Vienna, in 2022, was touted as the most liveable city by the Economic Intelligence Unit, and Mercer accorded it top honours in its annual Quality of Living Index survey in 2019. The route to this was by its eschewing all ambitions of great power status, pledging itself to perpetual neutrality, which minimized the possibility of superpower meddling, and concentrating on development. Austrian ambitions of a great power status were deftly substituted by its endeavours to make Vienna an important international centre, as exemplified by its becoming the headquarters not only of the International Atomic Energy Agency (IAEA) and United Nations Industrial Development Organization (UNIDO) but also of the Organization of the Petroleum Exporting Countries (OPEC) secretariat and more recently of the Comprehensive Nuclear-Test-Ban Treaty Organization (CTBTO).

Austria's economic development owes much to its focussing on its strengths, such as tourism, for which it is exceptionally well-endowed on account of its rich cultural heritage and unmatched scenic beauty, as well as the manufacture of specialized products ranging from glassware and porcelain to high-quality pressurized container vessels and specialized steels and assorted alloys. This exercise was, of course, facilitated by the fact that having been at the heart of the Austro-Hungarian Empire, Austria was well-equipped with many of the skill sets and infrastructure that go with a developed country, such as an excellent transport system and high-grade manpower in diverse spheres, including in relatively esoteric areas like ophthalmology.

In the mid-1960s, unlike in many other West European countries, basic living in Austria was relatively cheap, but luxury items and imported manufactures like cars, electronics and even clothing were prohibitively expensive. My meagre allowances, which amounted in all to about ₹1,600, or 5,500 Austrian schillings, made it a struggle to make both ends meet, even though I had a fairly frugal lifestyle. The only luxuries I indulged in were to employ a maid, to eat out and to acquire a small car. The maid came five days a week, whilst I was at work, to do the dishes, polish the floors, clean the windows, and wash and iron my clothes. Her salary and fuel costs for my car alone accounted for almost 40 per cent of my salary!

◆

The Vienna mission was relatively small with an Ambassador, a First Secretary, two probationer Third Secretaries, three Attachés, four or five India-based clerical staff, and three or four local staff.

I was lucky to have Mr R.G. Rajwade as my first Ambassador. He joined the IFS in 1948 through lateral entry at the age of 31 and belonged to an affluent princely family. Competent, friendly and outspoken to a fault, he was deeply respected by everyone, and the atmosphere in the mission was relaxed and friendly. He came into office for only about three hours in the morning and left the day-to-day running of the mission to the First Secretary. A man of means and style, he was always impeccably turned out, and his suits and shirts bore the Savile Row mark.

It is testimony to his uprightness that when offered the highly prestigious and lucrative job of Deputy Director General (DDG) at the IAEA by Sigvard Eklund, the Director General (DG), he unhesitatingly turned it down with great finesse. He is reported to have responded that he could not possibly accept the offer, as it would mean the end of a wonderful friendship because as the Indian Ambassador, the DG had to pay careful heed to whatever he said, but once he became DDG, the nature of the relationship would change, and he would have to take orders from the DG.

Within a couple of weeks of my arrival in Vienna, Mr Rajwade took me out for lunch to the Sacher Hotel, one of the most exclusive hotels in town. When I ordered a relatively simple dish, notably a wiener schnitzel, Mr Rajwade, noting that I was being parsimonious, suggested that he be permitted to order for me. On my agreeing, he queried as to whether I was averse to beef. Delighted to note that I had no such inhibitions, he proceeded to order a fantastic meal that must have cost him an arm and a leg.

Mr Rajwade took a keen interest in me, and I was a frequent invitee to his house, often to make up a fourth at bridge or to fill a gap at his sit-down dinners on account of an unexpected dropout. A stickler for etiquette, Mr Rajwade made it known that at his formal dinners, black tie was de rigueur. A suit or the officially prescribed bund-gala was not good enough. Accordingly, I invested in a black tie outfit, which I never had occasion to use in any of my subsequent assignments!

Mr Rajwade was succeeded as Ambassador in Vienna by Mr V.C. Trivedi, a more staid but nevertheless amiable officer. While always correct in his dealings with me, he lacked the charm and warmth of his predecessor and I was, therefore, never really close to him.

◆

Soon after my arrival in Vienna, Mr J.N. Dixit, a 1958 batch IFS officer, joined the Embassy as First Secretary. A brilliant officer and a fine human being, he was endowed with an infectious sense of fun that made him a joy to interact with. He was the pivot around which the Embassy functioned, and as I got to know him better, he became my friend, philosopher and guide. Indeed, over the years and decades, this friendship deepened and encompassed our respective families.

At the very outset, Mr Dixit told me that unlike third secretary probationers elsewhere, who spent their initial posting mainly on language training, he expected me to put in a full day's work at the Embassy, and learning the language would essentially have to be an after-office activity for me. At the same time, he clarified that he expected me to complete my language training within a year and a half or so and pass the required examination. Accordingly, I had inordinately long working days and nights at Vienna commencing at 9 a.m. and extending right up to midnight, as language study demanded at least four hours of work each day. I welcomed Mr Dixit's approach, as under his constant guidance, I was introduced to the entire gamut of an embassy's activities and, even more importantly, I was encouraged to arrive at my own conclusions after careful study and analysis. In the process, I inculcated the habits of sticking to timelines, paying meticulous attention to accuracy in reportage and of standing up for one's convictions, even if it meant going against one's superiors or against conventional wisdom. I also learnt that a good diplomat is akin to a finely calibrated two-way transmitter, on the one hand, conveying to his superiors the true state of affairs in the host state and, on the other, projecting their own country in the best possible terms. The former demands objectivity of a very high order, which is often not easy, as local influences are always at work, which militate against it. It is, therefore, not uncommon for some diplomats to exhibit signs of localitis—a disease that manifests itself in their tendency to become the mouthpiece of their host country and to see things from its viewpoint rather than arriving at objective assessments. As to the projection of one's own country to the best advantage, this, though easier, demands not only an in-depth knowledge of all the relevant facts but also articulation of a high order.

Mr Dixit's insistence on adhering to timelines is what, funnily enough, broke the ice betwixt us. While soon after his arrival he had indicated that I should feel free to visit him whenever convenient for a meal, I had taken this as a pro forma assertion and initially refrained from taking him up on his offer. It was only some weeks later, on completion of a lengthy and time-bound report late one evening, that I invited myself to Mr Dixit's home for dinner. He was delighted, and we were up chatting till midnight. Thenceforth, I was a frequent visitor to the Dixit home for a drink or dinner, particularly towards the end of the month, when I was low on funds! As our friendship grew, I often accompanied him and his family on excursions in the neighbourhood and, occasionally, even took the liberty of inviting friends to his house for an Indian meal.

Learning French in Vienna was a serious challenge. Normally, IFS officers learnt their allotted languages in countries where those were spoken. In my case, I was required to learn French in a German-speaking country. This was not easy, as focussing on French was exceedingly difficult, since I was all the time bombarded with German, which, too, was alien to me. I took French classes three times a week from 4.00–6.00 p.m. at the Berlitz school, which was located a couple of kilometres from the Chancery. Instruction was in the main through conversation with my teachers, notably an elderly gentleman in his late 60s and a sprightly lady in her 20s. While it was relatively easy to follow what the gentleman was saying, as he spoke slowly, with relatively little liaison between his words, the lady's diction was infinitely more difficult to comprehend as she spoke far more rapidly. These conversation classes were supplemented by about two hours of written work each night at home, which were submitted to the school for correction. Additionally, I also made it a point to spend some time in the language laboratory whenever I had any free time. The hard work paid off, and I passed the departmental French examination on schedule. Though my examiner is reported to have observed that my French had a somewhat peculiar accent! It is a reflection on our system that through my four-decade-long career, it was only some 10 years later, when I was posted in Algiers, that my knowledge of French was put to professional use!

One of my regrets whilst at Vienna is that my involvement in IAEA-related work was minimal. This was handled directly by the Ambassador, the First Secretary and an Attaché on deputation from the Department of Atomic Energy. I am sure that had I made a pitch for being involved in IAEA work, this would have been readily acceded to, but I refrained from so doing on account of an already very heavy workload that kept me busy till late at night. This was, however, compensated to an extent by being able to meet socially with some of the senior persona who visited Vienna from the Department of Atomic Energy, like Dr Vikram Sarabhai.

◆

Consular matters and political work were the main areas of activity allocated to me at the Embassy. The latter entailed keeping minutes of important meetings between Mr Dixit and those he met, drafting the monthly and annual political reports, and preparing special despatches to the Ministry on important developments. One of the more notable developments that occupied me was the Soviet move into Czechoslovakia, with about half a million troops on 20–21 August 1968. The move was triggered by the Prague Spring, which entailed an across-the-board liberalization and decentralization process initiated by Alexander Dubcek after assuming the office of First Secretary of the Communist Party of Czechoslovakia in January 1968. Czechoslovak opposition to the Soviet action, though deep-rooted, was non-violent and extended for months on end. Faced by the might of the Soviet Union and little material international support, it was, however, doomed to fail, and most of the reforms initiated by Dubcek were gradually reversed. In 1969, Dubcek was replaced by hardliner Gustáv Husák, who brought back communist orthodoxy in the country.

I tracked these developments through discussions with Austrian Foreign Office officials, interactions at the border with tourists moving out of Czechoslovakia, a weekend visit to Czechoslovakia on a tourist visa and media reports. My visit to Czechoslovakia, which entailed much pub-crawling, was the most useful, as I could see first-hand the depth of opposition to the Soviet invasion. One also discovered at one's cost that reports of the Czechs having tampered with the signboards to mislead the Soviets were correct, as on returning to Vienna, I was misled by the road signs and instead of reaching the Austrian border, I found myself scores of kilometres away at the German border. India's neutrality in the matter was not well-received by many, and our Ambassador received some hate calls.

On a subsequent visit to Prague some months later, I attended a cocktail organized by Second Secretary Harinder Singh, a colleague from the 1964 batch. At the cocktail, amongst the rather diverse guests, I met was Emil Zatopek, who had won the marathon gold medal at the 1952 Olympic Games. Mr Zatopek had since become a member of the Czechoslovak Communist Party but, belonging to the liberal element of the party, he had been suspended soon after the Soviet invasion of the country. Notwithstanding his suspension, he still enjoyed much clout and popularity and was held in high esteem. This became evident from the fact that at very short notice, he secured three tickets for me and my sisters for the famed one-of-a-kind Czech show Laterna Magika—combining elements of film, live acting and music—bookings for which had, normally, to be made months in advance. I was saddened to learn that around mid-1969, he had become a non-person and was packed off to a labour camp.

◆

My Austria posting is so deeply etched in my mind not only because of the many pleasant memories that it evokes but also because of the tragedy that struck me while there. My father, like me, was a reluctant traveller, but I prevailed upon him to visit me and take a trip through Europe. He and my mother arrived in Vienna on 2 July 1968. Though a heart patient, he was in perfect health till the evening of 13 July, when he succumbed, within seconds, to a sudden heart attack. The extremely supportive role of the Embassy and, in particular, Mr and Mrs Dixit greatly eased our situation and ensured that the cremation and last rites were not only undertaken without any glitches but also with calm and dignity.

Following my father's death, I took a month's leave to accompany my mother to India and to attend to sundry personal issues relating to my father's demise. I returned to Vienna on 20 August 1968 and requested to be relieved at the earliest so that I could be with my mother, who was alone in Delhi, as my siblings were in other parts of India. I had already taken this up with the Ministry whilst in Delhi and had been assured that my transfer to Delhi would be effected in a few months. The mission, at my request, also assured me of this and took up this matter with the Ministry. In this backdrop, I was aghast to receive orders on 1 May 1969 for my immediate transfer to Karachi. As a disciplined civil servant, I decided not to contest these orders, though I did protest, pointing out that I had expected the Ministry to show greater sensitivity to my request for a transfer to headquarters, which would allow me to be with my mother when she was all alone and in need of support. Instead of responding with a modicum of sympathy, the Ministry took the line that it had specially posted me to Karachi, as it was close to Delhi and that I would be in a position to visit my mother frequently!

My unhappiness with the Ministry was aggravated by the fact that two of my batchmates had received similar transfer orders to Karachi before me and had managed to get out of that posting on one ground or another due to their connections. Indeed, one of them along with his wife had holidayed in Vienna in April 1969 and been my house guest. Whilst in Vienna, he confided that he stood transferred to Karachi and was trying to get out of that posting, as he wished to continue to stay on in his current assignment in Bonn!

With hindsight, I am glad that I gracefully accepted the Karachi posting, as I not only enjoyed it but also because it coloured my future career profile to my benefit. My assignment to Karachi once again revealed that the hand of God was guiding my destiny. I was, after all, not the first choice for this assignment but the third and was being placed there by my Maker.

3

IN HOSTILE TERRITORY: KARACHI

After a short spell of leave in New Delhi, I joined duty at Karachi as second secretary towards the end of June 1969. The approved mode of travel to Karachi from India for junior officers like me was by surface route. I, therefore, travelled by train from Delhi to Bombay and from there by sea to Karachi.

The India–Pakistan passenger sea link in those days was serviced by three or four vessels of the British India Steamship Navigation Company as a part of their forays into the Gulf. The vessel I travelled on was the *SS Dumra*, a relatively small 5,000-tonne ship carrying 40–50 first- and second-class cabin passengers, and about 1,500 deck passengers. Apart from the rough monsoon seas, the one-and-a-half-day journey was uneventful.

My stint in Karachi from June 1969 to November 1971 coincided almost exactly with General Yahya Khan's period in power as President and Chief Martial Law Administrator (CMLA). General Ayub Khan's rising unpopularity and failing health compelled him to ask General Khan to take over from him as President in March 1969. The latter held office till 20 December 1971, when he was displaced by Zulfikar Ali Bhutto in the wake of Pakistan's disastrous war with India.

General Khan presided over, perhaps, the most tumultuous period of Pakistan's history, which included events such as the December 1970 elections, the January 1971 hijacking of the Indian Airlines aircraft, Ganga, and the consequent suspension of Pakistani overflights across India, the March 1971 crackdown in East Pakistan, followed by the ensuing genocide and civil war in that part of the country, which led to the India–Pakistan 1971 conflict. Whilst in office, Yahya Khan also acted as a bridge between US President

Richard Nixon and Mao Zedong, the leader of the People's Republic of China, and sabotaged India's participation in the 1969 Rabat Islamic Summit Conference, which set the ground for India's non-admission to the Organisation of Islamic Conference (subsequently known as Organisation of Islamic Cooperation). India–Pakistan relations during this period were, accordingly, extremely strained, which naturally had an adverse impact on the lives of those posted in our missions in Pakistan. The exciting and rapidly evolving political developments in the country, however, ensured that all Pakistan watchers like us never had a dull moment and were constantly kept on our toes. To add spice to this was Yahya Khan's fondness for the bottle and for women, and there were innumerable stories and jokes afloat in this regard in the country. Indeed, one of his mistresses, who also reportedly pimped for him, Aqleem Akhtar, popularly known as General Rani, emerged as one of the most influential persons in the country and was an important power broker.

◆

In the late 1960s, there were several Indian missions in Pakistan, notably the High Commission in Islamabad, Deputy High Commissions in Dhaka and Karachi and, perhaps, also Assistant High Commissions in Rajshahi, Sylhet, Khulna and Chittagong. The High Commission in Islamabad, set up in 1965 or 1966, was much smaller than the Deputy High Commissions on account of the fact that its visa issuance was a fraction of the latter. For instance, as compared to the 30–40 visas per day issued by the High Commission in Islamabad in 1969, the Deputy High Commission in Karachi issued around 1,000 and, thus, its staff requirement was far greater.

In contrast to the Indian Embassy in Vienna, which had a handful of India-based officials, the Deputy High Commission in Karachi had about 100 India-based officers and staff and over 20–30 local staff. Additionally, while the Embassy in Vienna merely owned a single property, notably the Ambassador's residence, the Deputy High Commission in Karachi owned several properties—such as a new tastefully constructed chancery at 3 Fatima Jinnah Road, which overlooked the residence of the Nawab of Junagadh; a gracious residence previously occupied by the High Commissioner and later by successive heads of post, known as India Lodge, at 63 Clifton near the Bhutto residence; half-a-dozen flats for senior officers, collectively known as Hindustan Court, at 42-43 Kurrie Road; a bunch of flats for junior officers, collectively known as Shivaji Court, on McNeil Road; around two dozen flats for staff, collectively known as Panchsheel Court, in Frere town; and even a small cottage on the beach at Hawke's Bay!

Apart from the head of post, designated as Deputy High Commissioner, the Karachi mission had a slew of other officers, notably a Counsellor, a Naval Attaché, four first Secretaries, a second Secretary and three or four attachés. As Second Secretary, I was amongst the junior-most officers and was designated as Head of Chancery, with the task of administering the mission, managing its accounts and looking after its properties. Within a few months of my arrival, I was also asked to engage in political reporting, and a little later, to handle security-related issues. Thus, I had my hands full, and the Karachi assignment was an excellent learning opportunity in a highly challenging environment.

Within a couple of days of my arrival, the Deputy High Commissioner, a very senior officer of Ambassadorial rank, very kindly invited me for lunch at the Sind Club, even though he was shortly scheduled to leave Karachi on transfer as head of mission. Since it was the height of summer, I had presumed that it would be in order for me to wear a bush shirt as one did at the Delhi Gymkhana Club but, fortunately, I had the presence of mind to check with him on the dress code and learnt that the old British traditions were still very strong at the Sind Club and it was de rigueur to wear a suit. Accordingly, willy-nilly and with great reluctance, I donned a suit in the sweltering Karachi heat for lunch at the Sind Club. One did not, however, regret it as it was a pleasure to see such a well-maintained club and partake of an excellent meal in a setting not too dissimilar to what presumably prevailed in the days of the Raj.

Apart from the very agreeable luncheon with the Deputy High Commissioner, my interaction with him was limited, as he left on transfer a couple of weeks later. I did, however, have one other not-so-pleasant exchange with him. This happened when I was proceeding on courier duty to Delhi for a couple of days. On learning of this, he asked me to carry some of the artworks acquired by him in Pakistan for deposit at his residence in Delhi. I was constrained to refuse, as I feared that this could cause a problem at customs, either while leaving Karachi or on arrival in Delhi. The Deputy High Commissioner, though perplexed at my approach, did not, fortunately, hold it against me.

♦

On the Deputy High Commissioner's departure, he was succeeded as head of post for a few months by Mr S.E. Joshi, who was a Counsellor, with the designation of Acting Deputy High Commissioner. I had a very good equation with Mr Joshi, who, several years later, went on to become the head of the Research and Analysis Wing (R&AW). Mr Joshi was succeeded by Mr K.N. Bakshi, with the designation of Assistant High Commissioner of India. A thorough professional endowed with innate kindness and understanding, Mr Bakshi ran an effective and happy mission in a most challenging environment. He had the rare quality of thinking of the well-being of all he interacted with, irrespective of rank, and of resolving their problems in the most practicable manner. Within a few months, we became very good friends. This was, perhaps, not only due to mutual respect but also because he was just four years my senior and thus there was no generation gap between us. Most of the other officers in the mission were much older and none was a direct recruit to the IFS (A).

As with the mission,so too my lodgings were much larger than in Vienna. While in Vienna, I had a one-bedroom apartment, and later, just a tiny studio apartment, in Karachi, I was allotted a three-bedroom house at Hindustan Court with a separate drawing and dining room in which, as a bachelor, I could not but feel lost. Fortunately, unlike in Vienna, where I had to make do with some part-time help, I came to Karachi equipped with an excellent India-based domestic help, who was not only a wonderful cook-bearer but also good at overseeing the work of the local help so that my house was always spic and span. While in Vienna, I was constantly short of funds, as I usually ate out, in Karachi, I not only had the luxury of having home-cooked meals of my choice and a better lifestyle but also made some savings.

As Head of Chancery responsible for attending to the administrative needs of one of India's larger missions as well as the management of its finances, I found my hands full and saw in it an opportunity to make life better for all our officers and staff. One of my first moves was to have all our buildings repainted, changing the colour from the depressing PWD yellow, so common all across India for government properties, to a more pleasing pastel greyish blue. Furthermore, I made available some of the better furniture and carpets lying unused in storage to officers and staff as per their requirements and entitlement. Additionally, badminton and volleyball courts were built for our officers and staff within our residential complexes so that we could engage in some sporting activities so necessary to keep one healthy in hostile surroundings. Our hut on the beach at Hawke's Bay, which was in a state of total disrepair, was completely renovated, and officers and staff were encouraged to spend time there on holidays. An unforgettable Hawke's Bay-related memory was the sight of scores of turtles coming out of the sea to lay their eggs on the shore. Some months later, an equally remarkable sight was witnessing hundreds of hatchlings trying to make their way to sea.

Personnel management in a hostile country posed its own special problems, particularly in regard to staff. While the officers were, by and large, better geared to handle stress, clerical and Class IV staff were not. Accordingly, I made a special effort to ensure that they were made as comfortable as possible. I sought to achieve this by maintaining a continuous interaction with them, providing them with sporting equipment, permitting them judicious access to imported liquor, cigarettes and other supplies, and generally being supportive of their legitimate needs.

Notwithstanding this, harsh steps had to be taken in a few cases. In one case, a Class IV staff member was detected maintaining illicit relations with a Pakistani woman. He was promptly repatriated to India. In another case, one of our security staff, while trying to sell Indian saris, had been caught by the local authorities, beaten up and tasked to provide mission-related intelligence. Fortunately, I learnt of this the day it happened, and on sustained interrogation at my residence, late at night, the concerned official broke down and made a complete confession. He, too, was quietly repatriated to India a few months later, but whilst still in Karachi, we had to carefully control his movements to ensure that the local authorities did not get to him.

My income tax training was of great help in enabling me to handle the mission's accounts-related matters. One of these was the long-pending reconciliation of accounts, which essentially entailed the ironing out of differences between the balance shown in the Assistant High Commission cash book and the related bank statement. Such monthly reconciliation is essential for effective financial planning and management. On noting that the accountant was unfamiliar with even the basic methodology of accounts reconciliation, I patiently explained the same to him and, in the process, personally reconciled some of the pending accounts. The accountant, however, was incorrigible and failed to reconcile the remaining accounts. This led me to resort to something that I have rarely done—notably, record an adverse entry in his confidential report. The reviewing officer, the Head of Post, agreed with my assessment. Nevertheless, on returning to India, the accountant moved heaven and earth to try and get the adverse entry expunged. As a result, the Ministry took up the matter with the Head of Post, asserting that I had been too harsh, on the grounds that the accountant had served with very senior officers, including from the ICS, who had given him glowing reports. Accordingly, they suggested that the adverse entry be modified. I, however, refused to do so, reiterating that as an accountant, his work had been substandard and that the excellent reports received in the past by him may have been on account of his involvement in another line of work. The incident brought home to me that recording an adverse entry carried the risk of having to waste a lot of time in defending it. A more sophisticated if sneaky way of achieving the same objective, which is the norm in our bureaucracy, is to give a colourless report rather than one that honestly damns an official with subpar performance!

◆

Over the months, with the addition of political reporting and security-related matters to my areas of responsibility, I was on duty more or less 24/7. This did not, in any way, faze me, as I was a bachelor and keen to learn as much as I could. I suspect I was a pain to many, as I would show up in office at odd hours, including late at night, and drop in unannounced at the homes of colleagues and staff. This enabled me to keep my finger on the pulse of the mission and check up on the alertness levels of those on duty, particularly the security personnel. Indeed, from around September 1971, as the possibility of war became increasingly imminent, we instituted a system of officers sleeping at night in the chancery on a rotational basis. Being single, I did so more often than others. This was no inconvenience, as I had equipped the chancery with a cosy sleeping area, a well-stocked refrigerator, a table tennis facility, television and radio.

Personnel in Indian missions in Pakistan are a constant target of hostility and harassment by the Inter-Services Intelligence (ISI) at the best of times, and this is all the more so in times of high tension as prevailed in the period 1969–71. Both stationary and mobile surveillance by the ISI, even on junior officers like me, was on a round-the-clock basis. Stationary surveillance was exercised by ISI personnel located in the vicinity of our residences and around the mission. Mobile surveillance was exercised by ISI operatives either in cars or on motorbikes. Additionally, all our phone lines were tapped. To make matters worse, there was the ever-present threat of being abducted and beaten up by the ISI. The only check to the latter was the certainty that prompt retaliatory action would be taken against our Pakistani counterparts in India. As a result, there were only a couple of incidents in Karachi when our officials were roughed up.

I took the all-pervasive surveillance in my stride, but some of my older colleagues found it harder to come to terms with it. In fact, the mobile surveillance to which I was subjected to had its lighter side. On one occasion, while going out to a party, my car had a flat tyre, and not wanting to get my hands dirty, I requested my minders to help change the tyre, which they willingly did. On another occasion, I had enormous difficulty in locating an address to which I was headed for the wedding of an Indian friend who was marrying a Pakistani girl. Since my endeavours to shake off my minders had failed, I stopped my car and sought their help to find the location. They helped and smilingly told me that I should have done so, ab initio, as the address to which I was going was that of a senior Pakistani police official and that efforts to shake them off were quite unnecessary!

In purely professional terms, the intense surveillance and hostility inevitably impaired our operational efficacy, as it made it well-nigh impossible to engage in meaningful interaction not only with Pakistanis but even with foreigners. Our parties were, therefore, very poorly attended. Fear of the ISI taking adverse note of their interaction with Indian diplomats led many Pakistanis and some foreigners to keep their contacts with us to the bare minimum. Indeed, even Pakistani doctors were reluctant to see us at our homes, and we had to seek medical aid in their clinics. A German working in Siemens with whom I had struck up an acquaintanceship frankly told me that he saw no point in continuing our association, as he was in Pakistan for business and his meeting me would jeopardize his continuance in the country.

The extremely hostile environment, which was palpable not only by the constant surveillance imposed on us but also by the unremitting and high-pitched anti-Indian media tirade, inevitably brought Indians serving in Pakistan much closer together than happens in missions located in more friendly environs. Going together for movies, on walks, to the beach, to restaurants, like Bandoo Khan, etc. were the norm, not to speak of playing badminton, bridge or simply partying in our residential complexes amongst ourselves. Accordingly, there was much camaraderie within the mission, which enabled us to successfully cope with the stresses and strains of working in Karachi.

Despite the strained security situation, one of my most-cherished memories of Karachi was attending a live concert by Begum Akhtar. She was a guest of Rashid Khan, the head of the Gramophone Record Company of Pakistan, and since public recitals by Indian artistes were prohibited in the country, he organized a private recital for her at which the invitees numbered well over a hundred. While her performance was a tour de force and everyone was awestruck, what impressed me most was the manner in which she acted as an exemplary envoy of India. For instance, when quizzed about her sentiments about India, she asserted that she was proud to be an Indian, that she had received much love in India and that she owed all her success to India.

◆

Whilst posted at Karachi, barring a visit to Islamabad on consultations soon after my arrival, I was unable to visit any other city, as permission for travel from the Pakistan Foreign Office was hard to come by. The visit revealed the sharp contrast between the work content and living conditions for our diplomats stationed in Islamabad and those in Karachi. It also enabled me to re-establish contact with Deb Mukharji and Naresh Dayal, both second Secretaries from the 1964 batch, whom I had known for some time.

Karachi had been the capital of Pakistan from August 1947 to the late 1950s, when Ayub Khan decided to locate it elsewhere, as he felt that its climate was unhealthy and that its business community was a pernicious influence on the government. Accordingly, he appointed a Commission under General Yahya Khan to recommend a new location for Pakistan's capital and, meanwhile, temporarily shifted the capital to Rawalpindi. In early 1960, the Commission recommended that Pakistan's new capital should be built from scratch about 15 kilometres away from Rawalpindi at a new site, with the Margalla Hills as a backdrop. It was decided that the new capital be called 'Islamabad'. Soon after Islamabad came into being, the High Commission of India in Pakistan shifted there from Karachi in 1965–66.

Accordingly, when I visited Islamabad in 1969, it was still a work in progress and no more than a small township made up largely of civil servants with little by way of cinemas, clubs, hotels or restaurants, in marked contrast to what was on offer in thriving and bustling cities like Karachi or Lahore. The chancery in Karachi was infinitely superior to that in Islamabad, which was essentially located in a couple of houses and not in premises specifically tailored for the purpose. While the officers in Islamabad had more modern homes than those occupied by officers in Karachi, they were disadvantaged from a security perspective, since these were not located next to each other as in Karachi, where we lived in Indian-owned complexes with infinitely better security.

In these circumstances, life for our diplomats in Islamabad was not only more claustrophobic than for those in Karachi but also less secure. Furthermore, the grid layout of Islamabad and its miniscule size facilitated more intense surveillance on our officials than was possible in sprawling Karachi. Finally, hostility levels against India were much higher in Islamabad as compared to Karachi, since it was a Punjabi-dominated and government-controlled town, whereas Karachi was a cosmopolitan and business-dominated city. The high hostility levels in Islamabad were amply demonstrated a few months prior to my visit to Islamabad, when the house occupied by Naresh Dayal was stone-pelted by an irate mob at the instigation of the ISI. His wife and infant twin daughters were alone at home at the time, and the latter must have been traumatized by the event.

The work style of our diplomats in Islamabad was radically different from us in Karachi. Their interactions were in the main with the Foreign Office and with the diplomatic community with the focus on the warp and woof of bilateral ties. In Karachi, on the other hand, our work involved consular-related matters, trade issues, and interaction with the media and the business community. Interaction with the diplomatic community or the Foreign Office was negligible, as both were miniscule. Officials in both missions, however, devoted much time to examining and analysing media reportage and basing assessments thereon. In retrospect, we were mistaken in so doing, as the media at the best of times is an unreliable creature.

It is ironical that during my Islamabad visit, I was accommodated at the Scheherazade hotel, which was later used to house the Pakistan Foreign Office, which I was destined to repeatedly visit over the decades!

◆

Relations between the High Commission in Islamabad and the Assistant High Commission in Karachi were exemplary. While instructions from the former to the latter were relatively few and usually couched in the form of requests, compliance was instantaneous. Many of these requests were administrative in nature, involving the despatch of carpets and furniture from the more richly endowed Assistant High Commission, which had been the original seat of the High Commission, to the recently set-up High Commission in Islamabad. It is noteworthy that not only was the Assistant High

Commission accorded complete independence in terms of its reporting to Headquarters, but the High Commission was also generally supportive of its requests.

Interaction between the High Commission and the Assistant High Commission was frequent through exchange of communications and visits. While the High Commissioner and the Deputy High Commissioner visited Karachi a couple of times, the more junior officers from the High Commission visited Karachi much more often. Similarly, officers from the Assistant High Commission also occasionally visited Islamabad for consultations.

The High Commissioner, Mr B.K. Acharya, ICS, was one of India's senior-most officers who knew Pakistan well, as he had earlier also served as our Deputy High Commissioner in Dhaka. A workaholic and a strict disciplinarian, he fortunately had a human side to himself and fully empathized with us in the context of the difficult circumstances in which we were working. Indeed, he made known that young IFS officers ought not to be posted to hostile countries like Pakistan, as it militated against their professional growth. Elaborating on this, he argued that initial postings should be in friendly environments conducive to positive and productive engagement rather than in hostile ones like Pakistan, where such engagement was an impossibility and where one's role was reduced to perpetually block its inimical moves against India.

The fulcrum of interaction between the two missions was the Deputy High Commissioner, Mr A.S. Chib, a 1953 batch IFS officer who knew Pakistan like the back of his hand. Endowed with an innate maturity and wisdom, he set the tone for the interaction between the two missions and played the key role in the tasking of the Assistant High Commission. It was, for instance, at his initiative that my role in the Assistant High Commission was enhanced soon after my arrival from merely looking after administrative work, as done by my predecessor, to also engaging in political work.

◆

One of the most hotly debated and closely watched events during the Yahya Khan regime was the December 1970 election. This was only natural, as it was Pakistan's first foray into a countrywide direct election for the national assembly. No one had predicted the Awami League's landslide victory in East Pakistan, where it secured 160 out of 162 seats, or the Pakistan People's Party's (PPP) emergence as the majority party in West Pakistan, with 81 out of 138 seats. The most popular pre-poll assessments were that no party would emerge as a clear winner, leaving enough scope for the Army to create a coalition government of its choice. Amongst the diplomatic community, the British were the closest to the mark on the PPP's performance, estimating its obtaining 30–40 seats, with the rest guessing that it would do much worse. Our own estimates were that the PPP would at best bag around 25 seats, as we felt that Bhutto's '*roti, kapda, makaan*' (food, clothing, shelter) slogan was gaining traction. These estimates were somewhat higher than those projected by our Islamabad mission.

Political developments in Pakistan following the 1970 elections took place at a frenetic pace, and I was witness to the country's precipitous slide to disaster. This was, in large measure, due to the West Pakistan leadership's obduracy in not conceding power to the Awami League as warranted by the election outcome. Naturally, Yahya Khan bore much of the responsibility for this, but Bhutto, too, was complicit, as in his lust for power, he did his utmost to obviate the possibility of transfer of power to Mujibur Rahman. However, at a more subliminal level, West Pakistan's aversion to the acceptance of the Awami League's leadership, its campaign of genocide in East Pakistan and its justification thereof may be attributed to the racist psyche of its leadership and indeed its people. This was brought home to me in a brutally frank exchange in October 1971 with a PPP journalist, who was a fellow Stephanian and a friend, when he blithely justified the brutalities committed in East Pakistan on the grounds that Bengalis were not North Indians like the two of us and fully deserved the treatment meted out to them! It goes without saying that this was our last conversation and our friendship floundered thereafter.

We kept a close track of what was transpiring in East Pakistan through the foreign media. Indeed, the Reuters correspondent in Karachi, Howard Whitten, had given me a carte blanche to visit him at his Clifton residence to see his despatches in the matter. He frankly told me that he was giving me full licence to make whatever use I wished with his inputs, as he was not sure whether his reports were making it through the Pakistani censors to London and by letting me in on his reportage, he expected that some of it would make it to the free world through another channel.

◆

Following the crackdown in East Pakistan in March 1971, India–Pakistan ties rapidly deteriorated, and by June–July 1971, it became evident to many of us that war was on the cards. Accordingly, at around this time, the mission went into high gear to destroy all classified records, tighten security, repatriate wives and children, thin out staff, and prepare ourselves for being interned by stocking up on essential supplies. The bulk of this work fell upon me and, accordingly, though I was under orders of transfer, I decided to stay on for a few more months till most of the aforesaid activities were completed.

While repatriation of families and thinning down of staff proved relatively easy, elimination of classified material was much more time consuming than anticipated. While some of our records were sent to the headquarters through diplomatic bag, most had to be burnt, and as one proceeded to do so, one realized that paper in bulk takes a long time to burn. We had open fires working 24/7 for several weeks before this process could be completed. Additionally, on each floor of our chancery, we installed small improvised steel incinerators for destruction of records by each wing of the mission. By November, we had more or less completed this exercise and were in a position to tell the Ministry when they referred to an earlier classified message that they would need to repeat that message, as the same had been destroyed and was no longer available with us for reference!

That India and Pakistan were on the verge of war was graphically brought home to me sometime in September 1971 when one of my doctors—a Parsi—asked to see me urgently. When I reached his clinic, he took me to his anteroom and told me that war was now imminent, as he had noted troop movements to the Punjab from the Sind area and that Pakistan was getting additional aircraft from friendly countries. He was convinced that India needed to make peace with Pakistan, as it would not be able to stand up to the latter. He based this on his sense that in 1965, Pakistan had given India a drubbing and, with its refurbished capabilities, it would repeat this in 1971. Efforts to convince him that his reading of the realities of 1965 was inaccurate proved unavailing, indicating the extent to which people had been brainwashed in Pakistan.

I left Karachi for Delhi by air on transfer on 21 November 1971, just three days before all transport connectivity between India and Pakistan was severed! My car was flown out from Karachi to Delhi on 24 November 1971 on the last flight out of the city to India. I had, frankly, little hope that I would ever get back my car, and the fact that I got it so promptly is testimony to the loyalty of my colleagues and the staff that worked under me at Karachi.

4

ADMINISTERING AID AND DEALING WITH THE ENEMY: NEW DELHI

In December 1971 or early January 1972, I went to the Ministry to report for duty and duly met the desk officer in charge of Administration to enquire as to what assignment would be given to me. He told me that no decision had been taken so far and that I should meet the Joint Secretary Administration but that slots were open in the UN and Europe divisions and sought my preference. I responded that I would be happy to join either.

Later in the day, I called on the Joint Secretary Administration. As I entered his room and before I could even sit down, he informed me that I should report to the Department of Economic Affairs (DEA), Ministry of Finance, and then launched on a tirade on the importance of this assignment. When I, unhesitatingly, indicated my readiness to take the suggested assignment, the Joint Secretary underwent a dramatic behavioural transformation, requested me to be seated, offered me tea and biscuits, and was all honey and sugar. Clearly, the administration had been facing difficulties in finding takers for this assignment, and I am sure that there must have been others who had been sounded in the matter and had turned it down. The reluctance of IFS officers to proceed on deputation to other Ministries continues and is a serious shortcoming in the MEA. In retrospect, my move to the DEA was an inspired decision, as it provided me with insights on matters economic, which I could never have obtained in my own Ministry, and paved the way, subsequently, to a posting in the Economic Wing of our Embassy in Washington, which turned out to be a rewarding experience.

I served in the DEA for a little over a year and dealt with West German, Danish and Swedish assistance to India. This essentially entailed participation in the negotiations leading up to the relevant loan agreements, allocation of amounts out of this assistance to our industrial units, oversight of the disbursal of the loans sanctioned and follow-up discussions with representatives of the countries involved to ensure that the assistance was being effectively utilized. The size, nature and terms of each of these loan agreements differed as did the extent of oversight exercised by the concerned donor.

While the quantum of the West German assistance was, by far, the largest, the terms of the Swedish loans were the most generous. Moreover, while German credits were tied to imports from Germany, Swedish assistance was not specifically tied to imports from Sweden. The Germans also exercised an eagle-eyed oversight on the manner in which we utilized their loans, and every quarter, their teams would come to Delhi for discussions in this regard. Such oversight, however, never acquired a political overtone, and I did not, therefore, resent it, recognizing that what was being done was to ensure the optimal utilization of the loans, which was in the mutual interest.

I had considerable discretion in allocating funds to particular industrial units within specific limits. In case the demand was for an amount higher than the aforesaid limit, clearance had to be obtained from a more senior officer. Throughout my tenure in the DEA, I never felt pressured or hassled on any account. The only occasion when the Joint Secretary to whom I reported to asked me to make an urgent allocation of funding by the end of the day was in respect of the famous Mother Dairy project, in which Mrs Indira Gandhi had shown a direct interest. This demand was eminently legitimate, and by the day's end, I was able to report that I had booked a fairly substantial amount of the funds required under the Swedish credit, which, because of its largely untied nature, was akin to free foreign exchange. The balance funds required were met through the government's free foreign exchange reserves.

The group of officers I served under comprised Joint Secretary Thirumalai, the topper of the 1947 IAS batch, Director W.S. Tambe and Deputy Secretary M. Godbole. I developed a particularly close friendship with the latter, an extremely upright, industrious and courageous officer who later became our Home Secretary.

There was never an occasion when I was pressured to record a note favouring a particular line of action. On the contrary, I was encouraged to express an honest opinion after due study and analysis of the issue under consideration. Differences of opinion up the chain of command were aired from time to time and were taken in their stride. If anything, this bred mutual respect between the concerned officials.

◆

Unlike the MEA, where notes were usually initiated by the Under Secretary, in the DEA this was done by the Assistant or the Section Officer. Such notes were submitted to the Under Secretary by the Section Officer for further necessary action. Thus, it was not unusual for a file on a particular matter to carry notings by the Assistant as well as all the other officers all the way up to the Secretary. If the issue was complex, the notings by each officer could run into several pages and the differences in viewpoint would come out into the open. In the MEA, with its more collegiate functional style, such differences of opinion were relatively rare, and notings were more concise. Indeed, on reversion to the MEA, on seeing a one-and-a-half page note from me, my boss told me that no note should be more than a page, as no one had the time to read lengthy notes! This was one of the major culture shocks I faced on returning to the MEA.

Yet another major difference was in the quality of staff. While in the DEA it was difficult to find fault with the noting of Section Officers and even Assistants, in the MEA, similar officials could not be relied upon to produce high-quality notes, and the best that one could expect of them was to maintain the files required in good order. This was, perhaps, because of the rapid turnover of staff in the MEA, as well as a system that required initiation of notes by the officer cadre and relegation of the clerical staff to the mere maintenance of papers and files. After working in the DEA and my own Ministry, it was my considered view that the former was superior and was, perhaps, the most efficient Department in the Government of India. The same could not, however, be said of the other Ministries, and the MEA was more effective than most of them. The latter scored over most other

Ministries on account of its officer-oriented system, collegiate style of functioning and culture of time-bound output—often the product of discussions without written orders—which facilitated quicker decision-making than in most other Ministries.

Soon after my move to the DEA, the Joint Secretary (Pakistan) in my parent Ministry, Mr A.S. Chib, who had formerly been Deputy High Commissioner in Islamabad when I was in Karachi, suggested that I return to the Ministry to work under him. I informed him that I was quite happy where I was and would only consider moving to the Ministry on completion of a year in my current assignment. Accordingly, in early 1973, I joined the Pakistan division as Under Secretary, and a year later, I was promoted as Deputy Secretary.

Dealing with the Enemy

In terms of my physical work environment, the MEA scored handsomely over that in the DEA. Though in the latter, I did have the luxury of having a room to myself, it was no more than a remote cubbyhole with inadequate cooling. In contrast, in the MEA, I had a spacious and effectively cooled room shared with two other colleagues. Location wise it was far superior to my second-floor room in the DEA, being on the ground floor at the very entry of what is now the Prime Minister's Secretariat. I also had the luxury of being able to park my car right outside the room.

As explained earlier, working in the MEA after my stint in the DEA took some getting used to due to their differing ethos, manner of functioning and the fact that one did not enjoy the same degree of independence as in the latter. Face-to-face interaction with one's colleagues and superiors was much more in the MEA than in the DEA. I was also under greater pressure for time-bound output. All this, though a little irksome at the outset, was compensated by the fact that it made my work more exciting and enabled me to get into the groove of working in my own parent Ministry and amongst my own service colleagues.

◆

My adjustment to the radically different work culture was greatly facilitated by the fact that most of those in the Pakistan Division were well known to me from my Pakistan posting, notably Mr A.S. Chib, Joint Secretary and Head of Division, Mr K.N. Bakshi, Deputy Secretary and my former boss in Karachi, and Naresh Dayal, Under Secretary. In fact, the latter and I shared a huge three-seater room, of which the third incumbent was R.K. Kapur, a Senior Research Officer, specializing on matters relating to Kashmir. All four were sound professionals and easy to interact with. Mr Chib's understanding and knowledge of Pakistan was unmatched, and all of us greatly benefitted from his insights and guidance on matters related to Pakistan. One of his most important pieces of advice that has always informed me in my dealings with Pakistan was never to trust it or show it undue magnanimity, as in so doing, we would open ourselves up to betrayal.

It would not be out of place to mention here that Mr Chib, Mr Bakshi and Mr Dayal were all part of our delegation for the India–Pakistan discussions that led to the conclusion of the Shimla Agreement in July 1972. I am also given to believe that their hard-line views on Pakistan and, in particular, about the fact that Bhutto could not be trusted were made known to the senior-most levels in our system. It is unfortunate that these went unheeded, and we concluded the Shimla Agreement, whereunder we conceded much and gained little and lost a golden opportunity of settling the Kashmir issue once and for all. Being in occupation of over 5,000 square miles of Pakistani territory and holding around 93,000 Pakistani soldiers in joint custody with Bangladesh, it is a no-brainer that it should have been possible for us to have made Pakistan at least accept the conversion of the ceasefire line in Kashmir into an international border, with marginal adjustments.

Our inability to do so can only be attributed to our leadership being woolly headed and bereft of any sense of realpolitik. This is borne out in a discussion on 16 August 1973 in Dhaka between Sheikh Mujibur Rahman and P.N. Haksar, principal secretary to Mrs Gandhi, when in response to the former's observation that India had shown great generosity in vacating thousands of square miles of Pakistani territory the latter reportedly stated that 'be that as it may, any attempt at solving the pending problems by "dictating or stipulating conditions" will not meet with success in international politics. This is a lesson of history.' Elaborating on this, Mr Haksar attributed Germany's descent into the barbarism of Nazi philosophy to the diktat of the 1919 Versailles Treaty, despite its cohesion and a 'tangible cultural and ethnic background.' He concluded by asserting, 'So one should imagine the impact on Pakistan if it is confronted with such a situation, given Pakistani society's lack of cohesion and unity as a nation.'[5]

◆

At the time I joined the Pakistan Division in early 1973, with the Shimla Agreement having been concluded in July 1972, tensions between the two countries had diminished, but the process of restoring ties, which had been severed in the 1971 conflict, had to be addressed as also a host of Bangladesh-related issues. Amongst the latter were included the recognition of Bangladesh by Pakistan, the repatriation of the thousands of Bangladeshi officials and civilians interned in Pakistan, the Pakistanis stranded in Bangladesh, including non-Bengalis, and the Pakistani Prisoners of War (PoWs) held in India under the India–Bangladesh Joint Command, including the 195 PoWs held for war crime trials. The modalities of the repatriation process were addressed by the Delhi Agreement of August 1973 and the Tripartite Agreement of April 1974 and the entire exercise was underpinned by Pakistan's recognition of Bangladesh in February 1974. Under these agreements, as many as 300,000 people were repatriated. The process commenced in September 1973 and took around a year to complete. The entire exercise was addressed at stratospheric levels within the system with the Pakistan Division contributing a variety of suggestions and inputs.

It is regrettable that Bangladesh's demand for holding the 195

[5]'Record of discussions between the Prime Minister of Bangladesh and Shri P.N. Haksar on the 16th August 1973 at 6 P.M.' p. 2127 from Vol III of *India–Pakistan Relations 1947–2007: A Documentary Study,* Avtar Singh Bhasin (ed.), Ministry of External Affairs, https://bit.ly/3Vy8fEt. Accessed on 18 October 2022.

Pakistani PoWs for war crime trials was given up. Had we not pressured Bangladesh to give up on their insistence on the war crime trials while it is possible that an understanding on the repatriation process may have been delayed for some time, but ultimately this would have happened. More importantly, the holding of such trials would have prevented a patch up in Pakistan–Bangladesh ties in the immediate aftermath of Sheikh Mujibur Rahman's assassination, as they would have reopened memories of the enormity of the atrocities committed by Pakistan. This would also have given an enormous setback to the reactionary forces in Bangladesh, which were able to wrest power from the Awami League for decades.

Our pressure on Bangladesh for release of the PoWs arose in part from international pressure and in part from the hope this would help in arriving at a modus vivendi with Pakistan. This is amply borne out from a perusal of the discussion between P.N. Haksar and the Bangladesh Foreign Minister on 16 August 1973, wherein Mr Haksar, in response to the comment of the Bangladesh Foreign Secretary that all the concessions were being made by India and Bangladesh, responded that he would not repeat...

> His realistic, though somewhat cynical, assessment of international community's reactions in such matters. He added that if in spite of the reasonableness shown, the talks fail, then India and Bangladesh can discuss further steps to be taken. Mr Haksar remarked: 'We may cross that bridge when we come to it.' He added that while the UN will not pass any resolution endorsing or appreciating the concessions made by India and Bangladesh, it would certainly pass a resolution asking India and Bangladesh to return the PoWs. In the circumstances neither India nor Bangladesh should be sanguine about the world's reaction or willingness to bend Pakistan to India and Bangladesh's purposes.
>
> It should also be noted, that the pressure on Pakistan would be less because Pakistan is 'an available country.' India and Bangladesh have decided not to be compelled to play the role of concubines to super powers. So they face a more difficult and challenging

> predicament which requires greater dynamism and flexibility. Commenting on Pakistan's easy situation, Shri Haksar pointed out that though Pakistan has left the Commonwealth, none of the Commonwealth countries during the recent Conference at Ottawa passed any resolutions or made any statements supporting India and Bangladesh's cause *vis-a-vis* Pakistan. They did not ask Pakistan to recognise Bangladesh. In the circumstances the problem to be realised is that India and Bangladesh have to work together for the fulfilment of their own interests. If in spite of our effort, state of confrontation continues with Pakistan, we can survive it but the effort should be to avoid it. India's concern about Bangladesh is that it wishes to be a neighbour of Bangladesh with no domestic pre-occupations. The events of 1971 have generated political problems as well as economic problems. India has spent nearly 300 crores of rupees in drought relief in 1973. The period between the end of 1972 till today has been perhaps the most critical in the post-Independence history of India. But India is determined not to be swamped by these problems. With Bangladesh's cooperation and understanding, the political problems with Pakistan can be resolved. If India goes with a flexible approach to the forthcoming negotiations with Pakistan which clearly indicates to the world that, India and Bangladesh's motives are reasonable and genuine aiming at sub-continental stability and peace, there are prospects of some success. A greater amount of reasonableness is called for in such a situation as India and Bangladesh are dealing with Pakistan which is basically an unstable, troubled and oligarchic society.[6]

◆

Whilst in the Pakistan Division I had several dealings with the International Committee of the Red Cross (ICRC), who were

---

[6]'Summary of discussions held between the Foreign Minister of Bangladesh and Shri P.N. Haksar on the 16th August 1973, at 10 a.m.', *India–Pakistan Relations 1947–2007: A Documentary Study,* Avtar Singh Bhasin (ed.), Ministry of External Affairs, pp. 2119–20, https://bit.ly/3Vy8fEt, accessed on 18 October 2022.

maintaining an oversight on the treatment of Pakistani PoWs in India, and the Swiss Embassy, which was handling our relations with Pakistan. I found both to be excellent professional interlocutors. The ICRC would, every few weeks, share with the Ministry its reports and findings on the treatment of PoWs. On most occasions, the reports were favourable. Once or twice when there was an unfavourable report, which was unwarranted in my view, I found it possible to engage with the concerned ICRC officials and to convince them about the need to modify their findings, which was done. Similarly, the Swiss Embassy was meticulous in handling our issues in Pakistan and could be relied upon to strictly abide by our instructions and requests.

One of the issues we raised with Pakistan was the question of 54 missing Indian military personnel, both officers and men, believed to have been taken prisoner in the 1971 conflict. Pakistan, to this day, denies that these personnel are in its custody and, on the contrary, has raised counterclaims about their missing PoWs in India, who are not in our jails. Perhaps, a way out of this dilemma is to come to an understanding with Pakistan to permit the ICRC to visit jails in both countries to verify their respective claims about their missing PoWs.

A major area of work in the Pakistan Division was attending to Parliament Questions. This has always consumed an inordinate amount of the Division's time, as nearly 40 per cent of the questions for the Ministry are in regard to Pakistan. While initially I considered attending to this task as wasteful, Mr Chib placed it in the right perspective by pointing out that Parliament Questions were, in fact, an opportunity for civil servants to make policy. Replies to such questions, which were, after all, drafted by bureaucrats, once tabled in Parliament following Ministerial approval became policy!

I recall a particularly trying week when I had to attend to around a dozen questions of which three or four were starred questions requiring detailed notes to facilitate the Minister's response to possible supplementary questions. This happened because all the other officers in the Ministry were out of station, and I had to deal directly with the concerned Secretary and the Minister. Things passed off relatively smoothly as the Secretary concerned, Mr V.C. Trivedi, who was relatively new to dealing with Pakistan, had sufficient confidence in me, as he had been my Ambassador in Vienna, and even more importantly, the Minister was none other than the highly experienced and redoubtable Sardar Swaran Singh. Both made only slight changes to my draft replies, and while I spent an hour or so with the Secretary, briefing him in detail, the Minister called me in for only a few minutes for a couple of points of clarification. This relatively easy time I had with the Minister is in stark contrast to developments subsequently in the 1980s, when briefing Ministers required two or even three briefing sessions extending over several hours.

Around mid-1974, I was sounded out for a move to Bhutan as First Secretary, where a vacancy had just arisen and a hunt for an officer was underway. Having returned to India after serving in a C station, I thought this was unfair, as Bhutan, too, was a C station. Accordingly, I resisted the move and, perhaps, only succeeded as a batchmate and friend, K.V. Rajan, was in the Foreign Secretary's office. He was also kind enough to tip me off that a First Secretary's post was falling vacant in the economic wing of the Indian embassy in Washington, and if the DEA agreed, it should be possible to post me there. Impelled by this input, I contacted the officer in the DEA dealing with Administration, who happened to be Mr W.S. Tambe, a former boss. He was quite upfront and indicated that if there was any IAS officer in the DEA who wanted this job, he would have a preference over me, but that I would be the preferred choice if anyone from outside the Department made a bid for the same. As events panned out, there were two IAS officers in the DEA who were possible candidates for this job, but both were accommodated in what they considered were better assignments in Washington, notably in the World Bank and the International Monetary Fund (IMF). In these circumstances, when the MEA made a bid for this post and submitted my name as its candidate, the DEA acceded to the request. Here again, my posting was something of an accident, as it was attributable to my posting earlier to the DEA, which had, perhaps, happened because others had turned it down.

5

A RARE SPELL OF UNDEREMPLOYMENT: WASHINGTON

My wife and I reached Washington DC in October 1974 after a brief holiday in London. On arrival, we were lodged in the Jockey Club, a hotel located just opposite the Embassy. It took us nearly three months to find a suitable house. I was amongst the first of a bunch of Indian diplomats to settle on an independent house in McLean, Virginia, around 12 kilometres away from the Embassy. The existing practice had been to locate either in Washington DC or Maryland, much closer to the Embassy. I took a contrarian position, as houses in Virginia were newer and more spacious than those available within our allowance closer to the Embassy. With the passage of time, an increasing number of our diplomats opted for houses in Virginia. This was helpful, as it enabled us to organize car pools amongst ourselves for the to-and-fro commutes to the Embassy.

The Washington embassy was gigantic and dwarfed most other Indian missions both in terms of sheer numbers and the seniority level of the officers. The Ambassador was usually at the very least a secretary-level officer, if not a political appointee close to the Prime Minister, and there were around four Senior Joint Secretary-level officers, notably Minister (Political), Minister (Economic), Minister (Education) and Minister (Commerce and Supply). The latter was Mr J.N. Dixit, with whom I had served earlier in Vienna. Additionally, there were a gaggle of Counsellors and First Secretaries.

During my four-year tenure in Washington, there was a fairly rapid turnover at the senior-most levels. Thus, I saw three Ambassadors, notably T.N. Kaul, Nani Palkhivala and Kewal Singh; three ministers political, notably Eric Gonsalves, A.P. Venkateswaran and A.B. Gokhale; and three Ministers (Economic), notably G.V. Ramakrishna, J.S. Baijal and R.K. Misra. Ambassador T.N. Kaul, who served in Washington DC from 1973 to 1976, was clearly the most dynamic and colourful of the three Ambassadors. He had a fairly turbulent innings in the US, not just because he was a known sympathizer of the Soviet Union but also because India–US relations in the aftermath of the 1971 India–Pakistan conflict were near rock bottom. Notwithstanding the US write-off of about $2.2 billion worth of P.L. 480 dues while retaining $1.1 billion for US uses in February 1974, there was no upturn in the relationship due to our peaceful nuclear explosion in May 1974, the US lifting of the US arms embargo on Pakistan in February 1975 and, finally, our declaration of the Emergency in June 1975, which did not go down well with most Americans.[7] Though by no means blind to the downside of the declaration of the Emergency, T.N. Kaul handled a difficult situation very well. He made it clear to those in the mission that while we were free to have our own views on the matter, he would expect us to defend the move in public, and those not prepared to do so should put in their papers. In dealing with the US media on the Emergency, he was brilliant and took on the toughest television anchors on this issue, like Barbara Walters, with aplomb and more than held his own. At the same time, he minced no words with dignitaries from India in making it clear that the international community was looking askance at this move and it was imperative to restore normalcy in India at the earliest.

The other plus side of Ambassador Kaul was that he did not live in an ivory tower and made a conscious effort to interact with junior officers like myself. Accordingly, he took time out to attend our parties, with a view to assessing how we were performing our representational functions and, more importantly, took officers from each wing in the mission on a rotational basis on his tours within and outside the country. Accordingly, I accompanied him on a tour

[7]Kux, Dennis, 'India and the United States: Estranged Democracies', National Defense University Press, Washington DC, June 1993.

to the Bahamas and a couple of tours to some of the states in the Washington DC neighbourhood. Through this process, all the officers in the mission had a connect with the Ambassador, who, in turn, could form an objective opinion on them.

On the negative side, the Ambassador made no effort to discourage differences amongst some of the senior officers, which promoted the stovepiping of information—the bane of all bureaucracies. Being an IFS officer, reporting to the Minister (Economic), an IAS officer, I got the feeling that I was, initially, an object of some suspicion both with him and with the Minister (Political), who belonged to the IFS. The former, perhaps, felt that my service loyalties may prevail over my professional loyalties, and the latter that I may be prone to snooping for my immediate boss. These doubts and suspicions, however, gradually diminished once it became evident that all my reportage would go to my immediate boss but that relevant elements of it would be copied to those who could benefit therefrom. Indeed, over the months, the political and commerce wings would often request me to obtain inputs for them from my contacts on the Hill, which I had developed to keep a track of the hearings on economic issues.

The economic wing was fairly small, and apart from the Minister (Economic) and myself, there was only a Research Officer, an Attaché Economic and some clerical staff. This was only appropriate, as following the 1971 conflict, India–US relations were not exactly warm, there was virtually no US economic assistance to India barring some food aid, and bilateral interaction was relatively limited. The economic wing's role was, thus, mainly to monitor economic developments in the US, to service economic delegations that visited the country, and to liaise with our executive directors in the IMF and in the World Bank. The latter was done directly by the Minister (Economic), and I had no role in the matter.

I was initially left pretty much to my own devices and had a very light workload. Accordingly, I took it upon myself to visit the US Congress from time to time and listen to the innumerable hearings, some of which had a bearing on India. In the process, I cultivated friendships with some of the US Congressional staff, most of whom were relatively young and about my age. They were good sources of information, and some were influential. As a result of these contacts, I got useful inputs and, occasionally, had the opportunity to influence, in a small way, US legislation in the making. For instance, Senator Hubert Humphrey's aide, whom I got to know fairly well, readily shared with me the draft text of the new P.L. 480 legislation being contemplated. This was used by us to feed in our ideas about the changes that could be considered.

Contacts on the Hill were also useful in providing insights about why particular US legislators behaved in the manner they did and how we could promote our national interests. For instance, Congressman Clarence D. Long's viscerally anti-Indian posture had long perplexed me. This was hurtful to India, as he was a very influential member of the House Appropriation Committee and chaired its Foreign Operations Subcommittee. I, therefore, assiduously cultivated a friendship with one of his aides who, over a small dinner at his residence, bluntly told me that it was futile to try and get the Congressman to change his attitude towards India. According to him, the Congressman, initially, had no bias against India, but the same developed because he felt that he had been maltreated by Indian Customs during one of his visits to the country. In these circumstances, he suggested that instead of trying to influence Congressman Long, we should focus our attention on some other Congressmen who could be lobbied to counter the adverse legislation being developed on the Hill against India. In order to facilitate our efforts in this direction, he gave me a list of the Congressmen we could work upon. Such openness made working in the US easier than in many other countries and a rewarding experience if one learnt to press the right buttons.

Since the US is a government by lobby, India, like many other countries, had hired a lobbyist to influence opinion on the Hill. However, instead of employing a proven professional US outfit, this assignment had, for decades, been in the hands of a Kashmiri Pandit who had retired as press counsellor in the Indian Embassy in Washington in the 1960s. While he was extremely personable, had good contacts and many Congressmen readily came to his dinners, which were culinary treats personally conjured up by himself, his ability to decisively swing opinion in India's favour was questionable.

This is borne out by the fact that we have usually been in the doghouse in the US, and it is only recently that things have started to change on account of our emergence as an influential economic power. I feel that we would have been better served had we been more professional and employed a tried-and-tested lobbyist for our influence operations on the Hill as done by many other countries. This would, admittedly, have been much more expensive, as our Kashmiri lobbyist was being paid a pittance, but, clearly, we were guilty of being penny-wise and pound-foolish.

Dealings with the US State Department were limited, and though one had interacted with Dennis Kux, the Director dealing with India, they were, in the main, confined to my counterpart, Jay Grahame, who was somewhat laid-back but not particularly helpful. A far more friendly official was Julius Coles, my counterpart in the United States Agency for International Development (USAID). As an institution, the State Department did not inspire much respect. In this context, two episodes come to mind. On one occasion, the minutes of a meeting following delegation-level talks serviced by Jay Grahame and myself had to be typed out in my office in the Embassy, as the meeting lasted well into the evening and the secretarial staff at the State Department would not stay on beyond 5.30 p.m. This would have been unthinkable in India. On another occasion, during delegation-level talks led on our side by the then Fertilizer Secretary, Praxy Fernandes, the common courtesy of serving tea or coffee, which is standard practice, was not observed and instead a short break was taken at which this was available on payment through a dispenser.

An area which fell within the purview of the economic wing was the work relating to the Washington-based Committee on Surplus Disposal (CSD), which was a subcommittee of the Committee on Commodity Problems of the UN Food and Agricultural Organization (FAO). Its role was to monitor international shipments of agricultural commodities provided as food aid in order to minimize any adverse effects of these shipments on commercial trade and agricultural production. Each donor was required to keep the Committee informed of the assistance being shipped out by it. If any country had any objection, it was required to make known its concerns. Throughout the four years that I dealt with these issues, there were no serious problems, and the work of the CSD proceeded smoothly. I was left to pretty much handle this work on my own and to directly deal with our Ministry of Agriculture on all issues relating to it. During my stint in Washington DC, I was elected Chairman of this Committee, and in that capacity, visited Rome to present the Committee's annual report to the FAO.

Dealings with agriculture-related matters in the CSD inevitably led to my developing links with a host of agricultural attachés from a number of countries as well as officials from the US Department of Agriculture (USDA). In the process, I obtained invaluable insights into the US agricultural system. For instance, I learnt that while on the one hand, the US was critical of the agricultural subsidies provided by the developing countries, on the other hand, it, too, was no less guilty in this regard, even going so far as to pay its farmers to not grow anything and keeping their lands fallow!

The US representative to the CSD, Mr Doering, who was probably in his late 50s and was from the USDA, was something of an institution not only for his encyclopaedic knowledge on agriculture-related issues but also because he was a connoisseur of wines. Indeed, all members of the CSD periodically received from him a cyclostyled manual authored by him listing the wines available in various neighbourhood stores meticulously graded on a value-for-money basis. This was an eagerly anticipated publication not only by impecunious diplomats like me but also by those who were looking for genuinely good wines. I, however, only got the full measure of Doering's virtuosity on wine-related issues when he invited me to a wine-tasting function organized by him on a Sunday evening in Washington DC. He was, apparently, a part of a 12-member group that indulged in this exercise once each month, with the host serving a dozen different wines—six white and six red—as well as the bread and cheese to go with each of them. Far from being a drinking binge, as I had imagined, the wine-tasting exercise was an extremely business-like event lasting barely a couple of hours. The process involved each member being served the equivalent of a few sips of wine and asked to write down his assessment of it on several parameters, including point of origin, aroma, body, taste, appearance, etc. Thereafter, the host would enlighten the others of the precise details of the wine, inter alia, its provenance, price, where purchased, etc., and then engage in an animated discussion on the observations made by the participants. The wines served ranged from countries like Australia, Germany, France, Switzerland, South Africa, Chile and, of course, the US. But surprise, surprise, none of the red wines were from France, touted as the home of red wine, and none of the whites were from Germany, which is renowned for the same.

Given the fact that India–US ties lacked much substance, there were very few Indian official delegations to Washington DC, particularly on the economic side. The bulk of the visitations we received on the economic side were those related to dealings connected with the World Bank and the IMF, and involved in the main the Finance Minister and the Secretary, DEA. These visits were handled by the Minister (Economic) and by our executive directors in the World Bank and the IMF. Given the lukewarm nature of India–US ties, even getting a bilateral meeting for our Finance Minister with the Treasury Secretary was an uphill task. I recall an occasion when our efforts for such a meeting were fobbed off with the response that there was no need for it, as the two would be on the same table next to each other at one or another of the official luncheons being hosted by the World Bank or the IMF.

Though the purely bilateral economic work was limited, I had some interesting exposure to the world of industry and business during visits of the CEOs of some of our leading enterprises. An unforgettable experience in this regard was a one-week attachment to Mr N.B. Prasad, the Oil and Natural Gas Corporation (ONGC) chairman, during his visit to Houston for the annual World Energy Fair in May 1975 for purchase of drilling equipment. Having located oil at Bombay High, the ONGC was keen to operationalize it at the earliest and was in the process of effectuating purchases of the entire gamut of materials and equipment it required for this purpose. At Houston, Mr Prasad was engaged in meetings with diverse suppliers from early morning to late at night and, in the process, one learnt a lot about the oil industry. It was also gratifying to note the high esteem in which he and his small technical team were held by all the suppliers.

I came away from Houston with a much better knowledge about the oil and gas business, and a sense of confidence in our engineers and negotiators, who clearly were thoroughgoing professionals and went about their work with a great sense of dedication.

One of Ambassador Kaul's laudable initiatives was the development of a directory of Indian scientists in the US with the object of establishing contact with them and incentivizing them to enrich India with their expertise. This exercise was spearheaded by Dr Inam Rahman, Minister (Education), and Dr Ananda Krishna, Counsellor (Science). Indeed, a couple of interactions were organized at the Embassy with US-based Indian scientists and a scheme was evolved, under which, the latter would interact with select Indian scientific institutions for this purpose on a no-cost, no-loss basis while on holiday in India. It is unfortunate that this commendable exercise never really took off and somehow lost traction.

Whilst in the US, one had the occasion to visit some of the local universities on lecture tours, notably in Illinois, Ohio and Virginia. I was surprised to note the insularity of Americans and, in particular, their lack of knowledge about India. However, I could not but be impressed with the academic and extracurricular facilities accorded by these universities to their student community. Even common run-of-the-mill state universities far outstripped the best of Indian educational institutions in this regard. This explains why the US has always been an economic and technological powerhouse.

The visit of Prime Minister Morarji Desai to Washington DC in mid-1978 was unquestionably the most important event in India–US relations during my stint in the US. This was mainly handled by the political wing in the Embassy, with some of us chipping in with some liaison duties. Unfortunately, the visit did not result in any marked uptick in relations, and one gets the feeling that we missed a trick by not using it to our advantage. It was, of course, marred somewhat by the Prime Minister dwelling at length in his media interactions on the merits of urine therapy, which earned us much negative publicity. I was also amazed to note the Prime Minister's somewhat bizarre dietary requirements of the which, apart from an assortment of nuts, fresh fruits and paneer also included fresh cow milk!

Around May 1977, five months before my three-year term in Washington DC came to an end, I suddenly received orders from the MEA to immediately move to Bhutan on transfer. I informed the Ministry that I would be happy to proceed to Bhutan as instructed, but that I would do so only in October, as my wife was in the family way, and the delivery was scheduled for end July 1977. My boss was upset both at the Ministry's orders, which had been issued without any consultation with the DEA, and at my having accepted them without my apprising him of the same. Accordingly, he sent an angry letter to the Ministry asserting that any orders pertaining to me should be issued only after consultation with the DEA, as I was on deputation on the latter's post. In these circumstances, my move to Bhutan was cancelled by the Ministry, which reverted stating that I should have kept it informed that my wife was in the family way! My next posting orders came around a year later in mid-1998, asking me to move to Algiers as Counsellor. This missive came shortly after the arrival of my boss's successor. The latter, being new, was reluctant to see me go and urged me to allow him to intercede on my behalf for another year's extension. I, however, prevailed upon him not to take any such action, pointing out that I was an IFS officer and any such intervention was likely to be held against me by the MEA.

6

MY NORTH AFRICAN SAFARI: ALGIERS

Colonized by France in the 1830s, Algeria attained independence in 1962. This was only after a bitter and bloody eight-year-long struggle marked by extreme brutalities on both sides, in which Algeria lost around 1 million people, or a tenth of its population. Almost every family in the country suffered at least one casualty. The suffering and struggle that Algerians underwent to achieve freedom from colonial rule bred a fierce nationalism amongst them, which manifested itself in many different ways. First and foremost, it led to a clear Algerian-first attitude vis-à-vis foreigners, which meant that in the event of a dispute between an Algerian and a foreigner, it was presupposed that the former was in the right. Second, great attention was paid to the well-being of those who had suffered in the liberation struggle, which led to the State not only providing them free medical treatment but also compensating them through suitable employment. Finally, it created a sense of equality amongst the citizenry and the barriers that normally prevail between, for instance, the leader of a delegation and his chauffeur ceased to exist. Thus, it was not unusual for an Algerian secretary-level officer while taking his foreign counterpart through the country to ask his chauffeur to join him at the table for a meal. This never ceased to perplex Indian officials who visited Algeria!

From its independence till the late 1980s, Algeria was under the single-party rule of the National Liberation Front (NLF) and its armed wing, the Algerian National Army, which had spearheaded the liberation struggle. Indeed, from July 1965 till his death in December 1978, Colonel Houari Boumediene, a veteran of the liberation struggle and the Army chief, was the head of government. He ruled with an iron hand. None dared oppose him. The country was virtually a police state, and anyone, no matter how high-ranking, could become a non-person at the drop of a hat if he ran afoul of him. This is precisely what happened to Ahmed Ben Bella, a leading member of the NLF and the first President of the country, who was ousted in a bloodless putsch by Boumediene in 1965. Ben Bella remained under house arrest till 1979, and few even knew where he was being kept. In fact, one of our Ambassadors in Algeria was shot at and injured in the 1970s when he inadvertently strayed into a property on the outskirts of Algiers near Blida, where it is suspected that Ben Bella was being held.

The diplomatic community had a tough time in Boumediene's Algeria, as neither he nor his foreign minister, Abdelaziz Bouteflika, were easily accessible. Appointments sought with senior officials took inordinately long to materialize. Indeed, it took almost one year for a Pakistani Ambassador to present his credentials, as ceremonies for the same were fixed at short notice and after inordinately long intervals. Accordingly, each time a date for a credentials ceremony was fixed, the Ambassador happened to be out of station for one reason or another, and so it took him around a year to present his credentials.

An upside of living in a virtual police state was that the law and order situation was excellent. All and sundry were scared of the police. One could, thus, walk out in Algiers late at night without fear of being accosted by anti-social elements.

Stern of demeanour and reclusive, Boumediene was a staunch nationalist who sought to develop the country through socialist policies. Accordingly, he nationalized the oil industry and entrusted industrialization to state enterprises, much akin to what was done by Nehru in India. It is no surprise, therefore, that economic development in Algeria, as in India, was marked by low growth, corruption, bureaucratic sloth and inefficiency. Algeria could easily have grown much faster if it had focussed more on tourism rather than on industrialization, given its varied scenic wonders, ranging from splendid beaches, a beautiful corniche coastline, innumerable Roman ruins, the majestic Atlas Mountains and, of course, the exotic Sahara Desert. This would, of course, have required an efficient service sector devoid of state control—an impossibility in a socialist state. Under the existing dispensation, even a meal at the most prominent five-star hotel in Algiers, the Aurassi, was a nightmare, as service was painfully slow, with the staff quite disinterested in attending to its clients.

Boumediene was highly supportive of the Non-Aligned Movement (NAM) and of liberation struggles the world over. This was only natural, as during its liberation struggle, Algeria was the beneficiary of fulsome support and sustenance from NAM.

At the time of my arrival in Algiers, Boumediene was in a coma, and a few weeks later, in December 1978, was declared dead. He was succeeded by Colonel Chadli Bendjedid after a short power struggle and an interim government. Amongst those in the running for the Presidency were Bouteflika, the foreign minister, who had been very close to Boumediene. Chadli ultimately prevailed. In hindsight, this was, perhaps, inevitable, as he was the senior-most Army leader, and it was the latter who called the shots, albeit through the NLF. While Chadli was a far mellower personality than Boumediene, he did not dispense with the latter's dictatorial style of governance and of one-party rule. There was also virtually no change in the political and economic policies of the government apart from a slightly softer approach to dissent.

◆

The Indian Embassy in Algiers was one of our smaller missions with just two senior officers apart from myself, notably the Ambassador, Mr K.K.S. Rana, who was five years senior to me, and first secretary commercial, Mr R.K. Kapur, whom I knew well from my days in the Pakistan Division. Additionally, there was an interpreter and an attaché (administration) as well as some clerical staff.

On arrival in Algiers, my wife and myself along with our two small children were put up in a hotel, which went by the rather expansive name of Djamila Palace. I have rarely seen a shabbier or more run-down hotel, and to this day, I have not been able to fathom why the Embassy lodged us there, given that there were better hotels available. When I voiced my unhappiness about this, I was informed that Djamila Palace was the preferred option on account of its proximity to the Embassy. The wretched nature of the lodging was brought out by the fact that the bedsheets were full of holes and the steel-webbed beds were in the nature of cots twice the height of a normal bed. The fact that the beds were a bit of a health hazard was demonstrated on the very first night when one of our children toppled out of it on to the floor but luckily escaped without any serious injury.

On my predecessor's departure, we were located in the flat occupied by him, which was on the second floor of an apartment complex just one floor below the Indian Embassy on Rue Didouche Mourad. This was a boon, as it meant no commuting to office and I could go to office at all hours to attend to any urgent work. It, of course, had its downside as well, as my wife learnt soon enough when an expat showed up at our door and, on being told that the Embassy was located on the next floor, asked her to lug his suitcases above!

One of the first tasks assigned to me was to seek an exemption from a newly introduced regulation by the Algerian Foreign Ministry that all embassy officials on transfer out of the country must hand over the keys of the apartments leased by them from the government to the latter and that their successors must find new lodgings. Since there was a huge housing shortage in Algiers and since we had taken on most of our apartments from the government, we were seriously affected by this regulation and I, in particular, was most vulnerable.

While the task given to me was daunting, it was made even more difficult when the Ambassador told me that he would not make the services of our French interpreter available to me, as I was supposed to be a French-speaking officer. My pleas of having learnt the language in a German-speaking country and never having had the occasion to speak it since fell on deaf ears. Indeed, throughout my stay in Algiers, I had to make do on my own without the help of the interpreter as long as Ambassador Rana was in station.

In the event, I somehow succeeded in persuading the director dealing with this issue in the Algerian Foreign Office to desist from applying their new regulations to the Indian Embassy and allow us to continue to retain the accommodation provided to us. All the arguments possible were adduced to buttress our case, notably the close bilateral relationship, Third World solidarity, the hardship that this would cause, etc., but I have a feeling that more than these arguments, the official concerned was impelled to take a sympathetic stance on account of my heroic efforts at expressing myself in a language with which I was clearly not at ease. My scrappy French clearly saved the day for me far more than my arguments!

◆

My Algiers posting was, perhaps, the most uncomfortable in my career both on account of the living conditions and the work environment. Though categorised as a 'B' station it was much more difficult than all the three 'C' stations I served in.

The living conditions were trying, as we had to make do with a small, crummy and poorly furnished three-bedroom apartment equipped with rudimentary gas heaters, and cope with shortages of even basic items of daily use, ranging from toilet paper to butter. Accordingly, on occasion, we had to scour the market for even simple daily necessities, and when these became available, we tended to buy inordinately large quantities to safeguard ourselves from future shortages. Social contact was limited, as the locals were chary of interacting with foreigners, and the diplomatic community was tiny. In these circumstances, I was driven to socialization with colleagues in the Embassy and with the very small Indian community in the city. There was also little by way of entertainment in the immediate vicinity of Algiers apart from the beaches, which, though lovely, lacked infrastructural support.

Algeria was something of a purgatory for those who happened to be strict vegetarians, as the concept of vegetarianism was alien to the country and, perhaps, to much of the Arab world at the time. This was brought home to me when whilst accompanying an Indian cultural delegation through Algeria, in response to my remonstrations for not providing vegetarian fare despite our specific request for the same, our hosts reacted that they had taken note of it and had, accordingly, taken care not to serve beef or mutton, which had been substituted with fish and eggs! Luckily, my family and I faced no problem, as we were not vegetarians and also rather fancied the Algerian meat-rich cuisine, which had a Mediterranean touch and also included baguettes and cheese, which were something of a staple. As a bonus, strong locally produced red wine and beer were freely available. Indeed, substantial quantities of the former were exported, including to France. It would not be out of place to mention here that Algeria also boasted of excellent watermelons, figs and dates.

The observance of Ramzan in Algeria stood out in marked contrast to that in the subcontinent. While in the latter it is observed with great solemnity and with people going about their work more or less as normal, in the former, it is a fun time and all official work comes to a near standstill. Indeed, weeks in advance of Ramzan, the Foreign Office made it a point to inform all concerned that it would not receive any foreign delegations in the country during that period. All activity in Algiers would come to a near halt in the day time. However, at night, the city would spring to life, and the usually dour Algerians would engage in much merrymaking and revelry, the likes of which was rarely seen through the rest of the year!

◆

The work environment left much to be desired, as interaction with officialdom and the business community was at the best of times difficult due to the dictatorial nature of the regime and the opacity of the system. The diplomatic community could not be relied upon either for much, as it was also confronted with the same systemic difficulties and was very small. Indian diplomats were further handicapped by the fact that English was hardly spoken and all business was undertaken either in Arabic or French.

On the plus side, India–Algeria ties were excellent not just because of the absence of any bilateral political differences but also because of their ideological affinity arising from the fervent commitment of both to nonalignment and to socialist policies. Additionally, Algerian polity at that time was informed essentially by a secular outlook and not overly influenced by the Islamic factor. Indeed, a member of an Iranian delegation that visited the country shortly after the Iranian Revolution rather disdainfully referred to Algerians as Frenchified Muslims. Moreover, our movies had an enormous impact in terms of generating much goodwill for India at a people-to-people level. Accordingly, in a closed and somewhat xenophobic country, India was viewed much more favourably than most other countries and certainly those from the West. All of us in the Indian Embassy were beneficiaries of this. Thus, while colleagues from western missions were often fined for even minor traffic infractions, those from the Indian Embassy got off with just a mild verbal reprimand!

My workload in Algiers was extremely heavy, as I was dealing with all aspects of the mission's work: political, economic, consular, administrative and even ciphers in the absence of the cipher assistant. Additionally, for the first year, 1 had to work in the evenings for an hour or so to brush up on my rather rusty French. The fact that Ambassador Rana was a perfectionist did not help, as it tended to generate tensions in the mission which I had to help mitigate. This is a role I also had to play in my next assignment in Dhaka.

My relationship with Ambassador Rana was excellent. I admired his professionalism. He had assiduously developed good contacts with a range of Algerian ministers and senior bureaucrats, and used even chance meetings with them to push India's agenda. This was essential, as requests for meetings with officialdom often took time to materialize. Ambassador Rana's success lay in the fact that he was fully au fait with all aspects of the issues he raised. Pontificating on this, he explained to me that most knew the broad outlines of an issue they were addressing but only those who knew its fine details were best placed to attain their ends. Behind his harsh exterior, Ambassador Rana was helpful, well-intentioned and looked out after the interests of those who worked with him.

◆

The main endeavour of the Embassy under Ambassador Rana was to leverage our friendly relationship to maximize our economic and commercial ties. The latter were rather insubstantial up to the early 1970s, partly on account of the language barrier and partly because no serious effort had been made by both countries to cultivate this aspect of the relationship. As a result of the Ambassador's indefatigable efforts, India, by the early 1980s, was involved in as many as 26 projects in Algeria, and there were hundreds of Indian experts in the country, particularly in the fields of geology and medicine.

Several of the projects undertaken by us were in the hydrocarbon sector, mostly executed by Engineers India Limited. But there were also others for manufacture of blankets, production of water and gas meters, power generation, maintenance of buses, etc. The most impressive, however, was the construction of a rail track by IRCON, completed sometime after my departure, in very difficult mountainous terrain. As the Algerian authorities became familiar with Indian public sector companies, they consciously sought them out for additional contracts because of the Indian work ethic, which had a strong underpinning of altruism and was not based only upon purely commercial considerations as was the case of companies from most other countries. In fact, as one Algerian official put it, while western companies had no hesitation in billing the country for any piece of technical advice provided over and above that stipulated in the contract, Indian companies often provided such services free of charge simply as a matter of goodwill.

At one stage, over one-third of Algeria's health services were manned by Indian doctors who could be found in all parts of the country, including in small isolated and inhospitable desert outposts even in the deep south, where few locals were prepared to serve. The valuable contribution of the Indian doctors to medical services in Algeria was readily acknowledged by its health minister, who asserted that their dedication was worthy of emulation, as they were willingly working in the most difficult parts of the country and attending to the sick with great efficacy. We, at the Embassy, were also fortunate in having Dr Venga, a most competent and kind-hearted Indian lady doctor in Algiers, who was always at hand to attend to our medical requirements. She was a godsend, as medical assistance in Algiers did not inspire much confidence and was suboptimal.

◆

During my assignment in Algeria, there were many notable visits, including those of Foreign Secretary Jagat Mehta, Foreign Minister Atal Bihari Vajpayee, the Petroleum Secretary, the Prime Minister's special envoy Mr Mohamed Younus and, of course, the top managers of several companies that either had ongoing projects in

Algeria or were exploring new opportunities.

The most memorable of these visits was that of Foreign Minister Vajpayee sometime in 1979. One could not but be struck by his oratory of which one had a glimpse in his address to the Indian community during which he struck an instant rapport with them and won them over completely. However, in one-to-one exchanges, there was not the same charisma and sparkle, particularly with our Algerian hosts. In fact, in the over-one-hour meeting with the Algerian foreign minister, Mohamed Seddik Ben Yahia, it was the latter who dazzled with his fascinating and cerebral 40-minute overview of the prevailing international situation and the relevance of NAM. Mr Vajpayee could not engage on the same intellectual plane, and clearly, his grip on international affairs was not of the same order as that of his counterpart.

In terms of visits of business delegations, many came, and there were successes and failures. A bittersweet memory pertains to the visit of one of the senior-most executives of a public sector enterprise for supply of hosiery items to the Algerian Army. The visit was the product of relentless efforts by the Embassy to induce an Algerian Army delegation to visit India to source its supplies from India. The visit was well-organized, and the delegation was impressed with what it had seen. As a result, the Algerian Army invited the concerned Indian public sector company to Algiers for finalizing a contract for supply of its entire annual hosiery requirements. The nuts and bolts of the contract were tied up at a dinner at my apartment. This was no mean achievement, as the Algerian Army, in concluding the same, was departing from its normal practice of awarding contracts through tenders. Tragically, however, the Indian public sector enterprise dropped out of the contract at the last minute, as it felt that the scope of the order was too large and that it would not be able to fulfil it! Ultimately, it settled for an order only 25 per cent of the value of the order that it could have bagged, and that too after participation in a long-drawn-out tender process extending over a year. Clearly, the Indian business community of the time, particularly in the public sector, lacked the dynamism for optimal progress.

◆

One of my lasting regrets is that I did not travel as much as I should have in Algeria, which, about 70 per cent the size of India, has enormous variety and offers much to see. Apart from same-day excursions to the nearby beaches at Club de Pins and Boumerdes, the Roman ruins at Tipaza, and the hill resort of Chrea—60 kilometres from Algiers—I undertook only two or three major car journeys in Algeria. The most remarkable of these was to the Sahara. Much careful planning and preparation went into the exercise, as we had three small children, and for long stretches of the journey, there were no repair facilities, petrol stations or habitation. One had heard stories of people being stranded in the Sahara for hours on end due to blinding sandstorms, which acting like sandpaper caused massive damage to car paintwork as well as car engines if these were not switched off. We were, however, heartened by the fact that in even the smallest town through our journey there was an Indian presence by way of doctors from Andhra Pradesh who were working through the length and breadth of the country. We had also ensured that we had two cars, our own and that of Mr R.K. Kapur, who accompanied us along with his wife and teenaged daughter.

The scenery from Algiers to Ouargla, the furthest point south in our journey and a distance of about 760 kilometres, was ever-changing. The initial part of our journey was through hilly terrain, as it entailed crossing the Atlas Mountains and soon thereafter, we entered the rocky desert, which later assumed a reddish hue. It was not till we were in the vicinity of Ghardaia, around 600 kilometres from Algiers that we hit the sandy desert. The full majesty of this was, however, on view from Ghardaia to Ouargla. The sand dunes were massive—30 to 40 feet high. From Ouargla, we turned northwards and headed to Touggourt. It was in this section of the journey that we were caught in a sandstorm and had to drive with utmost care at slow speed, as parts of the road were covered with sand. I was aware that should we get off road, we would be stuck in the sand. The sandstorm was, fortunately, relatively mild, and we reached Touggourt without any mishap. Thereafter, we drove further north to Constantine and then eastwards to Algiers along the magnificent corniche coastline. This motoring expedition was made all the more pleasurable since the roads, which had been built by the French, were in excellent condition and conducive to smooth high-speed travel.

◆

Ambassador Rana left Algiers in late 1979, and I was chargé d'affaires for about six months till the arrival of his successor in April 1980. The latter was a complex personality, and working with him was not easy. Though very intelligent, he was inordinately cynical. He was also seriously afflicted by the successor-predecessor syndrome, as a result of which he did not bother to study the very thorough handing-over notes painstakingly prepared by his predecessor. These addressed both work-related issues as well as those pertaining to the Residence. Noting that my pleas that these notes be carefully perused were falling on deaf ears, I frankly told the Ambassador that while I would be able to brief him adequately on all official matters, I would not be in a position to do so on the fine details pertaining to the Residence, for which he would have to rely upon his predecessor's meticulous notes. He, however, did not do so. Consequently, he was not fully au fait with the various problems relating to the Residence, and a few weeks after his arrival, it was the scene of an easily avoidable gas explosion in which his wife suffered serious burn injuries, for which she had to undergo prolonged and painful treatment extending over several months. Fortunately, Dr Venga was on hand to shepherd her through her medical treatment, but I was sorry for the terrible ordeal that she had to go through.

The new Ambassador had a dictatorial bent of mind, which led to a souring of our relationship. The casus belli of our falling out was his insistence that I change the assessment in my report on an internal development in Algeria. As he was unable to convince me about the logic for the proposed change, I told him that I would not comply with his bidding, but that he was free to either suppress my report or send it to the Ministry with a covering note stating that he disagreed with my assessment and projecting his own viewpoint in the matter. At this, the Ambassador threatened to spoil my annual confidential report in case I did not comply with his bidding. I responded that he was at liberty to do as he pleased, but that I would not be browbeaten into changing my considered assessment.

As a result of my deteriorating relations with the Ambassador, I made known to the Ministry, whilst on leave in Delhi, that it would be in the interests of all concerned if I was transferred to Headquarters. Since I had already been out of the country for over six years, this was not an unreasonable request. I was assured by Mr S.K. Singh, the Additional Secretary (Administration), that there would be no problem and the needful would be done. Once again, however, the Ministry did not fail to surprise. Just as I was planning a holiday with my family to neighbouring Morocco for the summer, I was telephonically advised to leave for Dhaka immediately, where I had been posted as Deputy High Commissioner. I received this intimation with mixed feelings because, while on the one hand, my new assignment was an extremely important one, on the other hand, I would be working under a High Commissioner who was known to be a notoriously hard taskmaster.

7

IN AMAR SHONAR BANGLA: DHAKA

Flying into Bangladesh, I could not but be struck by its topography, which is characterized by miles and miles of totally flat terrain, lush with green vegetation and criss-crossed with innumerable rivers. The latter are, in fact, the lifeblood of the country, providing it with irrigation, an important means of transportation and freshwater fish, which constitutes a valuable source of food supply. As a north Indian, it was a revelation to note the critical role of rivers in Bangladesh's transportation system for moving both passengers and freight. Travel within Bangladesh inevitably required river crossings either by bridge or by ferry. For instance, road travel from Dhaka to Calcutta required at least two major ferry crossings. One of the ferry crossings, notably at the junction of the Padma and the Brahmaputra, was quite time consuming, as the river's expanse was such that the disembarkation point was not visible from the point of embarkation. The sense that one was at sea and not on a river was generated not just by the sheer expanse of water but also by the considerable wave action.

Whilst in Bangladesh, apart from my road journey to Calcutta at the end of my posting, I also motored to North Dinajpur, Chittagong and Comilla. The roads were in the main poorly maintained single-lane highways, akin to what existed in India in the 1950s. The country also presented a sad picture of poverty and underdevelopment.

◆

During my Bangladesh posting from 1981 to 1984, India–Bangladesh ties were strained. Abdus Sattar, who belonged to the Bangladesh National Party (BNP), was the President when I arrived in Dhaka. He was ousted in a putsch in early 1982 by the Army Chief, General

Hussain Muhammad Ershad, who took control as Chief Martial Law Administrator and subsequently assumed the office of President. Unlike his predecessor General Ziaur Rahman, Ershad was not a freedom fighter and was amongst the group of generals and officials who were interned in Pakistan in the 1971 conflict and who only made their way back to Bangladesh well after the freedom struggle. Like many of them, Ershad, too, had no deep ideological commitment to Bangladesh per se and was an opportunist who, though an alumnus of the National Defence College in New Delhi, aligned himself with reactionary anti-Indian and Islamist elements to keep himself in power. The resulting India–Bangladesh tensions naturally adversely impacted the functioning of the Indian diplomatic community in the country. Indeed, Bangladesh's relations with Pakistan, which had committed untold atrocities during the 1971 liberation struggle, were far better than with India, which had paid with the blood of its soldiers for the creation of the country. Bangladesh's negativity towards India was graphically reflected in the fact that its newspapers made it a point to refrain from even making a mention of the latter's role in the former's independence struggle. This is something that I was never able to come to terms with. The only rationale for it is, perhaps, that there were far too many Bangladeshis who had imbibed a Pakistani mindset.

Access to Ershad was available to the High Commission relatively easily, both through the High Commissioner and General Mazumdar, our Defence Attaché, who occasionally played golf with him. Notwithstanding his anti-Indian posture, Ershad was very personable. I had, on a few occasions, crossed fairways with him on the golf course, and he never hesitated to greet me. But the one occasion on which he went out of his way to interact with me was at a dinner hosted by him at his residence for a delegation led by Secretary Eric Gonsalves. Since his drawing room was small and could not accommodate all the invitees, the two junior-most officials from the two delegations, notably myself and the Bangladesh Additional Foreign Secretary, were seated in an adjacent anteroom. Half an hour later, I was pleasantly surprised to see General Ershad coming into the anteroom and sitting down next to me. He chatted with me for a good 10 minutes. Clearly, this example of good etiquette is attributable to the subcontinent's military traditions, which was also very evident in my dealings with the Pakistan military.

The uneasy India–Bangladesh relations at the time may partially be attributed to the many problems that beset them arising from disputed land and maritime boundaries, issues of water sharing with as many as 54 rivers flowing into Bangladesh from India, illicit migration of millions of Bangladeshis into India, policing the porous 4,096-kilometre land border, with areas in adverse possession and of enclaves within each other's territories, etc. In these circumstances, every now and then, there were border firing incidents, which, because of mutual mistrust, led to heightened tensions. Indeed, I was once summoned to the Bangladesh Foreign Office thrice on a single day by the Foreign Secretary to take note of its protests on a border firing incident resulting in some loss of life!

One of the most emotive issues in Bangladesh, pertaining to ties with India, was, perhaps, that related to the sharing of the Ganga waters. In this context, it is necessary to recall that the steady eastward shift of the main channel of the Ganga over the last two centuries had adversely affected the viability of Calcutta port on account of silting. With a view to addressing this problem, India had, in the early 1960s, commenced work on the construction of the Farakka Barrage with a view to diverting about 40,000 cusecs of water from the main stream of the Ganga to the Hooghly to flush out the silt from the Calcutta port. Pakistan had, of course, voiced its objections to the project, but India saw no good reason to abandon it, since well over 90 per cent of the Ganga flowed through India, and East Pakistan, being water surplus, was not critically dependent upon it for irrigation.

The Farakka Barrage was commissioned in 1975, and though Mujibur Rahman, then Prime Minister, too, had reservations about it, friendly and constructive discussions were underway between his government and India on what needed to be done in the matter in the best interests of the two countries. Towards this end, a Joint Rivers Commission (JRC) was set up between the two countries, test operations for the diversion of a part of the Ganga waters to the Hooghly were successfully conducted and India proposed that the waters of the Ganga itself could be similarly augmented by diverting some of the waters of the Brahmaputra through construction of a canal from Jogipara in Assam to a point upstream of Farakka on the Ganga. With Mujib's assassination in August 1975 and the setting up of a Bangladesh government inimically disposed towards India, the relationship took a sharp dip for the worse, and the construction of the Farakka Barrage by India was used as an instrument to whip up anger against it in Bangladesh. Indeed, the latter went so far as to internationalize the issue and launched a jihad against India in the matter, even raising it in the UN General Assembly (UNGA) in 1976.

Following intensive bilateral discussions, a memorandum of understanding (MoU) for a five-year period was concluded between the two countries in November 1977. The MoU set in place an arrangement for the sharing of the Ganga waters in the lean season, notably from 1 January to 31 May by 10-day periods, and recognizing the shortage of water, tasked the JRC with coming up with a proposal for the augmentation of the Ganga waters. The sharing arrangement was heavily weighted in Bangladesh's favour as, through the lean season, India, at 75 per cent flow availability, was allocated its requirement of 40,000 cusec only in the first 10 days of January and its allocation at its lowest went down to 20,500 cusecs in the last 10 days of April. The corresponding allocations for Bangladesh were as high as 58,500 cusecs and 34,500 cusecs, respectively. Additionally, the MoU had a guarantee clause stipulating that in case of decreased flows, Bangladesh's offtake would be frozen at 80 per cent of its allocated amount. While the water-sharing arrangement worked well for the stipulated five-year period, the JRC was unable to recommend an agreed proposal for the augmentation of the dry season flows of the Ganga, as India and Bangladesh had diametrically opposed views in the matter. India argued for the augmentation of the Ganga flows through transfer of the waters of the Brahmaputra, while Bangladesh contended that the additional flows be located within the Ganga basin itself by roping in Nepal. The Indian proposition made more sense, as the waters of the Brahmaputra were underutilized, while those of the Ganga were at near saturation point, as it serviced a much larger population. As a result of these basic differences of approach, the issue of the augmentation of the Ganga waters was stymied and has had to be virtually abandoned.

The approaching expiry of the aforesaid MoU and strained India–Bangladesh ties led to much posturing by Bangladesh through 1981 and 1982, with exaggerated claims of the damages suffered by it on account of India's water offtake at Farakka. Despite these antics, a fresh MoU was concluded in November 1982, soon after the expiry of the 1977 MoU on very similar lines. The only major difference was that the former had no minimum guarantee clause. However, as in the past, there was no progress on the issue of augmentation of the flows of the Ganga. This situation continued to prevail through the 1980s, with another similar MoU being concluded in 1985 for a three-year period. Thereafter, there was a hiatus in the matter till the conclusion of the 1996 India–Bangladesh Treaty on sharing of the Ganga waters at Farakka. This bore the impress of two friendly governments and was consequently a considerable improvement on the earlier understandings in the matter. Its duration was for 30 years, which put at rest the periodic bickering on this issue. The Agreement made for a much fairer allocation of the Ganga waters between the two countries and allowed each country to get 35,000 cusecs of water on an alternate basis over 10-day periods through the worst of the lean season. It further provided that Bangladesh get at least 90 per cent of its allocations during the lean season. It did not, however, have any provisions for the augmentation of the Ganga flows, perhaps because both countries recognized that their differences on this issue could not be bridged.

It is, however, clear that none of the differences between India and Bangladesh in themselves posed an insurmountable threat to the relationship, and the main factor responsible for India–Bangladesh tensions was that Bangladesh was governed by pro-Pakistan and fundamentalist elements averse to good ties with India. There has always been a deep polarization in Bangladesh between those supportive of the liberation struggle, as represented by Sheikh Mujibur Rahman's Awami League with its more secular and India-friendly outlook, and those opposing it because of their sympathies with Pakistan and their proclivity for a more radical Islam. Whenever the latter were at the helm of affairs, Bangladesh's relations with India were rocky.

◆

The Indian High Commission in Dhaka was amongst our bigger missions, with the number of officers and India-based staff running into three digits. Apart from a political wing, it also had economic, consular, information and military wings. Additionally, it ran a school for the children of our officers and staff and brought out, *Bharat Bichitra*, a monthly literary magazine in Bengali whose circulation, because of its popularity, ran into thousands. The magazine was started in the early 1970s by the Indian High Commission and I understand that it is still being brought out.

As the Deputy High Commissioner, I had direct responsibility for administering the mission as well as keeping abreast of local and bilateral developments. I had also to frequently deputize for the High Commissioner, who was often in New Delhi on consultations. In order to ensure that I was completely in the loop on all issues, all papers normally passed through me, both on their way up to the High Commissioner and on their way down from him. The price for this privilege was that one had to make sure that no file remained on my table for more than 24 hours so that work was not held up. The High Commissioner was deeply appreciative of this and the fact that immediately on his return to Dhaka from headquarters, I invariably gave him an in-depth briefing on all that had transpired in his absence so that he was fully au fait with developments before he stepped into office. 1, therefore, developed a very good rapport with him based on mutual respect.

My good relationship with the High Commissioner as well as with the other officers in the mission was helpful in smoothening inter se tensions. Being a perfectionist and a disciplinarian, the High Commissioner had occasional run-ins with one or another officer. It was my endeavour to try and prevent such occurrences and, when they did happen, to ensure that they were tactfully papered over and resolved.

I would rate High Commissioner Dubey as, perhaps, one of our best heads of mission in Bangladesh. He was both admired and feared by the locals and enjoyed access at the highest levels even at the worst of times. He was loved and admired not only because he was fluent in Bengali but also because he was steeped in Bengali culture, holding many soirees at his residence, assiduously cultivating local artistes, taking a personal interest in the publication of *Bharat Bichitra* and translating Hindi literary works into Bengali. Above all, it was readily acknowledged that he had Bangladesh's interests at heart and was deeply committed to its well-being. His popularity may be gauged from the fact that despite tense India–Bangladesh relations, our national day functions were the largest in Dhaka, to which invitations were eagerly sought. He was feared because he never hesitated in harshly castigating all those involved in anti-Indian antics. A graphic example of the latter was when an Indian paintings exhibition scheduled for our national day was sought to be sabotaged by ransacking the venue and slashing some of the paintings to be exhibited on the morning of the event. On learning of the incident and inspecting the site, the High Commissioner lost no time in storming into the Bangladesh Acting Foreign Secretary's residence and giving him a tongue-lashing. Mincing no words, he made out that the ransacking had occurred with the concurrence of the Bangladesh Government, that we were aware of the forces behind it, that we expected the Authorities to ensure that the exhibits were remounted in double quick time and that the exhibition take place as scheduled. The High Commissioner's aggressive and prompt action had the desired result, and the exhibition took place as scheduled, with the Bangladesh Government acting in a cooperative mode.

High Commissioner Dubey's successor, like that of Ambassador Rana in Algiers, was, regrettably, also one of those who suffered from a successor-predecessor syndrome. This manifested itself in his not only questioning many of the existing institutional arrangements in the mission but also viewing with suspicion those who had a good equation with his predecessor. I was, therefore, naturally one of the sufferers, and the practice of all papers being routed through me was discontinued. While professionally this was not a very happy development, at the personal level, it had its benefits, as I could devote more time to my personal interests like golf. It was ironical that the new High Commissioner was subsequently posted as Ambassador to a country that came under my charge as the Joint Secretary dealing with it. I, however, resisted the temptation to make things difficult for him and, on the contrary, was as helpful as possible on a variety of issues. This was facilitated by the fact that his performance in his new avatar was very good, proving the point that an officer's performance can vary from assignment to assignment and is governed, to an extent, by his work environment and circumstances.

◆

While at one level life in Dhaka was not easy, as relations were under stress and India was viewed with suspicion, at another level, things were not too bad because of a strong cultural connect and because those with Awami League leanings were positively friendly. Indeed, even many of those ideologically opposed to India were not averse to social interaction with its diplomats in the country. All manner of Bangladeshis flocked to India and the visa office in the High Commission was overworked. Furthermore, unlike in Pakistan, the intelligence agencies did not keep as intensive a watch on Indian diplomats, and there was not the same religious fanaticism in Bangladesh. Consequently, social interaction and contact with the locals was much easier for Indian diplomats in Bangladesh than in Pakistan. In these circumstances, I was able to interact with elements in Bangladesh firmly committed to the Establishment, such as Reaz Rahman, the Additional Foreign Secretary, the owners of *Ittefaq*, the largest-circulated daily in Bangladesh, and even Salahuddin Qader Chowdhury, the Member of Parliament from Chittagong who was hanged in 2015 for war crimes committed during the 1971 civil war. Additionally, there were several senior diplomats in the Bangladesh Foreign Office, such as Shafi Sami, Farouk Mustafa and Tariq Karim, who, with their Awami League leanings, were friendly towards India and readily accessible to me. All three were later appointed as High Commissioners to India. I also enjoyed a very warm relationship with Syed Kamaluddin, a senior journalist working for the *Far Eastern Economic Review*. Since he lived in my immediate neighbourhood in Dhanmandi, I could walk into his house for a drink and a chat even when the city was under curfew!

At the personal level, living conditions in Bangladesh, for me and my family, were infinitely better than in Algeria. As the Deputy High

Commissioner, I inherited a spacious, well-furnished five-bedroom bungalow with a lovely garden, which was a far cry from our shabby apartment in Algiers. I also had the luxury of a dedicated chauffeur-driven car at my disposal 24/7, while in Algiers, I had to share the official vehicle with colleagues.

As compared to Algiers, social life in Dhaka was hectic. Not only was there much interaction amongst colleagues in the mission but also with the locals. Additionally, the mission under High Commissioner Dubey was extremely active in regularly organizing cultural events with prominent artistes from India, which were invariably a great hit in Dhaka. All this entailed much wining and dining, and as a result, I put on several kilos in my Bangladesh posting. My culinary preferences also underwent a transformation—I not only developed a taste for Bengali sweets like sandesh, pranhara and mishti doi but also for river fish, which was a local staple but which I had hitherto tended to avoid.

8

DEALING WITH THE ARAB WORLD: NEW DELHI

My transfer to Delhi in mid-1984 after 10 years abroad on three postings in three different continents was a welcome development, as it is always good to get back to one's roots. On visiting the Ministry, my first port of call was naturally the Additional Secretary (Administration), Mr Bhutani, in order to ascertain what he had in mind for my assignment. He was candid and stated that this decision was in the hands of the three Secretaries and I should meet them in order to firm up my posting. In the event, I did not need to do so, as the following day, I happened to bump into Mr Romesh Bhandari, Secretary (West), with whom I had a nodding acquaintance in the men's room, who told me to join duty immediately as Joint Secretary (JS), West Asia and North Africa (WANA), under him. I was more than happy to do so, as I felt my Algeria posting would help me make a positive contribution to this assignment and as Mr Bhandari was known to be a very good boss and easy to work with.

The remit of the WANA Division extended to around a dozen countries comprising Morocco, Algeria, Tunisia, Libya, Egypt, Djibouti, Israel, Lebanon, Sudan, Somalia, Jordan and Syria as well as the Palestine Liberation Organization (PLO). The number of officers earmarked for the Division was totally out of sync with its responsibilities, as apart from myself as the Head of Division, there was only one Director, and three officers at the level of Deputy Secretary/Under Secretary. But this was the state of affairs all over the Ministry on account of a pitifully thin officer cadre. The paucity in the number of officers was made up to an extent by their quality which, inter alia, included J.S. Mukul, who later went on to become the Dean of the Foreign Service Training Institute.

Since my predecessor was rather laid-back, the kingpin in the division was the Director. He was extremely competent and enjoyed a special equation with the Secretary. Soon after taking over, I made it clear to him that while I had no problem with his maintaining a special equation with the Secretary, I would insist that all papers move through me both to and from the Secretary. The Director readily agreed to this, and we developed a very good relationship, and later, in another incarnation, I recommended him for a special commendation on account of his outstanding performance.

Within a week of joining the WANA Division, I was despatched to Algeria on a mission to persuade the Algerian authorities to revive a series of high-value contracts awarded to Indian public and private sector entities, which were under suspension. Algeria was threatening to cancel these, as we had not fulfilled our promise, made at the level of the Prime Minister, to import one million tonnes of Algerian oil. Our reluctance to import this oil arose from the fact that our refineries were not geared to processing it. It took protracted discussions to bring the Algerians around to not cancelling these contracts on the basis of a reiteration of our commitment to buy Algerian oil. Modalities for its purchase took a lot of my attention for the next few months. Since we could not process this oil in India, we had to bring all concerned on board to dispose of it through swap deals. This entailed the possibility of taking a loss. The Ministry of Commerce, which was one of the main beneficiaries of the amicable resolution of this issue, was adamant that it would not take the hit on this account and, in fact, refused to take the lead in the decision-making process in the matter. In these circumstances, I had to take all the initiatives on this issue which, inter alia, entailed preparing a note for Cabinet approval to lift 1 million tonnes of Algerian crude, to dispose of it through swap deals and to agree that any loss incurred on this account would be borne by the MEA. It is a matter of satisfaction that as a result of these endeavours, not only was our political relationship with Algeria safeguarded but also our economic and commercial links with it were enormously benefitted. However, this episode revealed the dangers of rash and ill-thought-out promises made by our leaders, the fulfilment of which imposed unnecessary burdens on the nation and reneging on which ran the risk of damaging bilateral relations.

◆

A few weeks after joining the WANA Division, I received a file from the PMO turning down a proposal made by it to permit the posting to India of an Israeli Consul General. I was perplexed as I recalled that it had, only a few days earlier, issued a clearance for the grant of a visa to the Israeli consul general designate to our missions, likely to be approached for the same. In the absence of the Secretary and the Director, who were together on tour, I countermanded the aforesaid clearance and simultaneously apprised the Secretary of the development. I, of course, had no knowledge about whether any of our missions had so far been approached for the visa and, if so, whether the same had been issued. Both the Secretary and the Director were naturally deeply disturbed and acknowledged that we had somehow erred but realized that all we could now do was to hope that the concerned Israeli diplomat had not already secured an Indian visa and was not en route to India. The Director, who was responsible for this goof-up, displayed commendable steel in clearly stating that should things go wrong, he was prepared to face the consequences. Happily, no visa was sought or given, and the WANA Division was fortuitously spared a Prime Minister's rightful wrath. There was, however, much panic in the WANA Division, and the idea of somehow 'losing' the relevant file was also, perhaps facetiously, mooted! I promptly shot it down and suggested that should the Israeli diplomat show up in India, the WANA Division had no option other than humbly plead mea culpa and take the medicine administered by the Prime Minister!

The tricky issue of granting an Indian visa to an Israeli was also instrumental in ending a friendship with an American diplomat, notably a counterpart in the US State Department from my days as first secretary economic in our Embassy in Washington DC. One evening, he phoned me at home indicating that he had just been appointed Consul General in Bombay and requesting me to help him get an Indian visa for his Israeli daughter-in-law, who would be accompanying him. After the usual exchange of pleasantries, while promising him all assistance, I told him that this would take a week or two, as the application would have to be vetted by our agencies. Instead of being grateful for a virtual assurance from me that the visa would be granted, he became vituperative and insisted that this be done immediately and that if this did not happen, it would have repercussions on India–US ties. I, however, refused to budge in the matter and went on to use the opportunity to remind him that whilst in Washington DC, I had approached him to help in the conversion of a single-entry US visa of an IAS colleague who was in the country on business into a double-entry visa, but he had flatly refused to do so. I had, however, not taken this amiss and understood his compulsions and counselled that he should take a similarly enlightened view regarding his daughter-in-law's visa. This failed to assuage him, and he banged the phone down. It is needless to mention that I never heard from him again.

◆

As Head of Division, I made it a point to read and respond to every despatch written to me by the heads of our missions in the countries under my charge. I undertook this practice to promote a dialogue between the various missions and headquarters with a view to ensuring that both were in sync on critical issues and, where this was not possible, to underline the rationale for the approach being adopted by the Ministry. This proactive approach was highly appreciated by our heads of missions in the WANA region, even those who may have had differences with the position taken by the Ministry on specific issues, and generated a greater sense of involvement on their part.

A collateral benefit of heading a Division dealing with several countries was that one became well-acquainted with the then Chief of Protocol (COP), Mr Hamid Ansari, and our relationship, over the years, blossomed into an enduring friendship. Since the COP dealt with all heads of mission on a regular basis, he was well-placed to know exactly what they were up to. Accordingly, he made it a point to drop into my office every now and then to brief me about the doings of my clientele. I found this useful and encouraged this practice. During these meetings, I would, in turn, share with him my impressions of each of the heads of missions with whom I had dealings. On occasion, we also acted in concert to ensure that our wards did not step out of line. One specific case in point that we handled was that of a chargé d'affaires, who was refusing to vacate a house located in Friends Colony (West) that he had leased from Mr H.C. Sarin, a Former Defence Secretary and later our Ambassador to Nepal, on expiry of its lease. In the normal course, this issue would have dragged on for months. However, joint and subtly applied pressure from the COP and me on the concerned diplomat led to the relatively prompt vacation of these premises.

◆

Shortly after reaching office on the morning of Wednesday, 31 October 1984, I started getting reports of Prime Minister Indira Gandhi's assassination. These were soon confirmed, and the mood all around was distinctly downbeat. On the morning of Friday, 2 November, I was summoned by Foreign Secretary M.K. Rasgotra along with Mr K. Srinivasan, Joint Secretary (North). We were instructed to proceed to Palam airport immediately to receive the foreign dignitaries who were pouring in for Mrs Gandhi's funeral and told to remain there till we were relieved in the afternoon. We could not, however, be relieved due to the disturbed conditions in the city. Relief was offered late in the evening, but I elected to stay on through the night, as I did not fancy my chances of going home since the city was engulfed in rioting. When I finally left the airport at around eight the following morning, rioting was still underway in the city. Before proceeding home from my office, I went to the roof of South Block and could see several major fires all over the city. My reflexive thought was that this is what Lahore must have seemed like during the 1947 riots.

Mrs Gandhi's funeral was a massive event and marked by an outpouring of grief by her many supporters and admirers. Scores of foreign dignitaries attended it, and it is a tribute to the organizers that it went off without any major glitch. The extent of personal rapport that she enjoyed with leaders across the world was brought home to me during a call on me by the leader of the Libyan delegation.

After the usual pleasantries, he, in all seriousness, told me that he had been asked by his President to ascertain from India as to who we felt was behind the conspiracy to assassinate his sister Mrs Gandhi so that Libya could eliminate him! This is one of the few formal official exchanges that I never minuted and merely reported it orally to the Minister.

◆

With the impending move of my boss Romesh Bhandari as Foreign Secretary in early 1985, I was asked by him to take over as COP from Hamid Ansari, who was on the verge of transfer. This suggestion was prompted by the latter's recommendation, who had earlier told me as much. Since I was happy in the WANA Division and since protocol work did not interest me, as it involved too much bandobast and ceremonial, I expressed my disinclination to take up the proposed assignment. Mr Bhandari was, however, adamant, arguing that the issue was no longer a matter of debate and that these were his orders. In a bid to persuade me, he went on to point out that as COP, I would have a lovely earmarked residence normally available only to more senior officers in the heart of Lutyens' Delhi and very close to the office. In response, I indicated that if ordered, I would naturally take on the proposed assignment, even though I felt that I did not have the requisite aptitude for it, but that I would continue to stay in my own Friends Colony residence. This was because my occupancy of the earmarked residence would always be in jeopardy, as the COP's assignment was at the pleasure of dignitaries like the Prime Minister, who could effect my transfer at a moment's notice. While I could accept such uncertainty as a professional, I saw no reason why I should expose my wife to the trauma of moving house at a moment's notice. The fact that I would not move into the house earmarked for the COP which the Ministry had obtained with some difficulty led to Mr Bhandari giving up on my transfer as COP. In retrospect, my decision not to accept the aforesaid appointment was an inspired one, as the colleague who was finally appointed as COP had to demit that office in a hurry because of a falling out with the Prime Minister.

◆

As Joint Secretary (WANA), I had the opportunity to be a part of Prime Minister Rajiv Gandhi's official party on his state visits to Egypt and Algeria in 1985. Both visits were fairly routine and uneventful, but they gave me the opportunity of interacting with the young Prime Minister and observing him from close quarters. In those early months in office, he brought a refreshing dynamism and modernity into the thinking and actions of our government, which had hitherto been led by a much older generation, with which officers of my generation found it difficult to strike a bond. Accordingly, most of us in those initial months of his leadership were immensely impressed with Rajiv Gandhi. Soon after the visit, he completely won us over by inviting all those who had been a part of his official delegation, along with their wives, for a small dinner at Hyderabad House as a token of his appreciation for the hard work put in by us. Both he and Sonia Gandhi were gracious hosts. One could talk to them as friends, without protocol and, above all, in the same idiom, as there was no generation gap between us.

Knowledge of the countries under my charge was somewhat limited in India, and accordingly, advice proffered on specific issues pertaining to them by the WANA Division was usually accepted. While the political content of the work pertaining to these countries was the exclusive domain of the WANA Division, much of my time was spent in promoting economic and commercial ties, which provide a critical underpinning to bilateral relationships. This entailed considerable contact with commercial enterprises engaged in business in the area as well as with our economic ministries and, in particular, the Ministry of Commerce.

◆

One of the highlights of my stint in the WANA Division was the historic decision to recognize the Sahrawi Arab Democratic Republic (SADR). The latter is a sparsely populated territory spread over around a quarter million square kilometres, bounded in the west by the Atlantic Ocean, in the north by Morocco, in the east by Algeria and

Mauritania, and in the south by Mauritania. The region was under Spanish colonial rule from 1934 to 1976, and with its decolonization by the latter, it was split between Morocco and Mauritania, with the northern phosphate-rich two-thirds going to the former and the southern one-third going to Mauritania. The Spanish move of splitting the area under Morocco and Mauritania was unjustified, as the people of the region had, since the early 1950s, been struggling for independence. Moreover, both during the period of Spanish domination and subsequently, the UNGA categorically recognized that the issue was one of decolonization. It further recognized not only the need for a referendum in Western Sahara but also the right of the Sahrawi people for independence and self-determination. The views of the UNGA were buttressed by the International Court of Justice (ICJ), which, in 1975, ruled that there were no ties of territorial sovereignty between Western Sahara and the Kingdom of Morocco or Mauritania that could affect the application of the UN Resolution on the decolonization of Western Sahara. In 1979, Mauritania gave up its claims to the area allocated to it in Western Sahara, and Morocco went on to claim the entire region. However, the Sahrawi liberation movement under the Polisario Front gradually acquired control of a substantial chunk of the territory, and the SADR, in 1982, was recognized by the Organisation of African Unity (OAU) and soon thereafter acquired membership of NAM. Indeed, by the mid-1980s, it was recognized by over 60 countries.

In this backdrop, India had, for some time, been under pressure from Algeria, which was strongly supportive of the Polisario to recognize the SADR. This pressure resonated strongly in India because while we enjoyed exemplary ties with Algeria, our relations with Morocco were under a cloud because of its dubious role at the Rabat Islamic Summit Conference in 1969, which saw India being first invited to participate and then being kept out of it on account of Pakistan's machinations. Furthermore, while Algeria was a pillar of NAM, Morocco was firmly in the western camp. Moreover, the Indian leadership of the older generation were well aware of the dynamics of the Polisario liberation struggle and fully sympathized with it. In these circumstances, when Rajiv Gandhi visited Algeria in June 1985, the latter made a strong pitch for India's recognition of the SADR and a commitment was made to do so in the near future if Morocco did not hold a referendum as had been promised by it.

In order to obviate the possibility of a break in diplomatic relations with Morocco when we recognized SADR, we engaged in detailed discussions with it to explain our position. In so doing, we underlined the fact that our decision was principled, as the Polisario movement was a genuine liberation struggle and was in control of considerable territory. Furthermore, the SADR was recognized by the OAU as well as by over 60 countries, it was also a member of NAM, and Morocco had failed to honour its promise of holding a referendum in Western Sahara. Morocco, on its part, argued that there was a parallel between India's position on Kashmir and its position on Western Sahara. This was a fallacious argument and was brushed aside by us, as Kashmir's accession to India was not open to challenge, either on legal grounds on account of the Instrument of Accession signed in its favour by the Maharaja, or on grounds of popular will, as its constitution explicitly recognized Kashmir as being an integral part of India, as did its participation in innumerable local and national elections. Ultimately, on the basis of Morocco's assurance that it would shortly hold a referendum in Western Sahara, India deferred its recognition of SADR for some time and even sent a special envoy, in the form of a recently retired Foreign Secretary, to Morocco to explain our position underlining that ours was a principled decision. It is, of course, another matter that our special envoy returned as Morocco's envoy, urging that we change our decision! Our Ambassador to Morocco was, similarly, all along, vigorously pressing Morocco's case with us and urging that we should not recognize the SADR. This tendency to plead the other country's case and to find fault with India's position is regrettably the bane of the IFS. This disease is, of course, not limited to the IFS and, perhaps, afflicts us as a people. Indeed, one of our prominent journalists spent an hour in my office arguing against our recognition of the SADR and pressing the Moroccan case in the matter. The IAS, too, is not exempt from this tendency, as one of our interlocutors with the Nagas who happened to also be a former Union Home Secretary bought the Naga argument hook, line and sinker and spared no opportunity to press for it.

With Morocco not moving forward on the promised referendum, Prime Minister Rajiv Gandhi, towards the end of September, approved the accord of recognition by India to the SADR, with instructions that the same be communicated to the latter through our Embassy in Algiers. Prior to this, on the directions of Foreign Secretary Bhandari, I had also secured the approval in the matter of the External Affairs Minister. In my interaction with the latter, I had gone prepared for being quizzed in detail on the issue. This proved to be quite unnecessary, as in discussing the matter with him, I felt that one was talking to the already convinced. Being an old Congress veteran, he was fully au fait with the Sahrawi liberation movement and, therefore, accorded his approval to the recognition of the SADR on file in a jiffy, with the comment that India should have done this long ago.

Immediately, on receipt of the formal approval for setting in motion the recognition process, I conveyed the same to Mr K.V. Rajan, our Ambassador in Algiers, through a cipher telegram. I had alerted him earlier in the morning to keep his cipher staff in readiness for an important message. Being fully clued up on the state of play on this issue, he realized the nature of instructions that were on their way.

Having participated in an unusually historic move in the day, I was settling down to a relaxed evening at home when at about eight I received a call from Foreign Secretary Bhandari directing me to hold up action on our recognition of SADR as desired by the Prime Minister, with whom he was on tour abroad. I informed him that this was not possible, as I had already conveyed instructions in this regard to our Ambassador in Algiers, who, knowing him as I did, was bound to have already conveyed the same to the Algerians and to the SADR representatives. Mr Bhandari, however, after expressing surprise at our having acted with such alacrity, asked me nevertheless to touch base on the phone with the Ambassador, ascertain if he had already acted thereon and, if not, countermand the instructions conveyed. I, accordingly, did the needful, but as I had figured, the Ambassador confirmed that he had already conveyed our decision to all concerned and that it had been joyously received. Mr Bhandari was more than a little put out when I informed him about the input provided by our Ambassador. In response to his query as to what he should tell the

Prime Minister, I suggested that he simply state that our recognition of the SADR was now a fait accompli and was irreversible.

The idea of reversing our well-considered and deliberate decision to recognize the SADR perplexed me. Though there was absolutely no proof, the attempted change in our stance did raise suspicions about a Moroccan hand behind it. This was all the more so as, ever since it was known that India might recognize the SADR, Morocco was in a hyperdrive to use all its influence to prevent it. Some Indian journalists were treated lavishly and won over, and even our special envoy, who had been sent to Morocco on the eve of India's recognition of SADR, had upon his return forcefully argued against our proposed move. In the instant case, I know that a senior member of the Congress party, on learning of our impending move, was upset, and it is possible that she, influenced by Morocco, had sought to prevail upon the Prime Minister to reverse or at least postpone our recognition of the SADR.

The suspicion that Morocco's influence was at work behind the 8.00 p.m. outstation call was strengthened 15 years later when the Vajpayee government, on 23 June 2000, suddenly announced the de-recognition of the SADR. The reason for this move is a mystery and the only logical explanation is that as in the past, Morocco's influence was again at work. The Ministry's announcement about this move as reported in the *Economic & Political Weekly* was vague, simply stating that,

> Keeping in mind all aspects of the evolving situation in the region and discussions currently on between the parties concerned, it has been decided to withdraw recognition from the Saharawi Arab Democratic Republic (SADR) with immediate effect. India continues to keep in touch with developments in line with its support for UN efforts and the warm and friendly relations traditionally existing with all the parties concerned.[8]

The half-baked nature of this announcement stands out in stark contrast to the statement issued by the Ministry on 1 October 1985,

---

[8]Dasgupta, Punyapriya, 'Recognition of Western Sahara Foreign Policy Volte-Face', *Economic & Political Weekly*, 12 August 2000.

as reported in the aforementioned issue of the *Economic & Political Weekly*, which provided an exhaustive rationale for our recognition of the SADR. The statement, inter alia, drew attention to the fact that the people of Western Sahara had, for over two decades, been struggling for independence and that the UNGA, recognizing that the issue was one of decolonization, acknowledged not only the need for a referendum but also the right of the Sahrawi people for independence and self-determination. It further noted that the views of the UNGA were buttressed by both the ICJ and the OAU. While the ICJ had ruled, in 1975, that there were no ties of territorial sovereignty between Western Sahara and Morocco or Mauritania, the OAU had called for the self-determination of the Sahrawi people through a peaceful and fair referendum without any administrative or military constraints. In this backdrop, our statement concluded that since the Polisario was a genuine liberation movement and since the SADR had already been recognized by 62 countries, India had decided to extend recognition to it. Such an approach was in conformity with India's policies on complicated regional issues, which are guided by representative recognized institutions.

9

DEALING WITH OUR WESTERN NEIGHBOURS: NEW DELHI

My enjoyable and carefree assignment as Joint Secretary (WANA) came to an abrupt end around mid-1986, when Foreign Secretary A.P. Venkateswaran told me to take over as Joint Secretary, Afghanistan-Pakistan (AP) from Mr S.K. Lambah (more commonly known as Sati), who was moving out on transfer. This was not a surprise, as I had been alerted by Sati, who had recommended my appointment to the Foreign Secretary. The former and I were good friends and used to commute together to the Ministry. I was delighted with my new appointment, not only as it was an important one but also because I felt that my Pakistan experience both in the Division and in Karachi earlier equipped me well to make an important contribution. I, however, always kept in mind the sobering advice given to me by Sati, on handing over charge to me, notably that in view of extensive India–Pakistan interactions across multiple channels, the Joint Secretary dealing with Pakistan may well not be the best-informed about it.

Shortly after taking over as Joint Secretary (AP), I needed to go to New York on a personal visit for a month to accompany my brother for cancer-related surgery. The Foreign Secretary was naturally loath to relieve me so soon after my taking over charge and indicated that my visit to New York could cost me my new appointment. On my replying that I was prepared to pay any price for my brother's well-being, the Foreign Secretary relented and stated that he was glad that there were still people around who were not out-and-out careerists and were guided by values. Accordingly, my leave to proceed to New York was acceded to with the caveat that I not ask for any extension.

In the event, I returned earlier than initially indicated.

The AP Division, though dealing with only two countries, was slightly larger than the WANA Division. Apart from a Joint Secretary, it had a Deputy Secretary, three Under Secretaries and a Research Officer. One of the Under Secretaries was expressly earmarked for Afghanistan and sundry Kashmir-related issues. My main concern on taking charge of the AP Division was my lack of knowledge on Afghanistan, to make up for which I spent, on an average 20–30 per cent of my time on the latter. On Pakistan itself, I had no such concerns, having served in the country and having dealt with issues pertaining to it as Under Secretary and Deputy Secretary. My concerns relating to Afghanistan proved to be unfounded, as I inherited an outstanding officer as the Under Secretary in charge of that country by way of Arvind Gupta. The latter remained with me in the Division till almost my entire stay in it. Indeed, all the officers who served with me over time in the Division, such as Prabhu Dayal, Ashok Kantha, Arun Kumar Singh, Deepa Wadhwa, Vijay Thakur Singh and K.J. Francis, were of exceptional ability and went on to acquit themselves with great distinction in the Service.

One of the more important activities relating to Afghanistan was the management of a modest assistance programme earmarked for it, all of which was in the nature of an outright grant. Apart from the upgradation of the 100-bed Indira Gandhi Children's Hospital to a 500-bed facility and the development of a small-scale industries park, the programme had a technical assistance and commodity component. The former entailed training programmes for Afghans in India in diverse areas as well as deputation of Indian experts, including medical personnel, to Afghanistan for varying durations for diverse tasks, including upgrading local expertise. As regards the commodity programme, this comprised provision of diverse products, ranging from tractors to machinery to edibles. Our assistance programme, though small, was deeply appreciated, as it was evolved not by diktat emanating from Delhi but on the basis of close consultation with the Afghan authorities.

◆

Soon after joining the AP Division, I was confronted by Arvind's contention that the Soviet Union was likely to withdraw from Afghanistan sooner rather than later. He persisted with this line of thinking despite my scepticism, which was coloured by conventional wisdom and the belief of many in the Ministry and, indeed, the world over that a Soviet withdrawal from Afghanistan was unlikely anytime soon. Given Arvind's feel for the Soviet Union based on his stint in that country and his persistence in the matter, I, however, committed myself to projecting his assessment to the highest levels, provided he could convince me of the logic of his views on the basis of a reasoned paper. Arvind readily took up the challenge. His only request was that he should be allowed to regularly receive two Soviet newspapers, notably *Pravda* and *Izvestia*, in order to fine-tune his argumentation, which was promptly acceded to.

By October–November 1986, Arvind produced the requisite paper, which was cogent, logical and well-thought-through. The paper, in a nutshell, detailed Mikhail Gorbachev's wish list, which, inter alia, included the Soviet withdrawal from Afghanistan and proceeded to argue that since many items on it were under implementation, this, too, was on the cards. Convinced of the logic of the paper, I submitted it to the Foreign Secretary, who commended it and had it appropriately disseminated within the Ministry as well as to the PMO. There was little reaction to this paper apart from an impassioned criticism from a senior colleague who had served in Afghanistan and who held fast to the conventional wisdom on the issue and was not prepared to countenance any fresh thinking in the matter. The absence of any reaction from higher levels of government led me, by way of abundant caution, to submit a variant of the note a few weeks later to the PMO channelled through the Minister of State. I was naturally surprised, therefore, when some months later, the Minister of State chastised me for not have alerted the government to the possibility of a Soviet pull-out from Afghanistan. He had no comeback when I told him that the Ministry had done so months earlier and a note in this regard had been sent to the PMO through his office!

Our assessment of the impending Soviet pull-out from Afghanistan and the possibility of the takeover of the Afghan government by elements of the Peshawar 7 led the AP Division to suggest that India should clandestinely reach out to the latter. This was accepted by government, and we established contact with Gulbuddin Hekmatyar through our High Commissioner in Pakistan. Indeed, arrangements were underway for the former's visit to India to meet with me. However, this never materialized, as Hekmatyar was put out as a result of a meeting of our Minister of State with the deposed Afghan king in Rome, news of which somehow leaked out.

Any possible chance of furthering contacts with the Mujahideen received a body blow, with President Mohammad Najibullah's India visit in May 1988. There was no call for such an invite, given that the Najibullah regime was clearly on its way out with the Soviet withdrawal a certainty. The invite was driven by the PMO and had little logic. The AP Division came to know of the visit only at the last moment, though a few days earlier, Arvind's contact in the Soviet Embassy, Second Secretary Ratzborinsky, had hinted at the same. What is even worse is that shortly after the visit, a Secretary in the PMO, who had recently taken over as Secretary, Ministry of Information and Broadcasting, discreetly met Najibullah in Kabul. I learnt of this only by accident as details on airline schedules were sought by his office from me. Soon after his visit to Kabul, I happened to run into him as he was emerging from the office of the Minister of State. He indicated that he had, at the Prime Minister's behest, invited Najibullah to visit India once again and that I should coordinate action with our Ambassador in Kabul to confirm dates. I was surprised and remonstrated that a second Najibullah visit would be counterproductive, since the fallout of even the first one had been disastrous, as it had ended up annoying the US and put paid to all our moves to reach out to the Mujahideen. He argued that we needed to demonstrate our support to Najibullah, to which I reacted that we could do so more effectively by upping our assistance to Afghanistan. To his riposte that the Prime Minister had already approved the invite, I urged that he should request the Prime Minister to reconsider the matter in the light of the aforesaid points and indicated that I would hold up any further action in the matter till he reverted. Fortunately, the PMO did not get back on this, and Najibullah's second visit did not materialize!

On returning to my office, I recorded a note on the aforesaid conversation and submitted the same to the External Affairs Minister for information. Interestingly, I did not get the note back from him immediately as per normal practice. It was only a week or so later that I received the note back commending the action taken. Clearly, this was yet another instance where he had not been kept in the loop and was unaware of the actions being taken by the PMO!

◆

As Joint Secretary (AP), I had the opportunity of visiting Kabul two or three times. The precarious military situation of the Najibullah regime was self-evident from the chatter of machine-gun fire that could be heard in the Intercontinental Hotel, where I was accommodated, from early evening onwards and from the fact that all functions were instructed to end by 7.00 p.m. so that all could get home before dark. Indeed, flights in and out of Kabul were susceptible to stinger attack and hence had to adopt dissuasive measures by way of flares and modified flight paths to minimize the possibility of damage. Notwithstanding this, the shops were full, and Afghan commercial ingenuity made it possible to secure a wide variety of merchandise at ridiculously low prices. When I commented on this to an Afghan official, he threw out the challenge that given the opportunity, he could deliver any Indian product in Amritsar at a price lower than what we paid for it.

While the bulk of the population was against the Najibullah regime and not hostile per se to the imminent takeover by the Mujahideen, the women were apprehensive, as they feared that they would lose their newly won liberties. These fears and apprehensions proved to be fully justified, as with the takeover by the Taliban, the position of women took a big hit.

◆

Developments following the sudden demise of Khan Abdul Ghaffar Khan, variously known as Badshah Khan and the Frontier Gandhi, on 20 January 1988 revealed Pakistan's churlishness, the huge popularity enjoyed by him not only in Afghanistan but also among the Pashtun people, including those in Pakistan, and Prime Minister Rajiv Gandhi's sensitivity and impetuosity.

Pakistan's churlishness was demonstrated by its merely sending a brief, wishy-washy condolence message to his family from Prime Minister Junejo. In contrast, the Afghan Government observed four days' state mourning, and President Najibullah, along with a large delegation, personally attended Badshah Khan's funeral, which was held in Jalalabad as had been desired by him. Additionally, the Afghan people who thronged in huge numbers for the funeral of Ghaffar Khan from both Afghanistan and Pakistan observed a ceasefire in the midst of a bloody civil war.

Rajiv Gandhi's sensitivity to the need to openly display India's close connect with Ghaffar Khan and his family was nothing short of exemplary. Regrettably, some of our subsequent leaders were found wanting in this regard. He declared five days' state mourning and decided to proceed forthwith to Peshawar to pay tribute to Ghaffar Khan. It was an impetuous move, as he was scheduled to emplane at around that time for his visit to Sweden for the Six Nation Summit. Even more importantly, there was the issue of getting the requisite flight, etc., clearances from Pakistan, and its officialdom, obdurate at the best of times, was proving to be difficult in this regard. Rajiv Gandhi was, however, not deterred and decided to emplane for Peshawar with or without the requisite flight clearance, confident that Pakistan would not be able to stop him. Throughout the morning, I was constantly on the phone with our mission in Islamabad, alerting it to the Prime Minister's plans, directing the Ambassador to proceed forthwith to Peshawar so as to receive him there, and most important of all, pressing for the requisite flight clearances at the earliest. To my knowledge, the latter never came till the plane had taken off and were, perhaps, communicated sometime later to the pilot. However, Rajiv Gandhi's instincts were right, and his special aircraft was allowed to land safely! He was accompanied by Sonia and Rahul Gandhi and made a short but dignified speech paying an eloquent tribute to the Frontier Gandhi and underlining the values of peace, harmony and non-violence to which the latter had dedicated his life.

Badshah Khan was buried in the backyard of a modest house

in Jalalabad, where he had stayed in his younger days. India sent a high-level delegation led by the then Vice President, Dr Shankar Dayal Sharma, which, inter alia, included the then Chief Minister of Jammu and Kashmir, Farooq Abdullah, and the then Delhi's Police Commissioner, Ved Marwah. The visit, undertaken on a special Indian Airlines aircraft, was coordinated by Arvind Gupta, who formed a part of our delegation.

The aircraft landed in Kabul around noon, and the delegation was received by our Ambassador and a senior Afghan minister. It was taken to a guest house, where it remained for several hours till well after sunset. Thereafter, the delegation was split into two groups and flown to Jalalabad, along with some Afghan leaders, in two military aircraft in pitch darkness and at high altitude to evade any missile attack.

The Indian delegation spent the night at Jalalabad in a somewhat cramped accommodation. There was much confusion and commotion, and the nervousness of the security personnel accompanying the Vice President was palpable.

The funeral took place in the afternoon. Since the numbers of those attending the funeral was large and the approach roads narrow, there was a virtual stampede. To add to the confusion, as the procession was in progress, there was a bomb blast a couple of kilometres away. In this situation, the Vice President's security personnel were unable to maintain the prescribed security perimeter around him and, indeed, some stumbled and fell into a nearby ditch.

Clearly, the Indian delegation's visit to Jalalabad for Badshah Khan's funeral was a risky venture. Although a ceasefire had been declared by both sides, it was not fully observed, and it is fortuitous that the members of our delegation came back unscathed. On the flip side, there can, of course, be no denying the fact that the presence of Dr Shankar Dayal Sharma at the funeral was greatly appreciated not only by the Afghanistan government but by all Pashtuns.

◆

An upside of being Joint Secretary (AP) was that it entailed dealing directly with Foreign Secretary Venkateswaran, who was, perhaps, one of our most incisive, warm-hearted, outspoken and dynamic officers. He was accessible 24/7 and was highly supportive of all those working with him, thus inspiring intense loyalty amongst all his juniors. On a couple of occasions, I phoned him late in the evening for guidance on a tricky issue. Not only did he unhesitatingly come on line but graciously invited me home for detailed discussions over a drink on the issue at hand, and I invariably left with precise instructions on how to proceed further. Additionally, he was highly protective of turf even from an overly interfering PMO. In this context, I can never forget an occasion when I submitted a note to him in which, while recommending a particular line of action, I also suggested that the PMO be consulted in the matter. The note came back directing that action be taken as proposed. Since the issue had a policy implication, I queried the Foreign Secretary as to whether the PMO had been sounded in the matter. He responded in the negative, stating that there was no need to do so if one had the courage of one's convictions!

◆

Through my tenure in the AP Division from mid-1986 to mid-1989, activity was frenetic and the workload heavy. During this period, India–Pakistan interaction, though unproductive, was intense and entailed a plethora of meetings and exchange of delegations across a wide spectrum of issues, ranging from Siachen to water and from terrorism to Sir Creek, not merely at the official level but also at the level of leaders. Apart from participating in these exercises, the AP Division continued, as per tradition, to be snowed under a very large number of Parliament Questions, which had to be handled in a time-bound manner with great sensitivity. This took a huge toll on our time, particularly as all the Ministers concerned insisted on innumerable lengthy briefing sessions. Some idea of the volume of Parliament Questions to be handled by the Division may be garnered from the fact that 35–40 per cent of all the questions for the MEA fell to the lot of AP Division.

But apart from the daunting workload, there was too frequent a change of critical personnel both within the Division and at the level of the Foreign Secretary. Thus, while I was Joint Secretary (AP),

I saw three Foreign Secretaries and three Deputy Secretaries. Such changes inevitably militated against continuity, which is essential for smooth functioning. The complexity of my task was exacerbated by an overactive, secretive and overly intrusive PMO which, over time, debilitated the Ministry. It often took steps without keeping the Ministry in the loop, which inevitably led to embarrassment and missteps. From time to time, there were also telephonic requests for notes from the PMO tailored to a particular viewpoint, short-circuiting the normal chain of command with the Ministry. While I invariably turned down such requests, colleagues from other divisions complied with them, as not doing so was a risky proposition.

On the flip side, despite the tense relations with Pakistan, I enjoyed an excellent personal equation with the senior officials in the Pakistan High Commission. During my time as Joint Secretary (AP), I saw two Pakistan High Commissioners, notably Dr Humayun Khan and subsequently Niaz Naik, and two Deputy High Commissioners, notably Aziz Khan and Shafqat Kakakhel. While I had a very good relationship with all these officials as well as with Counsellor Kamran Niaz, who were all professionally high-class and thorough gentlemen, my dealings with Aziz Khan were particularly intense. This was all the more so as on transfer from the High Commission, he became my counterpart in the Pakistan Foreign Office as Director General South Asia. Since we knew and trusted each other, we took to sorting out many issues at our level, like the scheduling of meetings, the level at which they should be held, grant of visa clearances, etc., directly on the phone rather than through our respective missions. Much of this would be unthinkable today.

A funny incident in this regard was on the convening of the border ground rules committee, which had been decided upon during the India-Pakistan Home Secretaries meeting held in May 1988. Since the issue primarily concerned the Border Security Force (BSF), I had assumed that our delegation would be led by the Home Ministry, as in the past. Home Secretary C.G. Somiah, however, insisted that I lead the delegation despite the fact that the Home Ministry and BSF representatives outranked me. Accordingly, while fixing the dates for the border ground rules committee meeting scheduled to be held in

Lahore, I informed Aziz Khan that our delegation would be led by me. He reacted that this was not possible, as on the Pakistan side, the delegation was to be led by the Director General Pakistan Rangers, who outranked him. I responded that this did not concern me, as our delegation would be led by me and it was for Pakistan to field whom it pleased as the leader of its delegation. Aziz Khan, in a moment of transparency, indicated that he could, perhaps, use our decision to his advantage to get himself appointed as the leader of the Pakistan delegation. This is exactly what transpired, and both of us led our respective sides for the border ground rules meeting in Lahore. I can take satisfaction from the fact that though this meeting was unable to finalize a revised agreement on border ground rules, this was so because of the irreconcilable positions of the two sides on this issue. During our discussions, both of us were quick to come to this conclusion and to pinpoint our differences, which, to date, have kept the two sides apart and prevented agreement on this issue.

◆

In mid-1988, Niaz Naik succeeded the outgoing Pakistan High Commissioner, Dr Humayun Khan. Within a few days of his arrival but before the presentation of his credentials, a Pakistani defence delegation was scheduled to visit India for Siachen-related discussions. The dilemma before me was whether to permit Niaz Naik to participate in the talks and accompany the leader of the delegation in his customary call on the Prime Minister, as normal practice did not permit this for heads of missions who had not presented their credentials. I reasoned that we need not go by normal practice in this matter, as there was little that we could ever do as a favour to the Pakistan High Commissioner, given the sorry state of our relations, and that this small goodwill gesture might go some way in influencing the new incumbent to look upon us a little more favourably. My recommendation in the matter was promptly accepted by the Foreign Secretary.

However, this decision invoked the ire of the COP, who barged into my room, which was next to his, and hauled me over the coals for this move. I heard him out patiently and told him that I had the Foreign Secretary's clearance for this step, and if he had any complaints in the matter, he should raise these with him. Furthermore, I told him that protocol was merely a service function and was not the be-all and end-all of everything. It was ultimately subservient to the achievement of a greater end as defined by the line Divisions. The matter was, however, escalated to the President's office, and a written explanation was sought from me and duly provided. Happily, there was no comeback on this issue.

◆

A few months after Niaz Naik's arrival and just prior to Benazir Bhutto's swearing-in as Prime Minister, we were rocked by what could be termed as the Abbasi affair. Brigadier Abbasi was the military attaché in the Pakistan High Commission and, in that capacity, was also the ISI head in India. In an operation planned by our Intelligence, he was caught red-handed at a small sleazy New Delhi hotel receiving documents from an Indian contact. Instead of declaring him persona non grata as per normal practice, he was taken into police custody. I learned of this only at about 7.30 p.m. on television. Simultaneously, Counsellor T.C.A. Rangachari, the chargé d'affaires from our High Commission in Islamabad, was on the phone to ascertain the facts of the case. I told him that I, too, had just seen the news and had nothing definitive to say at the moment apart from suggesting that he should ensure that our Defence Attachés should remain at home to obviate any untoward retaliatory action.

Thereafter, following a series of phone calls to the top brass in the Home Ministry and after consultation with the External Affairs Minister, I was able to arrange the handing over of Brigadier Abbasi to the Pakistan Deputy High Commissioner, Shafqat Kakakhel, at around midnight. Early next morning, a meeting was called by the Prime Minister on this issue, and it became evident to me that the operation had been planned by Intelligence in close consultation with him without keeping the MEA in the loop and without taking into account the possibility of retaliation against the officials in our mission in Pakistan. Clearly, the matter should have been handled more deftly, and Abbasi, instead of having been taken into police custody, should have been handed over to the High Commission and, thereafter, declared persona non grata. This would have minimized the possibility of any retaliatory action against officers in our mission in Islamabad. It is significant that in May 1992, an Indian Counsellor was abducted outside his house in Islamabad by the ISI and tortured. Our High Commissioner in Pakistan at the time told me that he was given to understand that this was in retaliation for the Abbasi episode. Such retaliation did not take place immediately, as Pakistan was at the time at the cusp of a regime change. Incidentally, Abbasi was something of a fundamentalist, and Niaz Naik, many years later, confided in me that officials at the Pakistan High Commission, aware of his leanings, were careful to abstain from drinking in his presence. On return to Pakistan from Delhi, Abbasi was promoted as Major General, and in the mid-1990s, when I was High Commissioner in Islamabad, attempted a coup against Benazir Bhutto, for which he was sentenced to seven years' imprisonment.

◆

A major development while I was Joint Secretary (AP) was the eyeball-to-eyeball confrontation between the Indian and Pakistani forces around the third week of January 1987 as a result of Operation Brasstacks which constituted India's largest-ever military exercise around 100 kilometres from the Pakistan border. This led to a huge Pakistani military build-up, which, in turn, due to a lack of adequate communication and trust between the two countries, brought their armies face to face. In these circumstances, there was a potential for the outbreak of an armed conflict, and tensions ran high. Both sides, however, agreed to resolve the issue through dialogue. Two rounds of discussions were held in this regard, with the Indian delegation being led by Secretary West Alfred Gonsalves and the Pakistan side being led by Foreign Secretary Abdul Sattar. Gonsalves was pitchforked into this role, as Foreign Secretary Venkateswaran had, following a spat with the Prime Minister, demitted office on 20 January 1987, and his successor, K.P.S. Menon Jr, only assumed office some days later. While Sattar was an old India hand, Gonsalves had no Pakistan experience, and some feared that the former would dominate the proceedings. This did not, however, happen, as Gonsalves was a highly cerebral officer and well-endowed to hold his own even in difficult circumstances. Indeed, with his razor-sharp intellect, he was able to discern and exploit differences between the civilian and military components of the Pakistan delegation to our advantage.

The first round of discussions was held in Delhi from 30 January to 4 February 1987, and the second round in Islamabad from 27 February to 2 March 1987. At the first round, there was agreement on a number of points, notably that neither country would attack the other, that there would be some force pullback in the Ravi–Chenab sector, and that further force reductions and pullbacks would be undertaken sector wise. At the second round of talks, details of these were worked out largely due to the efforts of our Additional Secretary from the Defence Ministry, Mr N.N. Vohra, and his Pakistani counterpart, Major General (retd) Raja Iqbal Mahmood. The latter was an amazingly outspoken and irreverent officer who enjoyed the complete confidence of General Zia-ul-Haq. The rapport developed between Mr Vohra and General Mahmood played a critical part in their being able to iron out the details and the schedule for the de-escalation of the troop build-up at the India–Pakistan border.

This rapport was largely the result of the cultural connect between these two. Both were typical Punjabis. They not only revelled in dialoguing with each other in chaste Punjabi but did so with complete and often brutal openness, which inevitably bred trust between the two so necessary for the successful conclusion of any delicate negotiation. I have no doubt that, left to themselves, Gonsalves and Sattar would not have been able to work out the nitty-gritty of this intricate disengagement process, as there was little chemistry between them, which, along with a modicum of trust, is critical in such complex matters involving much give and take.

◆

In the midst of the India–Pakistan military stand-off, General Zia-ul-Haq visited India from 21 to 23 January 1987 at the invitation of the Board of Cricket Control for India to witness the India–Pakistan cricket match in Jaipur. The visit was set up at very short notice, and there was much hesitancy in India as to whether to arrange any bilateral meetings for Zia with the Indian leadership. Finally, Rajiv Gandhi received Zia and hosted a dinner for him, and the latter also called on President Zail Singh. The following day, Zia proceeded to Jaipur for the cricket match. While the talks did not achieve much, Zia successfully projected the visit as a move on Pakistan's part to promote peace. This served an important purpose, as Pakistan was deeply involved, at the time, in providing inspiration and support to the Khalistan movement. Moreover, skilful as ever at media management, Zia had the Indian press eating out of his hand, something which Pervez Musharraf repeated during his Agra visit 14 years later.

The only redeeming feature from my point of view was the opportunity that I had to see Zia squirming in an exchange with President Zail Singh during his call on him at Rashtrapati Bhavan. Always the aggressor, Zia, with his synthetic smile, stated in chaste Punjabi that he looked to President Zail Singh as the tallest regional leader to resolve the prevailing India–Pakistan tensions. The latter responded in equally chaste Punjabi that he was merely an elected President with limited powers in a constitutional democracy and that this task more appropriately fell on Zia, who enjoyed untrammelled powers, as he was not just a President but also the Chief Martial Law Administrator!

During my many visits to Pakistan, I had the opportunity to call several times on President Zia along with one or another leader of our delegation. On every single occasion, Zia exuded great warmth and courtesy. Though much of this was artificial and for effect, it nevertheless had an impact. How could our delegation not come away favourably impressed with Zia when he made it point to personally not only see off the Secretary-level leader of our delegation to his car but to open its door for him? More often than not, he would engage not only the leader of the delegation but also its other members. For instance, on learning that I was from Multan, he insisted that I visit it and if paucity of time was a problem, he offered to place an aircraft at my disposal to enable me to do so!

◆

On the eve of the India–Pakistan talks of January–March 1987 to ease tensions arising out of the military stand-off between the two, specifically on 28 January 1987, Kuldip Nayyar interviewed A.Q. Khan, who revealed that Pakistan had nuclear weapons and was prepared to use them against India if required. The interview had been arranged by Mushahid Hussain, the editor of the Pakistani newspaper *The Muslim*. Kuldip Nayyar's article on the matter, however, appeared only on 1 March 1987 in the *Observer*, a British paper. The suggestion that this revelation by Pakistan constituted nuclear signalling and was designed to deter an Indian attack is, therefore, untenable, as by the time this became public, tensions had already eased and talks all but concluded. However, from the AP Division's point of view, it triggered a study based on open information about Pakistan's actual nuclear capability. After a detailed analysis of all readily available published material, the AP Division put out a comprehensive paper meticulously fashioned by Deputy Secretary Ashok Kantha, projecting that Pakistan had, in fact, attained nuclear weapon capability and that it would be reasonable to assume that it already had some nuclear weapons in its possession. Such capability had been achieved not so much through any original scientific work done in Pakistan but through the assistance provided by China, in terms of weapons design and transfer of fissile material, and by clandestine acquisition of the necessary materials from the West, which had turned a blind eye to the same.

◆

Whilst in the midst of Operation Brasstacks and its fallout, the Ministry was struck by Foreign Secretary Venkateswaran's untimely demission from office in the third week of January 1987. Mr Venkateswaran's irreverent comments and lack of deference to the Prime Minister and his coterie, so alien to our darbari culture, led to an uneasy relationship between the two and was at the root of his unceremonious and untimely exit. The situation was triggered by a query posed to Prime Minister Rajiv Gandhi by a Pakistani journalist at a morning press conference in Delhi as to when he would be visiting Pakistan. When the Prime Minister responded that he would not be going to Pakistan, the journalist countered that this had been indicated by the Foreign Secretary, to which the Prime Minister retorted that there would soon be a new Foreign Secretary.

On learning of the aforesaid development, I was the first to call on the Foreign Secretary later that morning. He confirmed that what I had heard was indeed correct and asked me as to what I thought he should do. I responded that I would take long leave. He told me that this was not good enough and that he intended to put in his papers.

In my opinion, Rajiv Gandhi's brash and graceless way of getting rid of the Foreign Secretary was not only damaging to the Ministry as an institution but also to his own image. In fact, the downturn in Rajiv Gandhi's fortunes can be traced to this event.

While it was no secret that Rajiv Gandhi's relationship with Mr Venkateswaran was troubled, he could have eased him out in a much more tactful and dignified manner, which would have avoided any institutional damage. Moreover, there was no justification for sacking the Foreign Secretary on the grounds that he had spoken out of turn in asserting that Rajiv Gandhi would visit Pakistan, as there was a government decision to this effect. I had learnt of this in a somewhat convoluted manner and only through a proactive move by me in the matter resulting from a report that I had seen in the Pakistani media that Prime Minister Junejo, on his return to the country after the Bangalore SAARC summit in November 1986, had indicated at Lahore airport that Rajiv Gandhi would visit Pakistan. Not having seen any note to this effect on our side, I had raised the issue with the PMO and was asked to check with the External Affairs Minister, as he had been present at the Rajiv Gandhi–Junejo meeting. Accordingly, as suggested, I posed this issue to the External Affairs Minister, who confirmed that the Prime Minister would visit all the SAARC Countries, including Pakistan, in his capacity as the SAARC Chairman. I duly minuted this discussion but did not submit it to the Foreign Secretary, as I presumed that he was aware of it. My presumption was well founded, as Mr Venkateswaran not only confirmed this to the Pakistan leadership during his visit to Islamabad in late December 1986 but also made this point at a press conference there.

Rajiv Gandhi's pronouncement against Mr Venkateswaran aroused much anger, not only in the Ministry but amongst the entire bureaucracy since it was unwarranted and since the latter was a highly respected officer. Moreover, he inspired deep affection, admiration and loyalty from all, particularly his juniors. In these circumstances, the IFS Association passed a carefully crafted resolution signifying its fullest solidarity with Mr Venkateswaran, lauding his contributions to the Service and making known its unhappiness with the episode, which hurt its sentiments and undermined its morale. Much pressure was brought to bear on the Association by some former IFS officers who were still stalking the corridors of power in one capacity or another to desist from passing this resolution. Mr Gonsalves, who at the time was deputizing as the Foreign Secretary, clearly acting under pressure, also advised a watering down of the resolution and warned that it could lead to action against those who were promoting it. Being a thoroughgoing professional and a true democrat, he, however, made known that it was ultimately up to the Association to take a final view in the matter and refrained from any further participation in the ensuing discussions. During these discussions, Additional Secretary Peter Sinai fought a losing battle to try and dilute the resolution. It may be mentioned that the initial resolution was drafted by four or five Joint Secretaries, which, inter alia, included Prakash Shah, P.K. Singh and myself. However, in the discussions at the Association meeting, the lead in pushing through the resolution was taken by junior officers with 10 years of service or less. The only redeeming feature of the entire episode is that the Prime Minister did not take disciplinary action against those who had drafted and promoted the resolution as had been suggested by some who were close to him.

The fact that there was much angst in the bureaucracy in general against the Prime Minister's comment about Mr Venkateswaran's impending removal was brought home to me in a conversation that I had with the then Home Secretary. Late on the evening that the IFS Association passed its hotly debated resolution in support of Mr Venkateswaran, I received a phone call at my residence from the Home Secretary asking me to indicate to him its contents. When I queried as to how he knew about it, he laughingly reacted that he was not the Home Secretary for nothing. On my reading out the contents of the resolution, he cryptically retorted 'damn good'.

◆

Mr Venkateswaran was succeeded by Mr K.P.S. Menon, who had just a few months to go for his retirement and was our Ambassador in China. A complete gentleman, soft-spoken, upright and with decades of distinguished service, Mr Menon's appointment provided the much-needed balm to a Ministry that was licking its wounds. For me, working with him took some getting used to after having been associated with his warm, dynamic and effervescent predecessor. I particularly missed the latter's easy accessibility and ability to take decisions quickly. Meeting the more formal Mr Menon was not instantaneous and often took three or even four days. This inevitably led to delays in decision-making. Above all, while Mr Venkateswaran and I were on the same wavelength on how to deal with Pakistan, Mr Menon's softer approach led to differences between us on this issue. In these circumstances, Mr Menon and I did not have the best of equations in matters relating to Pakistan. However, despite this, I came to respect and admire Mr Menon for his having gone out of his way to shield me from the totally unjustified ire of an irate Rajiv Gandhi on account of a press release put out by our spokesman criticizing President Zia.

The aforesaid press release was triggered by a very harsh anti-India statement by President Zia. Our spokesman drew my attention to it and shared with me a draft press release for my reaction. While I felt that a press release countering Zia was necessary, I thought that the draft prepared by our spokesman was overly aggressive and, therefore, prepared a more diplomatic version thereof and, along with the spokesman, took both drafts directly to the Minister of State for consideration in the absence of the Foreign Secretary, who was out of station. The Minister, with a couple of pencilled modifications, approved the harder version prepared by the spokesman, which was, thereafter, released.

A couple of days later, which happened to be a Saturday or Sunday, I received a phone call from Foreign Secretary Menon, who told me that Rajiv Gandhi was furious with the press release issued on Pakistan and that I should, therefore, come to his house immediately and explain as to how precisely it came to be issued. I did the needful and showed him both the draft releases submitted for the approval of the Minister of State. After having heard me out, the Foreign Secretary telephoned Rajiv Gandhi in my presence and told him that he had looked into the matter and that he could not find fault with what I had done. He went on to point out that though the press release had not been vetted by him personally, as he was not in station, he would probably have cleared it with one or two marginal changes. Moreover, the release had been cleared by the Minister of State, and there was no call for contemplating any action against me. Mr Menon's conduct in this matter was in the best traditions of the Service, and my respect for him skyrocketed. It contrasted sharply with the reaction of the Minister of State who, on learning of the Prime Minister's ire at the press release, called me to his office the next day and asked as to how the offending piece had come to be published! He, of course, had no comeback when I showed him the draft of the press release approved by him with his own handwritten corrections made thereon.

The rationale for Rajiv Gandhi's annoyance at our press release critical of Zia's intemperate outburst against India was inexplicable to me for some time. The penny, however, dropped when, a few weeks later, at a dinner at Deputy High Commissioner Shafqat Kakakhel's residence, the latter innocently let out that two senior officials from the PMO had quietly visited the Pakistan High Commissioner. This came as a surprise to me, and on checking, I learnt that even Foreign Secretary Menon was completely in the dark in this regard. Clearly unknown to the Ministry, the PMO was in negotiation with Pakistan! This alone can explain why the Prime Minister was so upset at the Ministry's hard-hitting press release. It is possible that this outreach was in regard to the evolving situation in Afghanistan, where India was hoping to develop a common approach with Pakistan.

◆

Mr Menon was succeeded as Foreign Secretary by Mr S.K. Singh in February 1989. I had a very good equation with the latter by virtue of our deep professional interaction arising from his being our High Commissioner in Pakistan and our being on the same wavelength on most issues. Moreover, I not only extended all due courtesies to him but also attended to all his requests with sympathy and promptitude, given the inherent difficulties of his assignment. Indeed, I was the first to inform him of his selection as Foreign Secretary. He was, naturally, overjoyed and promised me a posting of my choice. It is another matter that my requests for a posting to Malaysia or Singapore were not acceded to, and I, thus, had to settle for a posting to the Philippines! The aforesaid posting was conditional on my finding a suitable successor. I was able to convince the Foreign Secretary that Naresh Dayal, who was a year senior to me, would be an ideal choice, as he had served both in Islamabad and in the Pakistan Division.

Dealings with Mr Singh were smooth, as we knew each other well and saw eye to eye on most Pakistan-related issues. His drafting was of the highest calibre and his initial assessments were usually sound. He could not, however, match the class of both his predecessors when it came to standing up for his convictions and his juniors. I was a witness to a telling incident in this regard involving one of our Ministers of State. On a Saturday morning, while attending to Parliament Questions, I was summoned to the latter's office. As I entered his room, he was agitatedly telling Mr Singh that I should be sacked. When I asked as to what was the issue, I was told that I had the temerity to submit a file to him pointing out the misbehaviour in Pakistan of some Sikh pilgrims who had been cleared for the visit on his recommendation. I responded that he needed to appreciate two points. First, that these individuals would normally not have been able to go to Pakistan, as their names had been submitted late, and it was only at my intervention with the concerned Indian agencies that their names had been cleared. Second, that it was these agencies which had reported that these individuals had misbehaved and not the AP Division. The latter was merely doing its duty in drawing the Minister's attention to this so that in future, greater care was exercised in making such recommendations. Above all, the AP Division had taken care in not calling for any action in the matter. This explanation did not mollify the Minister, who kept getting angrier, demanding action against the officers involved in the AP Division on this issue. Instead of standing up for the AP Division, Mr Singh stated that he would seek an explanation from the concerned Under Secretary and, as I started to speak, he held my hand under the table, signalling that I shut up. As we walked out of the room, Mr Singh asked me to get an explanation from the Under Secretary, assuring me that, thereafter, the matter would be hushed up. At this, I told Mr Singh that I would do nothing of the kind and that if he asked for any explanation, it must be addressed to me, as the file had gone under my signature and the concerned Under Secretary had only acted on my orders. On returning to my office, I informed the Under Secretary concerned, K.J. Francis, of the incident and told him that under no circumstances should he offer any explanation if asked for one, and any communication received by him in this regard should be put up to me for a response. Fortunately, the matter died a natural death, as on Sunday, the Minister of State was transferred. Another instance of the hand of the Almighty guiding one's destiny.

◆

During my tenure as Joint Secretary (AP), terrorism and Siachen were some of the major items of bilateral discourse.

On terrorism, India's main concern was Pakistan's fuelling of separatism in Punjab through encouragement of the Khalistan movement and the provision of support and shelter to Sikh terrorists. In respect of terrorism in Kashmir, we began to flag it only from early 1989 on the basis of a few Intelligence inputs, but Pakistan, as always, professed non-involvement. On the issue of instigating Sikh terrorism, Pakistan not only vigorously denied it but, as is its wont, made counter-allegations to the effect that we were instigating separatists in Sind. In fact, at the very end of a meeting on terrorism in Delhi, the Pakistan side casually handed over a note detailing the safe houses in India from where the Sindhi separatists were allegedly operating. Since the note was handed over at the end of the discussions, no detailed counter could be made from our side. On the basis, however, of a quick perusal of the note, while the delegations were at tea, it became obvious that this exercise was a propaganda ploy, as one of the safe houses listed was a house in upscale Friends Colony (West), where I happened to live and where no such safe house could exist. Much to the embarrassment of the Pakistani side, I drew their attention to this, adding for good measure that the Pakistan High Commissioner was also an occasional visitor to this area to see his good friend the Nawab of Rampur, who was one of my neighbours. In a more light-hearted vein, I said that I had high respect for the ISI and had expected a more polished dossier from it rather than one concocted in haste and so shoddy that one could catch it out after even a cursory appraisal!

Some progress was, however, made on the issue of Pakistani support to Sikh terrorists during Home Secretary Somiah's interaction with Pakistan Interior Secretary S.K. Mehmood in Pakistan in December 1986. While for much of the initial part of the discussion the latter denied any Pakistani involvement in Sikh terrorism, he could not do so when the former showed him videos in which Sikh terrorists detailed the extent to which Pakistan had helped them in the promotion of terror in India. He frankly admitted that there may have been some low-level help to Sikh terrorists in the past, suggested that we should let bygones be bygones and promised that in future there would be no such assistance. Regrettably, this apparent softening by Pakistan on this issue proved to be illusory, and there was no let-up in its support to Sikh extremists.

On Siachen, there were innumerable Defence Secretary-level talks preceded by intense internal debates on how to address the issue. The imperative on the Indian side to find some solution arose from the financial burden and casualty toll it was incurring by keeping its troops in a most inhospitable terrain. Over time, a view developed that we should strive for an understanding with Pakistan, which would ensure that the areas occupied by the two sides would be demilitarized and their respective forces would be withdrawn to mutually agreed positions. The Indian Army, of course, made it clear that in the event of Pakistan violating this understanding and occupying the commanding heights in the area, it would not be possible for it to dislodge the Pakistani forces in a localized action, and the only way of so doing would be by resorting to an all-out confrontation. A resolution of the Siachen issue along the aforesaid lines, however, stalled due to lack of agreement on the points to which both sides would withdraw as well as Pakistan's reluctance to authenticate the location of the points from which the troop withdrawals would be effectuated. The latter was essential to establish breach of faith by either side, and

India's insistence on the same was natural, given the manner in which Pakistan had time and again broken agreements.

With Benazir Bhutto's election victory in November 1988 and her being sworn-in as Prime Minister on 2 December 1988, there was an expectation that this offered a window of opportunity for improved India–Pakistan ties. Certainly, the PMO was gung-ho about these possibilities. It was in direct touch with Benazir Bhutto through intermediaries like the former Consul General in Karachi, Aftab Seth, and Joint Secretary in the PMO, Ronen Sen. The feedback as a result of these exchanges was, of course, not shared with the AP Division, though it had become apparent that Rajiv Gandhi would be visiting Pakistan for the SAARC Summit later in the month.

On the eve of the visit, the Secretary Security strongly argued at a meeting taken by the Minister of State for Home Affairs that it be cancelled because of the uneasy security situation in Pakistan. While most of the other officials present did not challenge the Secretary (Security), who was well known for his fiery temperament, I made a strong a pitch that the visit should not be cancelled, pointing out that the Pakistan Government had a vested interest in providing proper security to Rajiv Gandhi and a small newly built township like Islamabad was relatively easy to secure. The Secretary (Security) was, however, not convinced and stated that if the Prime Minister persisted with his plan to proceed to Pakistan, he would lie down in front of the VVIP aircraft! He further queried whether I could give him a written guarantee that no harm would come to the Prime Minister in Islamabad. I riposted that we should only go by probabilities and was it possible for anyone to give a written guarantee that no harm would come to Rajiv Gandhi in Delhi or elsewhere in India? At this stage, the Minister took charge and pointed out to the Secretary (Security) that I was representing the MEA and merely articulating its view, and a final decision could be taken after further discussions at a higher level. Clearly, the Secretary (Security)'s melodramatics did not carry weight and the visit proceeded as scheduled.

In preparation for Rajiv Gandhi's bilaterals with Benazir at the Islamabad SAARC summit in December 1988, the AP Division shortlisted as many as five agreements that could be signed. It was, however, felt in the PMO that this could jeopardize Benazir's standing with the Army and, accordingly, only three agreements were signed, notably on non-attack on nuclear installations, cultural cooperation, and avoidance of double taxation of income derived from international air transport.

Rajiv Gandhi's December 1988 visit to Pakistan was followed up by his visit in July 1989—the first bilateral visit to Pakistan by an Indian Prime Minister since that of Jawaharlal Nehru in 1960. Between December 1988 and July 1989, there was an almost unprecedented interaction and exchange of delegations between the two countries. However, the outcome of this frenetic interaction was an anti-climax, as Benazir, no doubt under pressure from the military, made normalization of relations between the two countries contingent on concessions by India on Kashmir, an issue on which Rajiv Gandhi could not compromise.

Following the Rajiv Gandhi–Benazir bilaterals, I was looking forward to travelling back to India as scheduled by commercial flight via Lahore, where I had planned a brief stopover to see my ancestral home in Model Town. This was, however, not to be, as I was directed at the last minute to board Rajiv Gandhi's special flight to Delhi in order to avail of the occasion to brief him on Siachen. An agreement on this had, for long, been on the anvil, but for reasons cited above had been put off. During my half hour one-on-one exchange with him, where, in addition to the two of us, only a silent Sonia Gandhi was present, I made a pitch for concluding an agreement thereon, provided we could get Pakistan to agree on the authentication of the current location of the forces of both sides on a map as well as the detailing of the withdrawal of both sides to agreed-upon points. Additionally, I suggested that we should make it clear to Pakistan that any breach of the agreement would inevitably trigger a wider confrontation. Our forces should not be expected to confine themselves to try and take back the areas lost due to any Pakistani action, as given the terrain, this would be overly costly in terms of casualties. There was no reaction from Rajiv Gandhi, and I felt that there was a strange disinterest in pushing this matter further, triggered possibly by the fact that following his interaction with Benazir, he no longer saw a bright future for the bilateral relationship.

On return from Pakistan, I proceeded on leave and started preparing for my departure for the Philippines. I was told by friends and colleagues, including in the PMO, that I should not have accepted this posting and should have held out for something more important. I, however, paid no heed to this, as I needed a break from the hectic work life in Delhi, and in any case, I always had an itch to move on to a new assignment when I felt that there was nothing new to be learnt in the existing job. Barely had my heavy baggage been shipped to Manila that I was summoned by the Foreign Secretary, stating that I rejoin duty immediately, as the Prime Minister desired that I should continue in my assignment. The same message was also given in my presence to the Joint Secretary, Bangladesh, Sri Lanka and Maldives (BSM). While the latter readily agreed, I remained adamant and requested the Foreign Secretary to prevail upon Prime Minister not to insist in a change of my plans, as I would be greatly inconvenienced. Fortunately, there were no further surprises on this score, and I was able to proceed to Manila on my first Ambassadorial appointment.

10

SOJOURN IN THE HAPPY-GO-LUCKY PHILIPPINES

My tour of duty in the Philippines from mid-September 1989 to mid-September 1992 lasted exactly three years and was, perhaps, the most enjoyable and relaxed phase of my career. Being my first Ambassadorial assignment, it was a useful learning experience on how to run an Embassy.

The background briefing on my assignment to the Philippines at the Ministry was not particularly illuminating. The Joint Secretary dealing with the Philippines did not have much to say apart from sharing with me some detailed despatches from Ambassador K. Raghunath, whom I would be shortly replacing. The Philippines was obviously at the bottom in terms of importance of the countries under his charge. This was evident from his request that I desist from sending lengthy dispatches, as he simply did not have the time to read them! The disinclination to read lengthy notes clearly continued to pervade the Ministry. It was something I could not empathize with, as I felt that detailed reports from our missions abroad were a huge value addition to the Ministry and, if anything, deserved to be encouraged. I myself, as a Head of Division, had found them invaluable and not only read them carefully but also responded to them.

Living conditions in metro Manila were excellent for the diplomatic community. It was a modern bustling city with a population of about 8 million with, of course, its share of slums. English was widely spoken, and the country had nearly 100 per cent literacy. Schooling was outstanding. High-quality local domestic help was available on tap by way of Filipina maids who were not only efficient but also did not charge too much. The city abounded with modern malls, clubs and golf courses. Housing was plentiful and much of it was located in gated communities, which afforded good security, so necessary in a country with a high crime rate. The only major downsides were the massive traffic jams, the near-year-around high humidity and the absence of top-quality medical care.

I inherited a lovely, spacious five-bedroom residence complete with a garden and a good-sized swimming pool located in the plush North Forbes Park, where several other Heads of Mission, including Nicholas Platt, the US Ambassador, as well as Philippine notables lived, like former President, Diosdado Macapagal. North Forbes Park was a gated community in the Makati area cheek by jowl with the famed Manila Golf Club, the Manila Polo Club and the Fort Bonifacio Golf Club. I was a member of both the Polo Club and the Fort Bonifacio Golf Club.

The residence was also located barely at five minutes' driving time from the Embassy, which was in the neighbouring gated village of Das Marinas. Our Philippine mission was small, comprising an Ambassador, First Secretary, Second Secretary, a couple of Attachés and sundry staff. I was fortunate in having Mr Swaranjit Singh and Mr Sodhi as First and Second Secretaries, respectively. Both, though from the IFS (B), were very good officers. Additionally, Ranjit Rai, the Naval Advisor based in Singapore, was concurrently accredited to the Philippines and would visit Manila every now and then. He had earlier been Director (Naval Intelligence), and was dynamic and resourceful.

◆

Filipinos were an easy-going, fun-loving people who, even in the midst of dire tragedy, were not unknown to take to song and dance when most others would withdraw into their shell. They were full of a joie de vivre, sadly, foreign to most Indians. Most Filipinos, even those in high office, were entertainers par excellence, and even at many official functions, singing was de rigueur, and those attending were expected to contribute with song or dance. Thus, Raul Manglapus, Foreign Minister in President Corazon Aquino's government, apart from being a playwright and composer, was an accomplished pianist and headed the Executive Band, which was often invited to play at events hosted by the President.

Beneath the joyous exterior of the Filipino people there, however, lurked a streak of violence, which could erupt quite unexpectedly. All in all, I found the Filipinos a fascinating folk with amazingly contradictory characteristics. For instance, while being staunchly Roman Catholic, highly superstitious and strict in the observance of rituals, they, at the same time, were surprisingly amoral. This was only to be expected, perhaps, of a people who, as was commonly said, had for over three centuries till 1898 been in a nunnery (read Spanish rule) and for half a century till 1946 been in Hollywood (read US rule).

Like many Asian countries, the Philippines was a male-dominated country in which women were hard-working and men indolent. The extent of male domination was exemplified by the fact that one of oldest golf clubs in the city, the Manila Golf Club, had an exclusive mens'-only area, which was strictly off-limits for ladies. This was the subject of quite a controversy when the German Ambassador, who happened to be a lady and was a member of this Club, protested against this practice. Not only was her request for entry into the mens'-only area flatly rejected but the Club, which had hitherto liberally accorded temporary membership to all Heads of Missions, immediately withdrew this facility for all new Heads of Mission! As I fell into this category, I was a sufferer, and membership of this prestigious Club was denied to me.

In keeping with the character of the Filipino people, protocol which governs diplomatic life was wonderfully relaxed. Access to dignitaries was relatively easy, provided, of course, the individual concerned wished to meet you. If not, the meeting took weeks to happen. Thus, personal equations or need were the determining elements on whether or not meetings sought materialized early. Similarly, the dress code was uncomplicated. Suits were virtually unnecessary. Even for the most formal event, all one needed was a dark trouser and a barong. If one wanted to be sharply turned out, the barong could be tailored out of pineapple fabric; otherwise, it could be made of cotton or synthetic fibre. All this was both convenient and practical, as Manila was uncomfortably hot and humid through much of the year.

◆

The diplomatic community in Manila was mid-sized, close-knit, and their frequent interactions centred around golf or simply around parties at each other's homes. There was, of course, the occasional highlight as, for instance, a lavish dinner organized by the Saudi Ambassador to celebrate his son's wedding, where a belly dancer specially imported from Egypt for the event regaled the invitees with titillating performances. I had good relations with nearly all my diplomatic colleagues and, in particular, those from the US, the ASEAN countries, Australia, Saudi Arabia, Bangladesh, China and even Pakistan.

The US Ambassador was clearly the most important because of the influence exercised by him, as exemplified by the huge US military presence in the country for the last several decades at Clark Air Base and at the Subic Bay naval base. I had occasion to visit the former, which was spread over several square kilometres, and on entry, I felt as though one was in the US and not in the Philippines. All the cabs were lookalike New York taxis, the food was typically American and the US dollar was the sole legal tender. At the time that I was in the Philippines, there was a deeply polarizing debate on whether or not the lease for these should bases be extended. In late 1991, in a closely contested decision, the Philippine Senate, by a margin of one, voted against the continuance of the US bases, and the following year, the US withdrew its forces from the country. It is understood that following Sino–Philippine tensions in the Pacific, US forces are now being allowed to use some of the earlier bases on a rotational basis.

The Japanese Ambassador was also amongst the more influential Heads of Missions, as Japan had, over the years, emerged as the largest source of economic assistance. However, Japan and the Philippines were in a love–hate relationship. Whilst on the one hand, the latter cultivated Japan for the economic aid emanating from it, on the other hand, at a popular level, there was a deep-rooted hatred for it on account of the atrocities committed by it during the Second World War. In these circumstances, the Japanese Ambassador had to take strict security precautions in his movements.

◆

Located in the ring of fire girding the Pacific Ocean, the Philippines, comprising over 7,000 islands and with a population at the time of about 60 million, was susceptible to a variety of natural disasters of gargantuan proportions. Through my stay there, I was witness to any number of typhoons that hit the country regularly as also the deadly Luzon earthquake of 1990 and the volcanic eruption of Mount Pinatubo in mid-1991.

The ferocity of the typhoons in the Philippines was scary, and at least one or two hit Manila every year. The Philippines had a well-worked-out drill to handle typhoons with an efficient early warning system. Nevertheless, the damage caused was considerable, resulting in massive flooding, power outages, and loss of property and life. Within a few weeks of my arrival in Manila, a severe typhoon hit the metro Manila region. I had never witnessed a storm with such high-velocity winds accompanied by very heavy rain, which lasted nearly two days, totally disrupting normal life in the city.

The Luzon earthquake in 1990, with an intensity of 7.8 on the Richter scale, was amongst the worst earthquakes to have hit the country, leading to over 2,400 deaths on the very first day. Its epicentre was not too far from Manila. It is a tribute to those who built the city that there was no major damage to the buildings in it, though in some cases, as in the one occupied by the Foreign Office, the floor had buckled. The intensity of the earthquake was such that it was not possible to stay indoors when it struck, and severe aftershocks persisted for a good hour thereafter. Water from homes that had swimming pools like ours spilled out onto the surrounding areas! Arun Adarkar, the Treasurer of the Asian Development Bank (ADB), who had a top-floor office, told me that while the earthquake was in progression, he could see the building tilting towards the adjacent high-rise.

Though the typhoons and the Luzon earthquake were frightening, they were not one-of-a-kind experiences for me, as I had seen milder versions of the same elsewhere, but the eruption of the Mount Pinatubo volcano, located barely 80 kilometres from Manila, was something totally new for me. It has been touted as the second-largest volcanic eruption of the twentieth century, sending clouds of volcanic ash 50 kilometres into the atmosphere and disrupting air traffic in the vicinity. The eruption caused tremendous loss of life and property in the country. Clark Air Base was rendered inoperational, and normal flight activity in the Manila area was disrupted for some days. Many house tops in the vicinity collapsed on account of the sheer weight of the descending ash accumulated on them, and all that stood in the way of the uncontrolled flow of molten lava was destroyed. For me, in Manila, I felt that something strange was afoot, as the sky started darkening around 4.00 p.m. Stepping out into the open a little later, I felt something falling on my head. It was whitish-grey volcanic ash, composed essentially of sand and silica. It is then and on some investigation that I realized that there had been a volcanic eruption at Mount Pinatubo.

◆

Apart from natural disasters, the Philippines was also prone to man-made disasters. Ever since President Corazon Aquino assumed office in 1986 through the People Power Revolution, which rid the country of its long-time dictator President Ferdinand Marcos, the Philippine government was plagued by several coup bids. The most serious of these occurred in December 1989 and was decisively put down only after a week's military action. It was led, as indeed was the case in many of the earlier coups, by right-wing elements under Colonel Gregorio Honasan, a highly decorated officer, who had a host of grievances against the government, notably that it was not sufficiently proactive against the communist rebel movement, that the military was getting a raw deal and that it had not lived up to its promise of providing good governance. As with the earlier coup bids, it also had the support of erstwhile Marcos followers and those against the Aquino government. The sneaking sympathy amongst many Filipinos for the earlier coup bids and for Honasan is reflected in the very mild punishment meted out to the rebels, which, in respect of one of the coup bids, was 30 push-ups, in which the then Army Chief, Fidel Ramos, also participated!

The December 1989 coup bid was, without doubt, the most serious one and came within a whisker of succeeding. In the wee hours of

1 December, the presidential palace was strafed by rebel jets and a fierce firefight lasting several hours took place on its outer periphery. However, by early afternoon, the tide had been turned against the rebels. Not only was the presidential palace successfully defended, but the rebel aircraft were also destroyed by loyal elements of the Philippine Air Force. Furthermore, US jets were scrambled from Clark Air Base in the vicinity of Manila in a show of support for the Aquino government. It nevertheless took quite some time for the government to restore complete normalcy in Manila, and the rebels were able to keep parts of the city, like the posh Makati area, under their control for quite a few days.

The coup bid and the measures to quell it came with Philippine characteristics, which had their funny side. For instance, going into office on 1 December 1989, I saw an inordinately large number of rebel soldiers marching out of Fort Bonifacio, which they had captured, to Makati, which they were planning to target next. On reaching the office, where I learnt of what was afoot, I requested my wife to immediately go to Makati and stock up with provisions. She was able to do this without any trouble from the rebels. In fact, a friend later related to me that whilst in Makati, he requested the rebels to pose with him and his family for photographs, which they readily did!

Through the stand-off between the military and the rebels, we could sometimes hear the chatter of gunfire. However, the exchange of all gunfire stopped with impressive regularity between 1.00 and 3.00 p.m., as this was lunch and siesta time. Such understanding was also on show when the contending forces agreed to hold off any military action in order to evacuate one of my Sri Lankan friends heading the local office of the UN High Commission for Refugees, Sri Wijeratne, who had been injured in the exchange of fire. The surreal atmosphere in the city was vividly brought home to me when I went to the airport to receive my son on his return to Manila from school in India. While there was a near-total shutdown in our part of the city on account of the military showdown underway, in other parts of the city, life was in carnival mode with bustling restaurants and fully operational shopping malls!

◆

My task as a diplomat was eased by the fact that India–Philippine relations were trouble-free. However, while there were many commonalities and shared values, such as anti-colonialism, South–South cooperation, a strong democratic polity, an independent judiciary and press, and the wide use of the English language, the relationship lacked depth and intensity. The latter was in large measure due to the fact that while India was committed to non-alignment, the Philippines was firmly in the western camp and closely aligned to the US, to which it even provided military bases. The divergent political alignment of the two countries was also not offset by any deep historical, cultural and civilizational linkages or by strong economic ties, which would have been possible had India been an economic powerhouse. In these circumstances, the bilateral relationship never really flowered, and the best that could be done was to try and promote a greater understanding of India, to cultivate traditional friends and to develop new linkages to the extent possible in diverse areas.

Two factors played an important role in the gradual intensification of India–Phillipine ties, notably the advent of the Aquino government in February 1986 and India's economic liberalization, coupled with its Look East policy, in 1991. The advent of the Aquino government, strongly rooted as it was in Gandhian ideals, automatically resulted in an Indian connect, which was totally lacking under the Marcos administration. India's economic liberalization and disavowal of its earlier socialist policies, which were an ideological anathema in the capitalist economies of the ASEAN countries, removed a critical impediment to the deepening of bilateral ties and provided an underpinning to the success of India's Look East policy. While Singapore took the lead amongst the ASEAN countries in India's emerging as a sectoral dialogue partner of ASEAN, the Philippines was always supportive of this exercise.

Through my stint as Ambassador in the Philippines, I made multifaceted efforts at increasing India's profile in the country, knowing full well that while these would not succeed initially, but over time, our outreach would yield positive results. For starters, I ensured that whenever there was any calamity in the country, India provided assistance, which usually took the form of medical supplies. Since the Philippines was constantly hit by disasters, I was a frequent visitor to the Ministry of Health, handing over gifts of medical supplies, which were deeply appreciated. In the process, I developed a very good relationship with Secretary Dr Alfredo R.A. Bengzon, the Health Minister. The MEA was fully supportive of my efforts in this regard and usually supplied much more than the quantum of relief supplies suggested by me. But apart from the health sector, I also sought to promote the commercial supply of several Indian products, ranging from military vehicles to milk powder. Though there was not any major breakthrough in this regard whilst I was in the Philippines, at least the possibilities of enhanced commercial exchanges began to be explored.

◆

The absence of any work pressure and the openness of Philippine society enabled me to benefit from interactions with many eminent local personalities. Some of the more memorable of these included F. Sionil Jose, Cardinal Jaime Sin and the former President, Macapagal.

Sionil Jose was a very well-known and prolific Philippine author. His novels, in particular, the five-volume *Rosales* series, are extremely readable and provided valuable insights into life in the Philippines. I called on him at his bookshop in Ermita, Manila, and he was at that time already in his 60s. His leanings were distinctly left wing, but he was a staunch nationalist and a keen commentator on political developments in the country.

Cardinal Jaime Sin was the leading Roman Catholic cleric in the Philippines. He carried considerable clout on account of his immense popularity garnered through his support for the poor and outspoken criticism of autocracy. His support to Aquino against the Marcos regime was a critical factor in the former succeeding in her struggle against the latter. The Cardinal had a great sense of humour as exemplified by his receiving me with the words, 'Welcome to the house of Sin.'

Access to former President Macapagal was facilitated by the fact that we were virtually neighbours in North Forbes Park. The attendees at his parties were from diverse sections of the Philippine elite as well as from the diplomatic community. He was a wise old politician, and it was a treat to listen to his observations and comments.

◆

The Indian community in the Philippines was relatively small, comprising in the main a few thousand Indian Sikhs and Sindhis mainly involved in moneylending, and a few score expatriates engaged in local business, the ADB, multinational companies and the academe, extending from the International Rice Research Institute to various well-established universities. Amongst the expat community, I developed good friendships with people like Aubrey Bout, the local head of Procter & Gamble, and Arun Adarkar from the IA&AS, who was the treasurer of the ADB and who had been a colleague many years earlier in the DEA. Additionally, there were a number of colleagues from the IFS and IAS on deputation with the ADB, such as Farrokh Kapadia, Kartik Sandilya and Prabhu Ghate, with whom I interacted every now and then. While those working with the ADB were very well-paid, they were, with the exception of Arun Adarkar, grossly underworked and often griped about it.

The Sikh community in the Philippines were descendants of the soldiers who had come to Manila as a part of the British forces during the Seven Years' War in the mid-eighteenth century and had chosen to stay on. While some had become security guards, the bulk had taken to the profession of moneylending. As a result, Indians were commonly known, in a somewhat derogatory fashion, as 'five-six'. The term meant that they lent 5 pesos in the morning and took back 6 pesos in the evening. Understandably, they had become wealthy over the decades and, in the process, sometimes aroused animosity and fear amongst the locals. Indeed, Senator Leticia Ramos Shahani, a good friend and an Indophile who had married an Indian, admitted that, as a child, she was told that if she did not behave, the five-six would take her away! By virtue of their wealth, these local Indians were, however, a source of support in times of need. Indeed, during the coup bid when cash supply was uncertain due to closure of some of the banks, I was approached by the Bangladesh Ambassador, Major General Mannaf, as to whether I could bail out his staff. I had no hesitation in responding in the affirmative, telling him that I could do the needful through the Indian moneylending community.

◆

For every Ambassador, the presentation of credentials is an important occasion. It usually comprises a brief but exclusive meeting with the Head of State made up essentially of pleasantries, following which the Ambassador can freely undertake his normal diplomatic activities in the country of his accreditation. In my case, I had the good fortune to have had a nearly one-hour audience with President Aquino along with my wife. While the meeting provided one an opportunity of providing the President with an exposé on India's foreign policy and the possibilities of mutually beneficial cooperation, she was primarily interested in learning all she could about Mahatma Gandhi. This was because both she and her late husband had drawn inspiration from Gandhi's non-violent campaign in their contest with the Marcos regime. President Aquino herself came through as a straightforward and sincere person and not one meant for the hurly-burly of politics. However, beneath her simplicity, there was the steely resolve to stand up for her beliefs.

◆

The high point of my stay in the Philippines was the state visit of President Ramaswamy Venkataraman in 1991. (The only other really high-level visit from India to the Philippines preceding this visit was that of Mrs Gandhi in 1981.) I had long been urging the Ministry to organize the visit of some dignitary so as to provide a higher profile to the India–Philippine relationship. In response to my repeated requests, I received a phone call from Himachal Som, the Joint Secretary in the Ministry handling Southeast Asia, seeking my opinion of the possibility of arranging the visit of President Venkataraman to the Philippines from 28 April to 1 May 1991, as the visit needed to be synchronized with his already-programmed visit to Vietnam. While welcoming the idea, I informed Himachal that I would naturally have to clear this with the Philippine side, and the only problem that I envisaged was that the dates specified may not suit our hosts. Himachal indicated that I would need to get a very early response, as time was running out. In the event, I contacted Foreign Minister Manglapus, who met me at short notice at his residence early the following morning. He reacted very positively to my suggestion, and formal clearance for the visit materialized in quick time.

In the lead-up to the visit, the Ministry, as is its wont, urged that I should rope in additional staff either from headquarters or from neighbouring missions in order to help with the increased workload resulting from the VVIP visit. I, however, turned down this offer, as I was confident of managing with my own resources and felt that additional staff would, in fact, be a nuisance, as the Mission, in addition to dealing with the presidential delegation, would also have to cater to the needs of the additional staff. Fortunately, the Ministry went with my advice and, apart from ensuring that Ranjit Rai, the Naval Advisor accredited to Manila, was on site, no additional officials were sent to us for the VVIP visit.

Happily, the President's visit was a great success and, inter alia, entailed the signature of an agreement on cooperation in the peaceful uses of atomic energy and an MoU on cooperation in agricultural science and technology. As per protocol, he had extensive meetings with President Aquino and the Philippine leadership. The President gave an address at the University of the Philippines, which conferred upon him an honorary degree of doctorate of Law. The visit constituted a step in bringing the two countries closer together and was a precursor to our Look East policy as well as a chain of high-level bilateral visits over the years.

I had the honour of hosting a big reception for the President at my residence to interact with the Indian community as well as a small private dinner for him and his delegation. In the process of the visit and our exchanges, I was deeply impressed by his simplicity, humility and knowledge. There was no trace of arrogance in him and not once did I note any annoyance on his part on any issue.

I would be less than honest, however, if I were to suggest that there were no moments of tension during the President's visit. One that began even before the visit was related to the seating

Austria: Ambassador V.C. Trivedi (front) and Mr J.N. Dixit (left) and myself: presentation of credentials for the Ambassador

Washington DC: With US Agricultural Secretary Earl Butz

Philippines: With President Corazon Aquino: presentation of credentials

Philippines: With Health Secretary Dr Alfredo R.A. Bengzon

Pakistan: With Sartaj Aziz, Pakistan's Finance Minister and later Advisor to the Prime Minister on Foreign Affairs

Pakistan: With Mushahid Hussain, Information Minister in Nawaz Sharif's cabinet

Pakistan: With Begum Naseem Wali Khan and Asfandyar Wali Khan

Pakistan: With Sahibzada Yakub Ali Khan, Foreign Minister in Benazir Bhutto's cabinet

Pakistan: With Sunil Dutt and Dilip Kumar at our residence in Islamabad

arrangement at the banquet to be hosted for the President by his Philippine counterpart. As per the plan conveyed to me by the Philippine protocol, the children of our President, who were accompanying him, were shown as seated at a table other than the main table. Our President's protocol insisted that this was not acceptable and that the children, too, must be accommodated at the main table. My suggestion to our protocol that the Philippine proposition was perfectly in order and that we should accede to it was brushed aside. I was instead instructed that I must hold firm and insist upon our position. Once our delegation arrived in Manila, it was explained to me by our protocol that our position was dictated by the views of the President's daughter and she would not accept being placed at any table other than the main one. I was also told that if the Philippine side remained adamant, I would personally have to do all the explaining to our President's daughter. I found this odd, as the officials in the presidential party were far better placed than me to appropriately explain the situation by virtue of their familiarity with the President and his family. In any case, with no other option before me, I took it upon myself to discuss the matter with the President's daughter, whom I found to be highly cultured and reasonable, contrary to what I had been given to understand. She readily understood the logic of the seating plan proposed and all the more so, as the table on which she would be seated included President Aquino's children, of whom one was a celebrated actress!

Another moment of tension arose when, just as I was turning in for the night, I received an indication that the President's children wished to go night clubbing. This was contrary to our decision that this be discouraged in view of the high crime rate in the city. Accordingly, I went to the hotel where the presidential party was lodged and had to tactfully persuade the President's daughter to desist from stepping out of the hotel so late at night, pointing out that not only was it risky but could lead to avoidable adverse publicity. This, again, was an exercise that should have more appropriately been undertaken by those accompanying the President rather than being left to the Embassy.

◆

One of my lasting regrets is that I travelled very little whilst in the Philippines. This was in large measure due to the pathetically low emoluments I received. Accordingly, all I could do was to take short day or, at most, weekend excursions restricted to the environs of Manila. A couple of the more notable ones were to the Hundred Islands and to Baguio city. The latter is a charming hill station, which provides a cool getaway from the heat and humidity of Manila and is endowed with an extraordinarily quaint golf course. It was severely damaged during the 1990 earthquake that devastated the country.

Sometime in August 1992, I received a message from Foreign Secretary Dixit intimating my transfer as the Permanent Representative (PR) of India to the UN Offices in Geneva and requesting me to move immediately. While I had been anticipating a transfer, as my three-year term was drawing to a close, I was surprised at my transfer to Geneva as PR, since I had virtually no experience of UN-related work. When I mentioned this to the Foreign Secretary, he told me that he had deliberately taken this step, as there was a UN mafia in the Ministry that had taken to treating such assignments as its own special preserve to the exclusion of all other officers. He felt that this was not a good practice and in posting me as PR, Geneva, he wished to make the point that any good officer could be effective in an UN assignment and prior UN experience should not be a prerequisite for a senior-level assignment to the UN. In this context, he informed me on a confidential basis that he would soon be posting Hamid Ansari, our Ambassador in Iran, who, like me, had no UN expertise, as PR, New York.

11

HIGH-STAKE MULTILATERAL DIPLOMACY: GENEVA

My posting as India's Permanent Representative to the UN Offices in Geneva (PR Geneva) was my most challenging appointment. This was partly because multilateral work was new to me, but more importantly because my assignment coincided with Pakistan's intense campaign against India on the Kashmir issue at a time when the country was wracked by terrorism and when it was at its weakest economically. My overriding concern was to neutralize the Pakistani move against us, and this left little time for savouring the scenic wonders of Switzerland or of the countries around it.

Prior to taking up my assignment in Geneva, on transfer from Manila, I stopped over in Delhi for a brief spell of leave and consultations in the Ministry. From my interactions with the UN Division, it became evident that Human Rights and Disarmament were the two major areas of interest to India. The briefings that I obtained on these two areas by the concerned Directors were a study in contrast. While the officer dealing with Human Rights took great pains in walking me through the technicalities of the issues involved, the one dealing with Disarmament was reluctant to part with much information, and his briefing was perfunctory. The latter typified the preponderant majority in the bureaucracy, who knowing that information is power, choose to keep it to themselves for as long as possible, even though sharing it is in the greater national interest. Regrettably, my interaction with the Additional Secretary heading the Division was also not particularly illuminating. Indeed, I got the distinct impression that the folks in the UN Division were a little miffed that I had been appointed as PR Geneva and that they felt that this appointment should have gone to someone from the UN mafia.

In retrospect, it does not reflect well on the Ministry that it failed to alert me to the impending crises that were to engulf me in the areas of Human Rights and Disarmament. On Human Rights, the Ministry had not envisaged the possibility of Pakistan's moving a Kashmir-related resolution against us in the United Nations Commission on Human Rights (UNCHR, replaced by the United Nations Human Rights Council in 2006), and on Disarmament, it was clueless of what needed to be done to promote the complete elimination of nuclear weapons and the extent to which India should be supportive of the Comprehensive Nuclear-Test-Ban Treaty (CTBT) or the Fissile Material Cut-Off Treaty (FMCT).

None of the aforesaid issues figured in my interaction with the Foreign Secretary. His major concern related to an audit objection arising from a property purchased for the Head of Mission's residence sometime in the mid-1980s under the watch of one of my predecessors. This had been acquired at an exorbitant price of 6 million Swiss francs but had since remained unoccupied. Accordingly, he underlined the importance of my moving into this property at the earliest.

Taking note of the Foreign Secretary's direction, my first official act on reaching Geneva even before stepping into my office was to undertake an inspection of the aforesaid property. A detailed examination led me to the conclusion that, though extremely well-located right next to the UN Offices and a heritage property as well, it would not be suitable for use as a Head of Mission's residence, since its entertainment area was too small. Besides, the house was very old and in need of extensive repairs. As a result of my report, plans for my shift to this property were shelved. Efforts to sell the property proved abortive, as the best price we could get was 20–25 per cent lower than what we had paid for it. Ultimately, it was a decade and a half later and after spending an arm and a leg that the property was finally made suitable for occupation by the PR, but fortunately, this did not happen during my tour of duty. Had the Ministry insisted that I move into this property, I would have probably spent more time on overseeing its renovation than on my work!

◆

The Permanent Mission of India (PMI) to the UN Offices in Geneva was a relatively large mission by Indian standards and certainly much bigger than that in Manila. Apart from myself, the mission included three Counsellors, notably Manbir Singh, Neelam Sabharwal and Anil Wadhwa. The latter was soon replaced by Ajit Kumar. All were high-quality officers. While Manbir Singh handled United Nations Conference on Trade and Development (UNCTAD), Neelam Sabharwal dealt with Human Rights and Anil Wadhwa looked after Disarmament. Debashish Chakravarty was a First Secretary looking after Human Rights and doubling up as Head of Chancery, and a Second Secretary, T.S. Tirumurti, looked after agencies like the World Health Organization (WHO), International Labour Organization (ILO), World Intellectual Property Organization (WIPO), etc. Subsequently, I was able to get one more outstanding officer by way of Navtej Sarna for Disarmament work. All the aforesaid officers belonged to the IFS (A).

Additionally, I was fortunate to have a dynamic Counsellor level IFS (A) officer by way of Bhaswati Mukherjee on deputation at the UN Centre for Human Rights. She was a valuable source of information on Human Rights-related developments as she was in the key position of Chef de Cabinet of the head of the UN Centre for Human Rights.

Unlike today, when Disarmament is handled by a separate PR, in my time, the PR dealt with both Disarmament- and human rights-related issues as well as a plethora of other organizations like the WHO, ILO, UNCTAD, WIPO, etc. It did not, however, deal with WTO-related issues, which were dealt with by another PR who was from the Commerce Ministry. The administrative work of our WTO mission was, however, handled by us. Some PRs, like my Pakistani counterpart, had an even wider charge than me and also dealt with the WTO.

I believe that the creation of a separate mission to deal with Disarmament work, which was the doing of External Affairs Minister Jaswant Singh in the late 1990s, was a mistake for two reasons. First, with no Treaty negotiations underway in the Conference of Disarmament, the Mission is grossly underworked. Second, and more importantly, the wider the work coverage of the PR, the more influential he becomes, as he is better positioned to bring to bear his leverages in one area of activity for gains in another area. Above all, his contacts and information, which are critical components of a diplomatic toolkit, increase exponentially if he has a wider work coverage.

My work style in Geneva was radically different from that in other Missions. This was dictated by the nature of the work, which required most of the officers to be away from the Mission for much of the day in meetings strung across a variety of organizations. Accordingly, I insisted that all officers come to office sharp at 9.00 a.m. for a half-hour meeting enabling me to give instructions for the day to all concerned and, in turn, to be briefed on the important activities underway. This was also the occasion to finalize my own schedule after assessing where I was needed most. Additionally, this meeting was also an occasion to clear up differences amongst the officers with total transparency. While the institutionalization of this morning meeting caused some unhappiness in the beginning, I believe it made for greater cohesion and effectiveness and nipped, inter se, differences in the bud.

◆

A couple of weeks after reaching Geneva, I was required to proceed to New York to attend the meetings of the UN first committee dealing with Disarmament-related issues. Normally, the officer exclusively dealing with Disarmament in Geneva accompanies the PR for these meetings to assist him. However, this facility was denied to me by the Ministry, even though I was new to this work, on the grounds that the concerned officer had already exhausted his deputation time in New York with my predecessor on other Disarmament-related work. I could only attribute such a cussed approach to being one dictated by the UN mafia, who would have been delighted to see me trip up. However, every such move on the part of the Ministry coupled with the Foreign Secretary's faith in me only led me to redouble my efforts to succeed through sustained hard work and, more often than not, I found that I was tripping up the folks at Headquarters for their less-than-professional performance. While this did not exactly endear me to them, it did tend to keep them on their toes and made for a more effective presentation of India's viewpoint.

On arrival in New York, I devoted the entire weekend prior to the 1992 first committee session carefully studying the over 50 texts cleared by the Ministry relating to the resolutions up for tabling. Surprised at the linguistic deficiencies in many of the texts cleared by the Ministry and the questionable positions taken on some of the resolutions, I proposed a variety of changes, most of which were accepted, though not sometimes without reference to higher levels. Clearly, some of the officials in the UN mafia were plain lazy and tended to blindly go by the language of the resolutions from the previous year without sufficiently taking note of the changed circumstances or the bilateral implications.

A classic example of this approach on the part of our UN mafia was their direction at a subsequent session of the first committee that we support, as in the past, a Palestine-related resolution tabled by the Arab countries against Israel. On an analysis of this resolution, I felt that this would not be appropriate as it, inter alia, was supportive of the Treaty on the Non-Proliferation of Nuclear Weapons (NPT) and went so far as to call on Israel to sign it. In these circumstances, I asked for a change in the Ministry's position. Since this was not acceded to at the Director's level, I raised this to the level of the Additional Secretary who, amazed at what had been proposed by his Division, suggested a 180-degree turnaround and held out that instead of supporting the resolution, we should oppose it. Based on my dealings with the Arab world as a former Joint Secretary (WANA), I, however, persuaded him that this constituted too radical a shift, which would alienate many of our Arab friends and that it would suffice to simply abstain. As it is, the moment the resolution was voted upon, a number of Arab Ambassadors came up to me expressing unhappiness at our not supporting their pro-Palestine resolution as we had done in the past. I pointed out that we were, and would always be, supportive of the Palestinian cause, but this did not mean that we would support resolutions which extolled the NPT, as the latter was an anathema to us. I further remonstrated that the Arab world had always taken Indian support for granted and, in future, if they wanted our support, they should consult us in the drafting of such resolutions. The Arab unhappiness aroused by our move was compensated to an extent by the Israeli representative coming across to me to express his country's deep appreciation for not associating with this resolution.

The aforesaid interactions with the officials in the Ministry dealing with Disarmament set the pattern of my dealings with them through my tenure in Geneva. While the relationship was combative, I am convinced that my refusing to be a rubber stamp was valuable not only in improving the quality of our output but also in placing on notice the officers at headquarters that a *chalta hai* attitude was not going to work in their dealings with me.

◆

Inter se differences are not unusual in organizations and bureaucracies the world over, but it is rare to actually witness one, as I did, which was so detrimental to our national interests. The case pertained to the proposed appointment of Mr Anil Wadhwa, who was working with me as Counsellor Disarmament, as Deputy Director General (DDG) in the about to be set up secretariat of the Organisation for Prohibition of Chemical Weapons (OPCW) in the Hague. Mr Wadhwa was a fine officer who had been actively involved in the negotiations leading up to the conclusion of the Chemical Weapons Convention (CWC). Though he had worked with me for only a couple of months, I had a high regard for his capabilities and, accordingly, after clearing the matter with the Ministry, fully supported the request made, amongst others, by my British and US counterparts for his aforesaid appointment. The British interest in his appointment arose from the fact that the person selected as the Head of the OPCW, who was from the UK, wanted him in that position, since the two had been colleagues in the CWC negotiations and enjoyed an excellent relationship.

Regrettably, despite all these favourable circumstances, Anil's appointment as DDG in the OPCW never materialized, as the Ministry subsequently restrained the PMI Geneva from openly campaigning in the matter. The reason for this was that equations between Anil and a Joint Secretary-level official who was very close to Foreign Secretary Dixit were somewhat strained. Indeed, I even received a couple of calls from our Minister's office questioning me for the rationale of my support for Anil. Through all this infighting, India lost the opportunity of having one of its officers appointed to the pivotal office of DDG in the OPCW. Ironically, this appointment ultimately went to an Iranian! Several months later, Anil was appointed to the OPCW, albeit at the much lower post of Director Information.

◆

Regrettably, towards the end of my stay in Geneva, I was also witness to a somewhat similar incident in which the then Foreign Secretary allowed his personal predilections come in the way of selecting the optimal Indian candidate for an assignment on the UN Secretary General's Advisory Board on Disarmament Matters. The story in this regard is both insightful and sad but, at a more philosophical level, somewhat amusing.

At one of the innumerable cocktails in Geneva, I was told by one of my colleagues in the diplomatic community that the UN Secretary General, who was on one of his visits to the city, wanted to speak to me. I duly met him and was told that Mr Muchkund Dubey, who was on his Advisory Board on Disarmament Matters, was about to demit office and that he was keen that another suitable Indian be nominated as a replacement. In this context, he asked me if I had any name in mind. While thanking him for wanting an Indian on the Advisory Board, I responded that a possible replacement could be the former Foreign Secretary, Mr J.N. Dixit, but that I would have to seek the approval of the Foreign Secretary before making any definitive recommendation. The UN Secretary General indicated that he would welcome the choice of Mr Dixit, with whom he was well acquainted, but that he would await our final response based on our Foreign Secretary's input.

On the following day, I apprised our Foreign Secretary of my exchange with the UN Secretary General. He was livid at my even contemplating the name of Mr Dixit as a replacement for Mr Dubey. My explaining to him that my suggestion was logical, as both had served with distinction as Foreign Secretaries and were well-versed with all the nuances of Disarmament-related matters, cut no ice.

Noting that I was getting nowhere, I told the Foreign Secretary that, since my suggestion was not acceptable, he should himself indicate the name to be conveyed as the replacement of Mr Dubey. He responded a couple of days later citing three or four names as possible Indian candidates and sought my opinion in the matter. When I responded that in my view none of these individuals fitted the bill, he once again lost his shirt and asked for an explanation as to why I was rejecting every name suggested by him. I retorted that I did so as none of the names proposed by him were from the IFS and were, therefore, unfamiliar with the diplomatic nuances of Disarmament-related issues. Moreover, I was a bit of a trade unionist and since the names suggested by him were not from the IFS, I found it difficult to agree that any of them should be nominated to the Advisory Board. As a result of these rather acrimonious exchanges, the Foreign Secretary got back to me the following day and suggested the name of Mr N. Krishnan, my first boss in the IFS, as our nominee, to which I readily agreed, given his considerable expertise in the matter.

I must confess that the aforesaid incident could have been averted by me, as I knew that the relationship with the Foreign Secretary and Mr Dixit was rocky, but I wanted to test the objectivity of the former, with whom I had hitherto enjoyed a fairly good relationship extending over several years. In the event, while the Foreign Secretary came up short in my estimation, I lost a friendship!

◆

My Geneva assignment was largely coloured by Pakistan's endeavour to pass a Kashmir-related resolution against us in the UNCHR at its 49th and 50th sessions in 1993 and 1994, respectively. Each of these sessions spanned six weeks. It also attempted a somewhat similar resolution in the UNGA First Committee, which was handled by me in October–November 1994.

It is relevant to recall that this was a time when India was in a very difficult situation. Militancy in Kashmir, aided and abetted by Pakistan, was at a high. Confrontations between the security forces and militants were an all-too-frequent occurrence. Moreover, India was far from being a rising power as at present. It had a minority government fighting for survival, hard put to address a myriad of serious problems, such as the demolition of the Babri Masjid in December 1992, the subsequent Mumbai riots and an economy on the brink of bankruptcy, compelling it to mortgage gold to keep the economy afloat. India's diplomatic standing was, perhaps, at its lowest ever. With hindsight, it is obvious that Pakistan had orchestrated its move to mount a resolution against us on Kashmir in tandem with its promotion of militancy there so as to internationalize the issue and push us to the corner when we were at our most vulnerable.

Had Pakistan succeeded in its attempts to pass a Kashmir-related resolution in the UNCHR and later in the UNGA First Committee, it would have paved the way for the passage of similar resolutions in the UNGA and the United Nations Security Council (UNSC). This would have effectively internationalized the long-dormant Kashmir issue as in the 1950s and opened up questions relating to its accession to India. In this eventuality, not only would all our diplomatic energies have been sapped in debilitating debates and lobbying in the UN and in capitals the world over, but the militancy in Jammu and Kashmir (J&K), instigated, supported and financed by Pakistan, would have gathered further strength, presenting us with an even more challenging politico-military situation.

Pakistan's moves against us in the UNCHR in 1993 were well thought through. They were initiated only after the separatist movement in Kashmir had gathered momentum and in the wake of the Babri Masjid demolition and the Bombay riots, when India was in the news for all the wrong reasons. They were also accompanied by vigorous lobbying, particularly in the Islamic world. In fact, in 1993, Pakistan fielded a very large delegation in Geneva. It was led by the highly articulate Mushahid Hussain who, if I recall right, was Minister of Telecommunications. He was in Geneva for the entire duration of the session and personally participated in many of the debates. In these circumstances, I inevitably had several exchanges with him. Prime Minister Nawaz Sharif also came to Geneva and addressed the UNCHR from the podium.

During the UNCHR debates, the Pakistani delegation raised the Kashmir issue under many of the over-20 agenda items, a sharp departure from past practice when it figured only under three or four agenda items. The idea clearly was to raise the temperature and to internationalize Kashmir. Pakistan was ably supported in this exercise by several non-governmental organizations (NGOs), some international, which it had carefully cultivated over the years, and some local or regional, which it had influenced. The main points made by the Pakistani delegation were that the non-holding of a plebiscite in J&K by India constituted a violation of UN resolutions, that the activities which India termed as 'terrorist' were a spontaneous freedom struggle, that it was Indian forces that were committing atrocities in Kashmir, that the accession of J&K to India was illegal, that the elections in the state were bogus, that India was not a secular state, and that Pakistan was not involved in what was happening in J&K. In this context, it called for a fact-finding mission to be sent to J&K. The demolition of Babri Masjid and the subsequent rioting in Bombay came in handy for the Pakistani delegation in buttressing its case on Kashmir, as it placed in question our secular credentials and our capacity to prevent Human Rights violations.

The Indian delegation was led by me for the first half of the session and subsequently by Dr N. Janardhana Reddy, who was an MLA and former Chief Minister of Andhra Pradesh.

We firmly rebutted all the Pakistani arguments. I was not overly worried about the points made by Pakistan in regard to J&K, as we had a very strong case on the legalities of its accession to India and had ample evidence of the former's massive involvement in terrorist activities there, which was the root cause of the problem. The destruction of the Babri Masjid and the subsequent rioting in Bombay were much more difficult to defend. The line we took was that these incidents were an aberration, that India was committed to the preservation of human rights, that its ethos, constitution and institutions were the best guarantors of the same, that suitable remedial action was underway and that the Indian system had self-correct mechanisms to rectify any wrongdoing.

◆

The resolution initially under contemplation by Pakistan in 1993 was more far-reaching than the one it later tabled in 1994. In the fourth week of February 1993, Pakistan circulated a very detailed draft resolution with as many as 11 operative paragraphs for comments of friendly delegations in Islamabad. It represented Pakistan's maximalist position and incorporated the following elements:

- a re-affirmation of the rights to self-determination of the people of J&K;
- condemnation of Human Rights violations by Indian security forces in J&K;
- urging India to allow international Human Rights groups to visit J&K and investigate the Human Rights situation there;
- calling for dispatch to J&K of a fact-finding mission nominated by the OIC Secretary General;
- demanding the withdrawal of Indian forces from J&K;
- urging India to allow the people of J&K to exercise their right of self-determination;
- seeking international support for India–Pakistan negotiations to promote a just and peaceful solution to address the J&K dispute as per UNSC resolutions.

Since such a maximalist resolution was not gathering traction, Pakistan drastically watered it down in early March 1993, limiting it to an expression of concern at Human Rights violations in J&K, calling for dispatch of an OIC fact-finding mission to the state and inscribing it as an item to be taken up at the next session. The inclusion of the last element was to give the resolution an afterlife so that India always had a sword of Damocles hanging on its head.

India left no stone unturned in defeating the Pakistani effort at promoting such a resolution. In Geneva, we worked non-stop in assiduously countering every Pakistani argument and in lobbying every delegation. This entailed explaining our case on Kashmir to everyone, in exposing the hollowness and opportunism of Pakistan's endeavours and losing no opportunity to highlight the extent of Pakistan's involvement in terrorist activities directed against India. This exercise was very well-backed-up by the Ministry through an extensive lobbying effort with relevant Heads of Mission in New Delhi and in their capitals. In terms of countering the resolution if tabled, we carefully examined all the procedural possibilities open to us as suggested by the Ministry.

It was our assessment that, apart from defeating such a resolution by organizing a majority vote against it, there were, essentially, three options available to us. One was by gutting it through amendments. The second was by negotiating a chairman's statement, which inevitably involved accepting some elements of the original resolution. The third was by calling for a 'no action motion' on the original resolution on grounds that it was ill-founded and/or politically motivated, which, if passed, would effectively stymie it. The Mission advised against opting for the amendment route or working for a Chairman's statement. It was felt that the former was a risky proposition, as the fate of amendments in an open debate is always uncertain. Moreover, even if we were able to get some elements of interest to us included in the resolution, we may equally not be able to exclude all those of concern to us and, in any case, the resolution, once passed, would internationalize Kashmir by opening it up to debate at future meetings. A Chairman's statement was also felt to be dangerous for, though not carrying the same opprobrium as a resolution, it would keep the issue on the UNCHR agenda for years on end. Accordingly, the Mission urged that the resolution be addressed frontally either through a no action motion or a direct vote.

Our assessment was that if there was a straight vote, we would win it with a relatively narrow margin—about 11-4—and if there was a no action motion, we would win it 15-4. A no action motion was, therefore, our preferred option. This was all the more so because we could convincingly argue that the resolution was politically motivated and that Pakistan did not really have the Human Rights interests of the people of J&K at heart. This was amply borne out by the suffering imposed by Pakistan on the people of Kashmir through its blatant and massive use of terror and its own abysmal Human Rights record, particularly in Pakistan-occupied Kashmir (PoK).

In fact, it was during this session that we openly, and for the first time, accused Pakistan at an international forum for its flagrant and gross violations of Human Rights in PoK. Doing so was not easy or risk-free as I was surprised to discover. As per my practice, I had informed the Ministry in advance of my intervention relating to PoK. The following morning, as I was headed to the UNCHR, my Deputy came rushing to me and told me at the doorway that the Joint Secretary in charge of the Pakistan Division had advised against the proposed intervention. I told my Deputy that I had not heard her and proposed to make the said intervention, which I duly did. Interestingly, there was no comeback on this issue from the Ministry! I chose to disregard the Ministry's instructions in order to underline the fact that Pakistan had no genuine Human Rights agenda and, in accusing India of Human Rights violations in J&K, it was merely engaging in crass opportunism.

The cut and thrust of the India–Pakistan debate over the six-week session was intense and heated. For instance, when Pakistan took us to task for the demolition of the Babri Masjid, we responded that while in India the government and people of India had deeply regretted it and acted against the perpetrators, in Pakistan, following this incident, as many as 300 temples were destroyed, including one in Lahore, where a minister had personally used a bulldozer to destroy it.

Our endeavour was to use the debates not merely to rebut Pakistan's charges against us but also to project India's case on Kashmir and its commitment to human rights. We argued that while India was not a perfect democracy, there were self-correcting mechanisms in the Indian system, ensuring that whenever an aberration occurred, remedial action was taken to set things right. In contrast, Pakistan was an autocratic state lacking any genuine concern for human rights, and its accusations of Human Rights violations by India, while grossly exaggerated, were simply a self-serving exercise to secure a reversal of the accession of J&K to India in its own favour, and it was a habitual and unabashed exporter of terrorism to India.

◆

Pakistan did not finally table a Kashmir-related resolution in 1993. This was in large measure due to the fact that we lobbied hard and skilfully with every country in the 53-member UNCHR. It was our endeavour that even if we could not get a country to oppose the Pakistani move, we must, at the very least, secure its neutrality. The critical player in 1993 turned out to be China, as it persuaded Pakistan not to table the resolution. The Chinese PR was the first to inform me that Pakistan would not table the resolution. China's move was dictated by pure self-interest, as it was facing a resolution mounted against it by a determined western group, and it was anxious to firm up each and every vote against the same. An Indian vote against the western-sponsored China resolution was, therefore, very important for it, and we had made known that this could be secured if it could keep Pakistan from tabling a resolution against us.

Our vote in support of China was also a part of a policy change we consciously made in the 1993 UNCHR session. Earlier we had, on occasion, supported country-specific Human Rights resolutions, notably against Myanmar and Sri Lanka. In 1993, we decided not to support any country-specific Human Rights resolution but to either oppose or abstain on it. This secured for us at least the neutrality of virtually all countries under threat of such resolutions.

The aforesaid policy change in respect of country-specific resolutions was dictated partly by the pressure we were under on account of the resolution on Kashmir being moved against us, and partly by the realization that Human Rights had come to be used as a political instrument. It had, over the years, become evident that such resolutions were often tabled in the UNCHR not with a view to improving the Human Rights situation in a particular country but to punish its government. This was counterproductive. Moreover, there was also the issue of double standards in the introduction of such resolutions. Human rights violations were common the world over, yet resolutions were rarely moved against developed countries. Moreover, in moving resolutions against developing countries where Human Rights problems existed, fingers were never pointed against the developed countries, which often bore part of the responsibility for the same for their sins of omission and commission as former colonizing powers.

Accordingly, apart from opposing the resolution on China, we decided to oppose similar resolutions if tabled on Iran, Indonesia and

Sri Lanka. We abstained on the resolution on Myanmar, even though we had supported it earlier. I recall that the Myanmar delegation was delighted with the change in our approach, which was in part also influenced in our overall policy change towards it. In keeping with this policy change, we withheld support for a Cuban resolution against the US and a US resolution against Cuba. I came under pressure from the leaders of the delegations of both countries on this account but was successfully able to explain to them the logic of our policy.

◆

The 1993 UNCHR session was a baptism by fire for me. I realized that it was not a one-shot affair, that it would happen again and that we needed to set our own house in order. The Government of India, in particular our own Ministry and the Home Ministry, with help of far-sighted officials like Home Secretary Mr N.N. Vohra, were most supportive and readily accepted the point that it was necessary for us to clean up our act at home in order to be able to more effectively face both international and domestic problems. Towards this end, I made a few recommendations having long-term implications, which were accepted. One of these was the establishment of a National Human Rights Commission (NHRC), which was set up in 1993. The other recommendations pertained to availing the services of the International Committee of the Red Cross (ICRC), inter alia, to impart Human Rights training to our forces engaged in Kashmir, to engaging with the OIC, and to opening up Kashmir selectively to visits by reputed NGOs and diplomats.

In recommending the ICRC's involvement, I was influenced by my dealings with it in 1973 and 1974 on the issue of over 90,000 Pakistani PoWs in our custody. Following the 1971 conflict, we had entered into an arrangement with the ICRC to visit them with a view to obviating any criticism regarding the treatment meted out to them. It was that experience which convinced me that the ICRC was a much better entity to engage with rather than some of the other international organizations and NGOs. It was my belief that the ICRC, unlike some other organizations, was genuinely apolitical, disinterested in propaganda and solely focussed on the observance of human rights, which was also our objective. Moreover, their reports are confidential and solely directed at sensitizing the host government to deficiencies and to the means of addressing them with a view to ameliorating the situation.

In these circumstances, we entered into an agreement with the ICRC, providing it access to Kashmir, including the jails there, and giving it a role in the sensitization of our Forces so that while the latter went about their work of addressing terrorism, they observed the required Human Rights norms. Its representatives freely visited the jails where terrorists were detained and furnished confidential reports to the government on the treatment meted out to them, bringing out the shortcomings so that remedial action could be taken. Furthermore, under its guidance, Human Rights sensitization modules were run for our security personnel to create greater awareness about Human Rights norms and the need to abide by them.

My recommendation on the need to stop shunning the OIC and engaging with it constructively was triggered by my exchanges with its representative in Geneva, Ambassador Nanguyalai Tarzi, who was an Afghan and who many years later was the Afghan Ambassador in India. At the 1993 UNCHR session, Ambassador Tarzi made a blistering attack on India—no doubt drafted by Pakistan—on behalf of the OIC, and I responded in kind. At the end of the meeting, late at night, as I was leaving the conference room, Ambassador Tarzi was waiting at the doorway to speak to me. He remonstrated against my having made such a harsh statement, to which I retorted that I had no option in the context of what had been stated by him. He reacted that as an Afghan, he had great respect for India, and Afghanistan enjoyed an excellent relationship with it, but he was speaking for an organization in which there was a 'vacuum'. Upon my asking what he meant by that, he elaborated that India had no contacts with the OIC, and Pakistan, being a member, could, therefore, say what it liked against India without fear of rebuttal and a contrary opinion was completely absent.

I felt that there was much merit in what he said, and his remarks festered in my mind. I discussed this issue with our PR in New York, Mr Hamid Ansari, who shared my view that we needed to revise our policy in regard to interaction with the OIC. Towards the end of the 1993 UNCHR session and after Pakistan had dropped the idea of a resolution, Ambassador Tarzi sought a goodwill call on me at the mission along with an OIC delegation. In the context of our policy of no contact with the OIC, I told him that this was not possible, but he persisted, pointing out that if India did not brief the OIC, how could its members challenge Pakistan. In the context of Ambassador Tarzi's impeccable logic, I rang up Foreign Secretary Dixit for clearance to interact with the OIC. Mr Dixit reminded me of our stated policy, but I was able to convince him of the need to appropriately brief the OIC and, inter alia, expose Pakistan's self-serving blitzkrieg against India, which was based on falsehoods. Even so, he initially insisted that the proposed interaction must be informal and not in the Mission. Upon my persistence, the Foreign Secretary finally relented and agreed to my interacting with the OIC delegation in the Mission. His only condition was that, immediately thereafter, we should appropriately brief the media, which I readily complied with. This decision marked the beginning of a change in our policy on dealings with the OIC, as some months thereafter, we sent a special envoy to Saudi Arabia—I think it was Salman Haider—to interact with OIC. But the first formal contact with the OIC in decades was in Geneva and was inspired by the aforesaid interaction with Ambassador Tarzi.

The OIC goodwill delegation that came to the Mission was led by Senegal and comprised seven members, including Iran and the OIC Ambassador. The Indian side comprised myself, the late Prof. A.M. Khusro and Second Secretary Tirumurti, a very bright and dynamic officer. The latter normally dealt with agencies like the WHO, ILO, WIPO, etc., and not Human Rights, but I drafted him in for this meeting, as the other two officers dealing with Human Rights were overstretched. Since it was the month of Ramzan, we made it a point not to offer any refreshments. While the OIC delegation stated that it had come to 'express goodwill', it made a strong pitch for dispatch of an OIC delegation to Kashmir. I firmly rebutted any possibility of our agreeing to such a visit and instead used the occasion, buttressed with appropriate documentation, to highlight our case on Kashmir and to dilate upon Pakistan's use of terrorism against us. Prof. Khusro, in turn, provided a brilliant and detailed exposé on the complete integration of the Muslim community in the warp and woof of India's multifaceted sociopolitical and economic fabric, pointing out that concerns about it in the Islamic world stoked by Pakistani propaganda were totally misplaced. On leaving, the Iranian Ambassador, Cyrus Nasseri, wryly remarked to me, 'We came to sell you our story, and instead you sold yours to us.' The meeting, however, marked a change, as we started to interact with the OIC, and as a bonus, Ambassador Tarzi became a very good friend. This served us in good stead, as he kept us informed of Pakistan's machinations in the OIC.

Finally, my recommendation that Kashmir be opened up selectively to visitors and NGOs also found favour, as it was becoming clear that keeping it off limits to the international community only lent grist to Pakistani propaganda. Accordingly, from 1994, an increasing number of foreigners were allowed into Kashmir, comprising both NGOs, like the ICRC, as well as Delhi-based diplomats, so that they could see the ground realities for themselves. We were confident that such visits would not only expose the malicious propaganda on the issue by interested parties but would also underline the extent to which Kashmir was living under the shadow of Pakistani-controlled terror.

◆

The heat generated at the 1993 UNCHR session and the deteriorating situation in Kashmir, coupled with the continuing India–Pakistan tensions, convinced me that the 1994 UNHCR session was likely to be even more difficult for us. I received confirmation of this from my Pakistani counterpart, Ambassador Ahmad Kamal, with whom I had a very good personal relationship. The confirmation came about in a rather strange way.

In October/November 1993 whilst in New York on Disarmament-related work in the First Committee, my British Disarmament counterpart, Ambassador Weston, teasingly told Ambassador Kamal at a luncheon meeting that I had given him a 'bloody nose' at the 1993 UNCHR session. The latter responded that things may be very different the next time. On my quizzing Ambassador Kamal in a subsequent one-on-one conversation as to what he meant, he informed me that while at the 1993 session we had fought with 'gloves', at the 1994 session, the fight may well be 'without gloves'. Elaborating further, he indicated that while in 1993 no resolution had been tabled, there was a distinct possibility that this may be done in 1994 and, for good measure, added that he would let me know about it in advance.

I duly apprised the Ministry of this conversation and urged the importance of appropriately preparing ourselves. In Geneva, detailed briefing folders were readied by us, containing everything under the sun, from A to Z, in defence of our case on J&K, on the Human Rights situation there, on the self-serving nature of Pakistan's moves against us, and of its own pathetic Human Rights record. Between 8 and 25 January 1994, I provided a comprehensive briefing on all aspects of the Kashmir issue to every Head of Mission in Geneva, underlining that Pakistan was likely to once again raise it in the upcoming UNCHR session and of the need to defeat it, since it was unwarranted and no more than a political gambit. Simultaneously, the Ministry was urged to similarly take up the matter with all concerned countries in their capitals, through dispatch of special representatives as well as with their Missions in New Delhi.

On 26 January, a few days before the beginning of the 1994 UNCHR session, Ambassador Kamal, true to his word, informed me, 'This time the gloves will be off and Benazir will come.' I informed New Delhi of the same and we were, much to my chagrin, soon inundated with a huge delegation, which enormously complicated my task.

In operational terms, the team addressing the Pakistani onslaught against us at the UNCHR in Geneva was quite different in 1994 as compared to that in 1993. In both years, while the officials handling the issue from the mission remained unchanged, the component from Headquarters and from other missions increased exponentially in 1994 from the levels in 1993. While in 1993 the political presence was limited only to Dr Janardhan Reddy and a few others who came for short periods, in 1994, we had a peak of 20 to 25 high-level delegates from India and other missions, including personalities such as Dr Manmohan Singh, Mr Vajpayee, Mr Brajesh Mishra, Mr Salman

Khurshid, Mr Natwar Singh, Dr Farooq Abdullah, Dr L.M. Singhvi, Mr Vinod Grover, Mr Prakash Shah and Mr Hamid Ansari.

Fortunately, all members of the delegation were on the same page and, on most issues, went by the Mission's advice. There was good understanding amongst the delegates and a great team spirit. Everyone realized that we were involved in a national effort of considerable importance. The sense I got from our VIPs from New Delhi was that Kashmir was on fire, but once we had addressed the issue internationally, we would quickly sort it out internally and find the appropriate solutions. Though we were able to quell the international storm in 1994, promotion of complete reconciliation in Kashmir has been more timeconsuming.

The presence of so many VIPs inevitably posed a management issue. In 1993, with a relatively small external component, the Mission was spared this management task, and I could be much more focussed on the debates and directly participate in most of the exchanges. In 1994, after having gone through the fire of 1993, I think Delhi was nervous and inundated us with many high-powered persona despite my recommendations to the contrary. One change that the presence of so many people resulted in was that while in 1993 I myself made most of the statements and interventions, in 1994, these were made by our representatives from Delhi and elsewhere, though they were, of course, prepared by the Mission. In 1994, we were also engaged in a much more massive lobbying exercise in committee rooms and at luncheons and dinners organized at restaurants or at my residence. VIPs like Dr Manmohan Singh and Mr Vajpayee were fielded for this purpose, but I was disappointed that they were unable to strike a rapport with leaders of other delegations, possibly because the latter were not politicians and since there was usually a huge generation gap.

The person who was the most effective in this lobbying effort and whom we, therefore, used to the hilt was Mr Khurshid, our then Minister of State in the MEA. While following the brief, he was highly articulate, able to strike a chord with the leaders of other delegations, project our viewpoint optimally and take on even the most difficult queries with great aplomb. Prima donnas and eccentrics like Dr Abdullah had to be fielded carefully, in short bursts. His histrionic talents were, however, handy in countering Benazir Bhutto's blistering attack on us in her address from the podium. The presence of senior professionals, far more experienced than myself, such as Mr Brajesh Mishra, Mr Prakash Shah and Mr Hamid Ansari, was very useful in strategy formulation. I was also backed by two very hard-working and dedicated colleagues dealing with Human Rights from the mission, namely Mrs Neelam Sabharwal and Mr Debashish Chakravarty.

As a management exercise, it was our job to use everyone the best we could in terms of determining what statements would be made by whom and who would be used for lobbying which group as also consulting them for advice and obtaining feedback. It also required us to ensure that each of our delegates was fully briefed on a daily basis and provided with the texts of statements that they were required to make. Everyone played ball, but the sheer size of the delegation, with so many prima donnas, certainly posed a problem. We addressed this to an extent by tactfully engineering that a few were kept away from Geneva by facilitating their visits to places of tourist interest like Chamonix, Montreux and Lausanne.

While I had come to terms with Pakistan's self-serving agenda in trying to pass a Kashmir-related resolution against us, the attitude of the West in using it to sanctimoniously pressurize India on human rights-related issues was galling. The approach of the West German delegation was particularly offensive. At a bilateral lunch hosted by it for our delegation, which was attended by Mr Salman Khurshid, Mr Natwar Singh and myself, its members spent nearly all the time on grilling us on the Human Rights situation in India. Both Mr Khurshid and myself fielded all their queries as best as we could, with Mr Singh maintaining a studied silence throughout. When towards the end of lunch some additional queries were made, we suggested to Mr Singh that he may like to respond. His reaction was nothing short of brilliant, and he was at his caustic best. After an inordinately lengthy pause, he cuttingly stated that he saw no reason to engage on issues related to Human Rights with the representatives of a nation which was responsible for millions of deaths and whose record in the matter was amongst the most horrific. He added for good measure that the Human Rights record of countries like the US and other western colonial powers was also deplorable and they had no business to lecture others in this regard. This abruptly ended all further discussion on human rights, and we moved on to more neutral topics.

◆

Innovation and improvization is the name of the game many a time in some enterprises when things are not fully thought through from the very outset, and the same was certainly applicable to the choice of the leader of our delegation for the 1994 UNCHR session. As per the Ministry's instructions, we had informed the UNCHR that our delegation would be led by Finance Minister Dr Manmohan Singh. On arriving in Geneva and noting that Benazir Bhutto had addressed the Commission from the podium, Dr Singh insisted on doing likewise. Since this privilege was not accorded to leaders of delegations and extended only to eminent persons, we had to appropriately re-designate Dr Singh as a statesman, which meant that he could not lead our delegation. Accordingly, we had to find an alternative at very short notice. My advice to the Ministry was that we should go strictly by protocol, and on this basis, our leader should be Mr Vajpayee, who, as Leader of the Opposition, outranked all others present. My proposal was accepted immediately, and I received confirmation in this regard within 24 hours. This is a reflection of how well New Delhi was functioning and of the strong rapport between Prime Minister Narasimha Rao and Mr Vajpayee.

Dr Singh's address from the podium was pedestrian, and the impact he made was not a patch on that made by Benazir Bhutto, who had spoken eloquently and created a very favourable impression. He, however, made up for this by his outstanding handling of the media in a press conference held shortly thereafter. His ability to effectively deal with all queries, which were wide-ranging and not merely confined to human rights, was masterly and impressive.

Though the 1994 UNCHR session was a difficult one, we were fully prepared for all eventualities, and the Ministry was magnificent in terms of support. Both Foreign Secretaries were very supportive: first it was Mr Dixit and later Mr Srinivasan, and they reposed complete trust in me. The points man in the Ministry dealing with the issue,

Director Dinkar Srivastava, was outstanding and was working on a 24/7 basis. Both in 1993 and 1994, there was a body of opinion that favoured giving up our hard-line position of frontally defeating a resolution against us and accepting a compromise in the nature of a Chairman's statement to get the heat off us. In a 1994 midnight phone call, the PMO flagged this possibility, urging me to give it serious thought. My consistent advice was that we should rule out any such move, as, once we went down the slippery slope of compromise, the chances of ultimate defeat would increase multifold. When countered on whether I could guarantee success, I responded, 'No, particularly if the resolution is diluted, but acceptance of a Chairman's statement or even an indication of readiness to negotiate one will in the end lead to a resolution against us.'

To be fair to Delhi, it was naturally thinking of worst-case scenarios. The fallout of a resolution on Kashmir would have led not only to a drastic increase in militancy in the area but would have had a terribly negative political impact for the government. In the short term, a resolution would have been disastrous. A Chairman's statement, on the other hand, would have been easier to explain away, and its immediate consequences would have been less severe. I, on the other hand, was thinking long term and was opposed to even contemplating a Chairman's statement, as within a year or two, it was, in any case, likely to lead to a resolution. The national interest, I felt, demanded that we defeat a resolution once for all, and should it be passed, we should flatly reject it as politically motivated and unjustified.

Pakistan was, perhaps, more hopeful of securing support for the resolution tabled by it in 1994 as compared to the one fielded by it in 1993, since it was a bare-bones resolution much watered down from the one initially contemplated by it in 1993 and more or less identical to the one that it was reduced to thinking of at the end of the 1993 session. It had only two introductory and two operative paragraphs. The introductory paragraphs reaffirmed the fundamental rights of the people of J&K and expressed grave concern at the violation of their human rights. The operative paragraphs called for sending a fact-finding mission to J&K and to consider the situation of Human Rights there at the fifty-first session.

Pakistan felt that a short and crisp resolution restricted only to Human Rights would garner broader support internationally than a more diffused and maximalist resolution with political overtones. I understand, with hindsight and after being assigned to Pakistan, that such a restrained resolution was not viewed very well internally in the country. However, we had several things going for us, most notably the Parliament resolution of February 1994 on Kashmir underlining that it was an integral part of India, calling upon Pakistan to vacate aggression and condemning it for its involvement in terrorism there. Moreover, our increased transparency on Kashmir, engagement with the ICRC as well as the International Commission of Jurists, and establishment of the NHRC demonstrated our sincerity in actively addressing Human Rights violations in the area. Together with our extensive lobbying, this greatly strengthened our hands.

◆

Naturally, this was a time of much tension for us in Geneva. Apart from monitoring the proceedings of the plenary committee and group meetings, which stretched from around 9.00 a.m. till late at night, preparing statements for various members of our delegation along with rights of reply, keeping track of the evolving thought processes of key delegations, and undertaking a vigorous lobbying effort, we were checking, twice a day, with each delegation on its position on the Pakistani-sponsored resolution. In this entire endeavour, Mr Vajpayee's presence as the leader was a great support. He not only went by most of our recommendations but, noting our fears and apprehensions, made it very plain that we should simply do our best and not bother about the outcome. In a lighter vein, he mentioned that the Prime Minister had been smart in nominating him as the leader as, in the event of a defeat, the government would not have to worry about the Opposition, which would have to take a part of the blame!

On the eve of the debate on the resolution, it was our assessment that we would win the no action motion on it by a narrow 7-4 margin, with all others abstaining. In a house of 53, this would only be a pyrrhic victory, but a victory nevertheless. The countries that we counted for

Pakistan were Iran, Libya and Syria. The position of some countries was in constant flux and hence the necessity of checking with each delegation twice a day. On the basis of our readout of a delegation's position, on many an occasion, I had to directly contact our Head of Mission in its capital to ensure the required outcome.

A good example of this was our interaction with the Costa Rican delegation. Traditionally, Costa Rica had, over the years, voted with Pakistan on Human Rights issues. But our Ambassador concurrently accredited to Costa Rica, namely Pramatesh Rath, had established an excellent rapport with the top leadership in that country and categorically informed me that he had persuaded the latter to vote against the resolution tabled by Pakistan. When I approached the Costa Rican delegation in Geneva for confirmation in the matter, it obfuscated and made out that it had not received instructions. I forthwith conveyed this to our Ambassador, who was camping in Costa Rica. This process went on a couple of times before I got a clear-cut confirmation from the Costa Rican delegation that they would oppose the Pakistani resolution.

Apart from Costa Rica, we had the support of only Cyprus, Russia, Bulgaria, Cuba and Mauritius. This is reflective of the meagre support we enjoyed and, though fractionally more than that of Pakistan, it was humbling and a cause of anxiety. In comparison, China could count on many more countries for support though, of course, it had the entire western bloc opposing it, which was neutral in our case.

As in 1993, I approached China in 1994 as well, urging it to influence Pakistan to abandon the idea of moving a resolution against us. However, on this occasion, the Chinese told us that Pakistan was not agreeing to their request and they could do nothing more in the matter. In these circumstances, I decided to approach Iran in the matter. I had a good equation with Ambassador Cyrus Nasseri and was aware of Iran's reservations about Pakistan's move against us. This had been brought home to me at the Asian Regional Preparatory Meeting in Bangkok on the eve of the 1993 World Human Rights Conference, where the Indian and Iranian delegations had worked closely together on the documentation developed therein and where the latter had brutally scuttled Pakistan's endeavours to embarrass us on Kashmir. Moreover, with Benazir Bhutto's assumption of power, it was logical to assume that Iran's influence in Pakistan would have increased.

Accordingly, shortly after the commencement of the 1994 UNCHR session, I called on the Iranian Ambassador and urged him to exercise his influence with Pakistan to cause it to desist from moving a resolution against us, much as China had done in 1993. In seeking his help, I pointed out that it was as important for Iran as for India that the issue did not come to vote. Elaborating on this, I told him that I knew that if there was a vote, Iran would willy-nilly vote with its Islamic brother, Pakistan, and if it did so, the Indian economic cooperation that Iran was so keen on would remain a dream. The Iranian Ambassador was non-committal and went so far as to suggest that we go for a compromise with Pakistan, which he could help broker, or that we consider a Chairman's statement. I, of course, turned down these suggestions and merely reiterated that Iran could not afford the Pakistani resolution going to a vote and that I would not speak to him again on this issue and that it would be he who would now seek me out in the matter. He concluded by indicating that we should wait and watch and let Pakistan 'give off steam' till closer to the end of the session.

As anticipated, three or four days prior to the vote, the Iranian Ambassador rang me up at my residence on a Sunday morning and sought a meeting. I called on him the following day, and he indicated that Iran would exert pressure on Pakistan and try to defuse the situation. The debate started at noon and soon Iran asked for an adjournment, primarily, I think, because it wanted to fine-tune the modalities of the Pakistani climbdown. I was apprehensive that the adjournment may be a ploy to gain time to secure some additional support for Pakistan or to further dilute the resolution and, therefore, wanted the issue to be put to a vote straightaway. Fortunately, my fears were unwarranted, and the adjournment worked out well, with Pakistan agreeing not to press for the vote, and the resolution dying a natural death. This was a moment not of celebration but of relief for me, though many friends and colleagues saw it as an occasion of great joy.

It has sometimes been suggested that the Hindujas played a role in obtaining Iranian support for us, and it is a fact that they offered to help out. But we kept them at arms' length. Far from soliciting their help, we made it amply clear to them that we were quite confident of dealing with the issue on our own. So, the Hindujas, in my view, from the vantage point of Geneva, played no role in this matter. It is, of course, possible that there were high-level governmental contacts between Delhi and Tehran. While I do not have direct evidence of this, it cannot be ruled out. However, it is undeniable that Iran played a very helpful role which, unfortunately, is often not sufficiently appreciated in India.

◆

Much of my being able to devote all my energies in successfully countering the Pakistani campaign against us on Kashmir must be attributed in no small measure to my wife, Beneeta. As at all my other postings, she not only took complete charge of looking after the household, including our three children, but also coped magnificently with my representational responsibilities. The latter had increased exponentially, both on account of the long-drawn-out UNCHR sessions and the inordinately large Indian delegation. While I did some of my entertaining at the local restaurants, the bulk of it was by way of innumerable dinners at home. Some of these were only for our delegation, but most were formal sit-down events to which others, apart from our delegation members, were also invited as a part of our lobbying effort. Through the six-week UNCHR session, we hosted many such events at home, to one or two of which I myself was late due to unexpected meetings at the UNCHR that required my presence. My only contribution to the work relating to the dinners at home was ensuring an adequate supply of appropriate hard drinks, cigarettes and cigars, as well as the preparation of seating plans and place cards. The innumerable other arrangements, including, inter alia, the drawing up of a menu, overseeing the preparation of food, ensuring that it was elegantly presented and served, taking care of the room décor, etc., were flawlessly conceived and executed by Beneeta. Indeed, as at Geneva, so too at all my other assignments, she was a pillar of strength, silently and uncomplainingly tending to the multifarious needs of our family and deftly managing our household, leaving me completely free to focus on my work.

◆

Through both the 1993 and 1994 UNCHR sessions, we had been under huge pressure, and once the resolution was tabled, this was all the more so. I, however, felt it was important from a psychological viewpoint that we should not let our anxieties show. Accordingly, I emphasized to all my colleagues in Geneva that they should maintain a relaxed and confident mien, go about their business in a normal fashion, and stretch themselves to the full by involvement even on issues which may otherwise have been ignored. Accordingly, we were active across the entire spectrum of developments at the Commission and indeed at other fora in Geneva, such as the Conference on Disarmament, UNCTAD, etc. In these circumstances, we made seminal contributions at the Commission during this period on issues that had nothing to do with Kashmir, like the push for the recognition of the 'Right to Development' as a human right. Such all-encompassing and across-the-board involvement stood us in good stead, as it opened up opportunities to strike deals with other countries on J&K-related issues, which were of more critical import to us.

An example of such activism was my election in 1994 as Chairman of the Working Group on Situations. This working group invariably had several countries, both developed and developing, under its scanner for grave Human Rights situations. Amongst those in the dock in 1994 were countries ranging from Germany to Saudi Arabia. Accordingly, the working group's members, and particularly its Chairman, had great influence on the recommendations made by it in regard to the countries under review. This provided me with a leverage vis-à-vis these countries on issues of concern to us. The short point is that I recognized that every issue opened up possibilities that could be used to our advantage and that it was thus imperative, even when under pressure and hard-pressed for time, that we be proactive on issues on as wide a spectrum as possible. This, inevitably, greatly increased our workload. We were stretched to full capacity, working till midnight and up again by five or six in the morning to prepare for the day's meetings. There were no weekends. It was fascinating, fatiguing and intensely stressful, but at the end of the day, we gave a good account of ourselves and successfully stymied the Pakistani move against us.

◆

In the midst of my hectic schedule, sometime in mid-1993, at the request of Mr Sanjeev Tripathi, our Consul General in Geneva who later went on to become our R&AW chief, I also involved myself in efforts to get the Khalistan Liberation Organisation (KLO) expelled from the Unrepresented Nations and Peoples Organization (UNPO), a rather influential NGO. Sanjeev had, over time, developed a very good relationship with the entire leadership at UNPO, including its Secretary General, Mr Michael Van Walt Van Praag. On Sanjeev's suggestion, we called on Michael Van Walt and provided him with detailed documentation on the KLO, highlighting the fact that it was nothing more than a terrorist outfit that enjoyed negligible support in India. We also organized a visit for him to India to see for himself the situation on the ground and make his own assessment in the matter. Due to these endeavours based upon Sanjeev's excellent groundwork, the UNPO expelled the KLO from its membership.

In my dealings with Human Rights-related issues in Geneva, I formed a rather negative impression of many NGOs in the business as well as some Indians in media and in high office.

As for NGOs, while I had no doubt that some like the ICRC were genuinely interested in the promotion and protection of human rights, many others were not and were in the game for a variety of other motives, namely to advance themselves, to make money and to make propaganda; many were also influenced by other players and countries. Some, of course, were created by countries to promote their agenda and derogatively came to be known as 'CONGOs'. Many NGOs that spoke against India on Kashmir were put up to do so by Pakistan and some were even created and funded for this purpose.

I had a particularly low opinion of Amnesty International as, lacking in objectivity, it was not even-handed and was solely focussed on advancing its own agenda. It seemed to want publicity somehow, anyhow. It is, therefore, no accident that its reports, often based on unverified material, would come out on the eve of the meetings of the UNCHR or some of its subcommittees. On Kashmir, while highly critical of India, it tended to look the other way about the atrocities committed by Pakistan-supported terrorist outfits and about the complete denial of Human Rights by Pakistan to the people of PoK and the Northern Areas as well as those in Balochistan. Moreover, Amnesty, unlike other reputed NGOs, did not observe the standard practice of sharing its reports in draft form with countries it was criticizing and incorporating therein the comments of the latter, which is so essential for purposes of balance and objectivity.

There were, of course, NGOs with a much better pedigree which also came out with negative reports on Kashmir. The International Commission of Jurists[9] for instance, came out with a very damaging report in March 1995 on the situation in Kashmir because of the palpable pro-Pakistan bias of its team leader, Sir William Goodhart. Its team visited J&K in August 1993 and was the first international Human Rights organization to be allowed into J&K in the 1990s. Clearly, we should have done a background check on Sir William, which would have alerted us to his bias and helped us to insist on a more objective International Commission of Jurists team leader. Fortunately, its practice of sharing its reports with the countries concerned enabled us to engage in a lengthy discourse with it, as a result of which we were not only able to secure some modifications therein but also have incorporated within it our dissenting note, which ran into nearly 50 of its 200 pages.

In the process of refuting the International Commission of Jurists's call for self-determination in Kashmir and its accusations of Human Rights violations committed there by Indian forces, our note drew pointed attention to the horrendous Human Rights violations committed by Pakistan-sponsored terrorism. In so doing it, inter alia, also referred to 'the targeted killing of members of the Hindu minority community which has led to the exodus of over 250000 members of the community resulting in a change in the very demographic

[9]International Commission of Jurists, *Human Rights in Kashmir: Report of a Mission,* 1995, https://bit.ly/3Gwb9EC. Accessed on 18 November 2022.

profile of the area and blatant religious cleansing.'[10] As a result of the aforesaid interventions with the International Commission of Jurists, we were able to delay the publication of its report beyond the crucial 1994 UNCHR Human Rights session. This entire exercise was greatly facilitated, as I enjoyed a good relationship with the Secretary General of the International Commission of Jurists, Mr Adama Dieng, who was fair-minded and held India in high esteem.

But leave aside NGOs, the absence of any sense of national interest in some of our media personnel and even those in high offices or positions of influence was a source of some concern. We had a couple of bright Indian media personnel in Geneva representing two of our leading national dailies, with whom I was in frequent touch. Regrettably, my pleas to them to not be taken in by Pakistani propaganda and desist from publishing reports based thereon fell on deaf ears. To my contention that what I was proposing was in the national interest, the response was that media freedom was supreme and above national interest! I could not, however, blame them, as Pakistani representatives, to substantiate their arguments denigrating India, would, every now and then, quote extremely critical assertions made by Indians who had held high office. This continues to be a bane to this day and one wishes that Indians in a position of influence are imbued with a greater sense of nationalism, which would lead them to be more discreet in their statements and thereby not hurt the national cause.

◆

In this context, one cannot forget an endeavour by the Secretary General of our NHRC to make a statement in the UNCHR in 1994, which contained some rather critical comments about our government. On seeing the draft statement, I requested that it be recast so that the offending elements therein were purged, or at least modified, as they would be used against us by those inimical to India. The Secretary General flatly refused, arguing that the NHRC was an independent body, and all my assertions that his statement was not in the national interest proved unavailing. The situation was

[10]Ibid. 106.

exacerbated by the fact that our Foreign Secretary Designate, who was visiting Geneva at the time, felt that I was 'over the top' in taking such strong objection to the aforesaid draft statement. Deeply agitated by this approach of the Secretary General and of the Foreign Secretary Designate, I conveyed my anguish in the matter to our Minister of State in the PMO, Mr Bhuvanesh Chaturvedi, on his arrival at Geneva airport next morning, inter alia, pointing out that such an absence of basic patriotism would prove to be our undoing. Mr Chaturvedi promptly pulled up the Secretary General, who later that morning sheepishly informed me that he was making the suggested changes in his statement.

My efforts at countering Pakistan's jehad against India did not go unnoticed by the Ministry. The latter was most generous in promptly acceding to my requests for an ad hoc increase in my representational grant to cope with my enhanced representational responsibilities, for the creation of an additional post to handle Disarmament-related activities and for the complete computerization of our Mission. Normally such requests take months of effort, but in my case, these received an across-the-table favourable response from Foreign Secretary Dixit. Clearly, the moral of the story is that if a Mission is perceived to be performing its duties well, its requests, if reasonable, will be viewed favourably by the Ministry.

As part of our UNCHR-related work, I was appointed as a Special Envoy of our External Affairs Minister and required to proceed to several countries as a part of our lobbying effort. I was not very keen to do so, as the action was in Geneva, which I felt was the place I should be in for much of the time. In the event, I visited only a select few countries like Cyprus, Iceland, Denmark, etc., and suggested to the Ministry not to send special envoys to countries where our accredited Ambassadors had the requisite seniority and competence to do the needful.

In much the same vein, I requested permission to be excused from a meeting of our Heads of Mission in Europe being convened in Paris, as it was being held in the middle of the UNCHR session. Though my request was turned down, I was able to get the Ministry to agree that I need not stay on in Paris for the entire duration of the two-day meeting and that the issue of human rights, which I was to address, be taken up as soon as I entered the meeting room and following termination of the discussion thereon I be allowed to return to Geneva. Accordingly, I left Geneva for Paris by a superfast train in the early morning of the aforesaid meeting chaired by our External Affairs Minister, reached the meeting room by mid-morning, briefed those present on the happenings in the UNCHR on Human Rights and, following a hasty lunch, caught the train back to Geneva early afternoon.

◆

Apart from the work relating to the UNCHR which formed the centrepiece of my activities relating to Human Rights, another important area of activity pertained to the UN World Conference on Human Rights held in Vienna in June 1993. The Conference was preceded by preparatory and regional meetings.

The Asian Regional Conference on Human Rights held in Bangkok in March–April 1993, inter alia, provided a fascinating insight into the dynamics of the Iran–Pakistan relationship, which was most instructive, and the lessons learnt proved invaluable for the 1994 UNHRC session, which has been dwelt upon in earlier paragraphs. At the Bangkok Conference, most of the Asian countries were clear that while Human Rights needed to be upheld, they should not be used by the West, as had long been the norm, for devising intrusive mechanisms as instrumentalities for political interference. Towards this end, we were fairly quickly able to develop a consensus paper. Anticipating that there was always the possibility of Pakistan playing the spoiler, at Mr Hamid Ansari's suggestion, both of us called on the leader of the Iranian delegation, Deputy Foreign Minister Javad Mohamad Zarif, at the beginning of the session. Mr Zarif was a good friend of Mr Ansari and later went on to become the Iranian Foreign Minister. He expressed appreciation at the thrust of our paper, stated that we should feel free to meet him at any time if we faced any difficulties in pushing it through and indicated that we should not be overly worried about Pakistan's machinations, as the latter was like a bird that could be put in or taken out of his pocket as required. As expected, our paper was at the end stage held up on account of Pakistan's insistence on inserting language calling for self-determination in Kashmir, which naturally was unacceptable to us. Having reached an impasse, we met Mr Zarif in the matter late at night, and the latter assured us that in the morning there would be no Pakistani opposition. This is exactly what transpired, and thanks to Mr Zarif's intervention, our consensus paper had a smooth sailing.

The World Conference on Human Rights was preceded by four preparatory meetings in Geneva from September 1991, the last of which was held in May 1993. Our delegation was led by Mr L.M. Singhvi, our High Commissioner in London and an eminent jurist. Whether or not to participate in this meeting was a dilemma with which I grappled for a few days, as it coincided with two other important meetings that required my presence, notably a meeting of the Disarmament Commission in New York, inter alia, to finalize a paper on Regional Disarmament, and a meeting of the G15 to be hosted by the Prime Minister in New Delhi. Since both the preparatory meeting for the World Conference on Human Rights and the G15 meeting had very high-powered Indian participation and since the Disarmament Commission had limited Indian participation but was of critical importance to us due to India–Pakistan differences on the issue of regional Disarmament, I, with the Ministry's clearance, decided to attend the latter.

◆

While in the last stages of the Disarmament Commission meeting in New York, I received an unusually panicky phone call from Foreign Secretary Dixit directing me to leave New York immediately and return forthwith to Geneva as, at the preparatory meeting being held there, some highly objectionable paragraphs calling for self-determination in Kashmir had found their way into the draft document. When I enquired as to how this had happened and that he might like to check with Mr Singhvi, the leader of our delegation, I was informed that the latter had left Geneva for London. At this, I told the Foreign Secretary that I would get back to him shortly after checking the position both from Mr Singhvi and from my Deputy in Geneva. Following detailed telephonic discussions, I discovered that this had happened due to our delegation's inattention, whose momentary absence from the meeting room where the discussions were being held was taken advantage of by Pakistan to insert the objectionable language. Though High Commissioner Singhvi had a long-standing friendship with the Conference Chairperson, he was unable to get the latter to expunge the offending language from the draft, which had been included through sleight of hand.

On completion of my enquiries into the matter, I reverted to Mr Dixit and informed him that my returning to Geneva at this point in time would be counterproductive, as my presence in New York was essential to clinch the gains made by our delegation in the paper on regional Disarmament, and my return to Geneva at this late stage would make no difference to the draft already finalized with the objectionable language. Moreover, the offending language in the draft was in square brackets and did not represent an agreed text. Accordingly, it would be up for renegotiation in Vienna, and I could assure him that I would ensure the offending language would not be a part of the final approved document that emerged from the World Conference on Human Rights.

The UN World Human Rights Conference was held in Vienna from 14 to 25 June 1993, with the participation of over 170 countries and with over 7,000 delegates. Our delegation was led by Finance Minister Dr Manmohan Singh and comprised many other dignitaries as well as senior officials, including Foreign Secretary Dixit. I was nominated as the Head of our Drafting Committee and was placed in charge of negotiating the final text. This onerous task, compounded by the imperative of removing the objectionable Kashmir-related paragraphs that had been inserted at the preparatory conference, put paid to any thoughts of revisiting any of my haunts in the city, which I had so loved and spent so many happy moments in my first posting. Indeed, all my waking hours from early morning to well past midnight were spent in the basement of the conference venue, where all the negotiations took place.

I recognized, at the very outset of the Conference, that the removal of the offending Kashmir-related language from the draft text demanded that I impose my dominance both on the proceedings and on the Chairman of the Drafting Committee, Ambassador Gilberto

Saboia of Brazil, so that unlike at the preparatory conference, where our viewpoint went by default, here, our consent would have to be taken on every issue of importance to us. This required a constant physical presence throughout the two-week-long proceedings and a proactive participation in all the issues under debate. With this in mind as a tactical ploy at the very first meeting, somewhat to the consternation of the members of my own delegation, I raised as many as six points of order, which compelled the Chairman to turn to me on every issue. This led to a comic situation, with the Chairman referring to me by error on one occasion as 'Mr Chairman'. To mount further pressure on the Chairman, I privately made it clear to him that there would be no consensus document if the offending language relating to Kashmir was not removed. Happily, as a result of these tactics and sheer hard work, I was able to fulfil my assurance to the Foreign Secretary and ensure the removal of the offending text pertaining to Kashmir from the final document.

◆

Through the conference, vignettes of the dynamics of India–Pakistan relations were on display, including the propensity of the latter to raise issues not on intrinsic merit but simply for embarrassing India. For instance, its proposal castigating the destruction of places of worship was clearly aimed at the destruction of the Babri Masjid. Some of my colleagues, noting this, argued that one should oppose it. I, however, felt that we should, on the contrary, support it as there was prima facie nothing wrong in it and, indeed, Pakistan was infinitely more guilty in the destruction of religious places of worship than India. Foreign Secretary Dixit, who happened to be in the room at the time, fully endorsed my viewpoint. Accordingly, we supported the said proposal, much to the consternation of the Pakistani delegation which, thereafter, lost all interest in the matter!

At the conference, I was also witness to how India had to bend to US pressure. Through the conference, India, while supportive of human rights, had been steadfast in its opposition to intrusive mechanisms purportedly designed for their promotion but used by the West for political ends. Towards this end, it had built up a strong coalition of mainly non-aligned countries for this purpose, with the Ministry's clearance, even though many of these countries had a terrible Human Rights record. One of the main targets by this India-supported coalition was the West-sponsored exercise to set up an Office of the Human Rights Commissioner. In the midst of a debate on this issue, I received a phone call from Foreign Secretary Dixit from New Delhi stating that he had heard that I was troubling the Americans and that I should be more accommodative on the issue of the establishment of the Office of the Human Rights Commissioner. My pleas that what we were doing was fully justified and was also with the express clearance of the Ministry were unavailing. Noting that he was adamant, I told him that it would be very difficult for me, personally, to do a volte face and, in view of his instructions, I would remove myself from all discussions in the matter, which could now, perhaps, be dealt with by Mr Ansari. On my return to the meeting, Cyrus Nasseri, my Iranian counterpart, observing that I was not participating in the discussions on the issue, with a knowing smile, posed the rhetorical query, 'Instructions from home?'

◆

If Human Rights absorbed much of my time in Geneva, the work relating to Disarmament, being more cerebral, was far more interesting. This was dealt with by the Conference of Disarmament (CD) in Geneva and, additionally, by the Disarmament Commission in New York as well as by the UN First Committee. The brains trust for Disarmament-related activity was unquestionably located in the CD. The latter was a cosy club of about 40 Ambassadors who inevitably got to know each other rather well and, by and large, had a very good personal equation with each other. It has since expanded to 65 and is probably not as well-knit a group any longer.

The opening session of the CD attended by me in January 1993 was a stormy one and quite unnecessarily so, as the Ministry, at the very last minute, instructed me to insist on the setting up of an ad hoc group for the complete elimination of nuclear weapons. Since the Indian stance had been adopted without any preparation and any lobbying and was in the teeth of P5 (Permanent Five or Big

Five) opposition, it had no chance of success. In effect, in adopting this position, India was telling the Disarmament community that it would hold up all work in the CD unless the latter also addressed the complete elimination of nuclear weapons. On feeling out the ground situation, I warned Foreign Secretary Dixit that we were completely isolated and that very soon, there would be enormous pressure on us to give up our hard-line approach. My warnings fell on deaf ears, but a couple of days later, exactly what I had predicted occurred, and the Ministry had to eat humble pie due to US pressure and concur with my initial advice. This unfortunate and unnecessary eventuality arose because those in charge of Disarmament in the Ministry were divorced from reality and disinclined to trust their man on the spot. They must bear the primary responsibility of putting one in such an unnecessarily awkward position, which did not do any good for India's image. If the Ministry really wanted the setting up of an ad hoc group for complete elimination of nuclear weapons, it should have lobbied for the same months in advance rather than sought to do so in the spur of the moment. Many countries, like Mexico and even Pakistan, may have come on board had we orchestrated our position more skilfully and with greater preparation.

◆

This style of functioning, which essentially entailed in keeping the man on the spot in the dark, was well-illustrated in a surprise visit that I had sometime in September–October 1993 from the Heads of the Disarmament and Americas divisions on their way back to India from the US. They had essentially come to inform me that they had just finalized with the US that our country, amongst others, would cosponsor both the CTBT and the FMCT. I was further told that I would now need to negotiate the nitty-gritty of both these resolutions, which we were to cosponsor at the upcoming First Committee meeting in New York. I was surprised because this implied an abandonment of our ambitions as a nuclear weapons armed state. While by some stretch of imagination, we could persuade ourselves to believe that having tested once, we did not need to do so again, to agree to a FMCT would mean capping our meagre fissile material stocks. I bluntly made these points and, for good measure, added that I should at least have been consulted. This was, however, water off a duck's back, as this breed of officers was riding high in New Delhi at the time.

I duly negotiated and cosponsored both the aforesaid resolutions in New York in October/November 1993. The history of subsequent developments on both resolutions does not reflect well on India, and particularly the Ministry, on more than one count.

As far as the CTBT is concerned, negotiations on it began in real earnest in January 1994 in the CD. The brief from the Ministry was that we should be active and constructive participants. Accordingly, we participated with utmost diligence and, in fact, as a tribute to the value we brought to the table, it was informally proposed in January 1995 by colleagues in the CD that I should accept chairmanship of the Verification Group for the Treaty. Since I had, by then, confidentially learnt of my impending transfer as High Commissioner to Pakistan, I declined the offer but my Deputy on Disarmament matters, Ajit Kumar, was appointed as a Friend of the Chair for Verification. In any case, while I was in Geneva, till July 1995, there was no hint from the Ministry that we had any second thoughts about the CTBT. However, soon after my leaving Geneva, we started distancing ourselves from the CTBT and to date have not signed it. The question then is: why did the Ministry decide to cosponsor it and ensure that India was a constructive participant? Indeed, even if we had been arm-twisted by the US into cosponsoring the Treaty, as may have been the case, we could surely have played the spoiler in the negotiations and forestalled its finalization for much longer. Clarity of thought and resoluteness of purpose have not always been distinguishing features of bureaucracies, and in particular, ours. Indeed, we seem to excel not in charting a clearly defined path but in landing ourselves in avoidable difficulties and then clumsily trying to find a way out.

On FMCT, the negotiations have not got off the ground to date due to Pakistan's intransigence. Moreover, due to our supine diplomacy, we allowed Pakistan to build a substantial measure of support around its position, which was to address not only future production of fissile material as mandated by the resolution but also its past production. Our position, like that of the P5 and a few other countries, was limited only to addressing future production. Regrettably, at a NAM ministerial conference in Cairo in mid-1994, our representative from the Ministry not only failed to develop a consensus around our position but also allowed the Pakistani position to secure acceptance. While the former was admittedly difficult, the latter was relatively easy to prevent since NAM decisions have to be based on consensus. Had we opposed it vigorously, this would have been possible. On learning of this development at the NAM conference, I was furious, and when I made known my unhappiness in the matter, our negotiator from the Ministry had the insouciance to argue that at such international gatherings, it is not done to stand in the way of consensus! This gave rise to an ironical situation of the Pakistan PR and I being deputed—he by NAM and I by the P5—to resolve the differences on the negotiating mandate for the FMCT. We did not, of course, succeed, but I found it strange that Pakistan should be representing NAM—a group of which India was the founder—and I should be representing the P5, against which we had taken up cudgels repeatedly!

◆

While the work relating to Human Rights and Disarmament took most of my time, I was also occasionally occupied with activities relating to WIPO, UNCTAD, ILO and WHO. In the process, I had the opportunity for very stimulating exchanges with our delegates from India who came to attend these meetings.

One of our representatives with whom I developed an excellent relationship and for whom I had the highest respect was our Labour Minister, Mr P.A. Sangma. He was a regular visitor to Geneva for the annual ILO meetings. Open, outspoken and endowed with a great sense of fun, one could not but admire and be drawn to him. We were on the same page on most issues and felt that we should adopt many of the ILO recommendations in regard to child labour regulations, on which many in India had reservations. On one occasion, he phoned me from Delhi to check whether I stood by my forthright approach in the matter as he wanted to quote me to the Prime Minister, particularly as my Ministry was being guarded in the matter. I stood my ground, and this further strengthened our equation.

The outbreak of plague in Surat, Bombay and Delhi in 1994 led to an embargo on our rice exports, particularly to the Gulf, and fears of the imposition of a cordon sanitaire around India. In order to defuse the situation, we had intensive discussions with the WHO Director General, Dr Hiroshi Nakajima. We had to work hard to persuade him that the WHO should refrain from off-the-cuff advisories that could hurt our exports and indeed our international standing. This was not easy, as two of his close aides were Pakistanis. Ultimately, we succeeded, and much of the credit goes to Second Secretary Tirumurti, who had good working-level contacts in the WHO and was finely tuned to its mechanics. Since we had nothing to hide and were interested in working with total transparency, we suggested that before issuing any adverse notifications, the WHO should send a team to India to make its own objective assessment in the matter rather than take its cue from random and often biased media reportage. This was done promptly, and the WHO team made out that there were no more than a maximum of 200 confirmed cases of plague in India, that there was no epidemic as such, that the situation had been brought under control, that no cordon sanitaire should be imposed around India, and that there was no evidence that plague could be transmitted through Indian exports. This report greatly helped contain the fallout from the plague outbreak in India and ensured that our exports did not suffer.[11]

◆

Though my work life in Geneva was tense and hectic, the assignment had its compensations. I inherited a lovely residence that had been selected by Mr A.P. Venkateswaran, who had been PR Geneva over a decade earlier. It was located next to Lake Geneva and was very close to the picturesque Geneva Golf Club, of which I was a member and which I frequented on weekends and sometimes even on weekdays, late in the evening. It was also only a 10–15-minute drive from office and so I could often come home for a hot lunch.

---

[11]'International Notes Update: Human Plague—India, 1994', CDC, https://bit.ly/3he4lAO. Accessed on 5 November 2022.

Despite time constraints, I had a fairly active social life, which was not merely confined to those I interacted with in my normal work life but also some others. Amongst the latter may be mentioned Gilbert Etienne, a Swiss economist and Indophile who knew more about Indian agriculture than most Indians; Arif Hussain, a former colleague in the IFS who had worked with me in Dhaka and subsequently joined the WTO; Sri Wijeratne from the UNHCR, whom I had known in Manila and was later to be with in Islamabad; and Ambassador Narendra Singh Sarila, who after retirement as our Head of Mission in Paris, had taken up residence in Switzerland and was Chairman of the Board of Nestlé.

My busy schedule also kept me from travelling very much. However, I was able to make day trips to neighbouring cities like Lausanne and Montreux as also short visits to Italy, France and Austria with my family. I, of course, visited Gruyere, the home of the renowned Gruyere cheeses, where we naturally partook of raclette and fondue, which have, for long, been a favourite of mine. I was also partial to the simple fillet de perche, a staple at restaurants on the banks of Lake Geneva. Additionally, a whole range of Swiss cheeses and chocolates became family favourites. It was also in Geneva that one came to appreciate its exquisite white wines and, in fact, I invested in a couple of cases thereof, which stood me in good stead for a year or so at my next assignment in Islamabad.

While having enormously enjoyed my Geneva stint, not only as a learning experience but also as an occasion to play a role in neutralizing Pakistani machinations against us, I must confess that multilateral diplomacy did not provide me with the same measure of satisfaction as offered by bilateral diplomacy. This is perhaps because in the latter, successes tend to be more tangible and meaningful, whereas in the former, they are usually less tangible and often ephemeral. Indeed, UN-based multilateral diplomacy may be likened to a series of one-night stands offering a momentary high but little lasting satisfaction, as it involves temporary issue-based linkages with all manner of players, even those inimical to one, which vanish overnight. It may also be pointed out that our multilateral experts lacked the rigour of bilateral specialists and were often innocent of the fine nuances of bilateral relationships that had a bearing on what was done or left undone at multilateral fora.

In this backdrop, I was very happy to informally learn in January 1995 that I was soon to be transferred to Islamabad to once again succeed my good friend S.K. Lambah as High Commissioner. The two of us were soon in touch to fine-tune our respective moves. I was able to inform him that I would be ready to move in July 1995, immediately on conclusion of the CD session in June. My successor in Geneva, Miss Arundhati Ghosh, who was moving from Cairo and was a part of the UN mafia in the Ministry, could not believe that I was willing to leave Geneva and phoned me on several occasions to confirm this.

12

IN THE ENEMY'S LAIR: ISLAMABAD

On leaving Geneva in July 1995, and after consultations in Delhi, I joined duty as High Commissioner in Islamabad in August 1995. Friends have often asked me as to whether this was my toughest assignment. I have always responded in the negative, as I came fully prepared, having served in Pakistan from 1969 to 1971, and having dealt with it from Headquarters in two spells: once from January 1973 to October 1974 and on the second occasion from 1986 to 1989. Moreover, I never felt that I was a stranger to Pakistan, as my parents were from Multan, Lahore was my birthplace and I came equipped with a spoken, though somewhat rusty, knowledge of Multani, also known as Saraiki, Punjabi and Urdu. Above all, with India–Pakistan relations perpetually at a low ebb, there was no chance of anyone being able to attribute the sorry state of relations to the High Commissioner!

As I started delving into the local scene, I was struck by the absence of any major changes since my earlier tour of duty in the country two-and-a-half decades ago. There was the same hostility to India, the same ISI surveillance and harassment of our diplomats, the same dominance of the military in local polity, and the same petty political infighting. Accordingly, in my very first cable to India as High Commissioner, I reported that the basics of the local scene in Pakistan appeared to be relatively unchanged from that which had prevailed decades earlier. While it is true that the military was not directly ruling the country, civilian rule was merely a façade. The only major perceptible change since my earlier assignment was that the media was somewhat freer and more open to occasionally criticizing the government.

The Indian High Commission in Islamabad, with over 100 India-based officers and staff, was one of our larger Missions. It had a strong high-quality officer component. Apart from the Head of Mission, it, inter alia, included Sharat Sabharwal, Deputy High Commissioner, Yash Sinha, Counsellor (Political), A.B. Mathur, Counsellor (Consular), and several First Secretaries, including Avinash Mohananey, Ruchi Ghanshyam, A.R. Ghanshyam and N. Parthasarthy. Its military wing included Brigadier Ajay Sood, Group Captain Pervez Khokhar and Captain Rakesh Pandit. All secretarial staff was Indian as also the chauffeurs and security guards. While the officers and secretarial staff had their families with them, chauffeurs and security guards did not.

Not only did my colleagues in the High Commission uncomplainingly put up with the daily pinpricks from the ISI and the palpably hostile environment, which is the lot of Indian diplomats in Pakistan, but they also provided me with excellent support. On-time reportage of local developments was the norm, very good contacts were maintained, and some high-visibility and popular cultural events were organized with participation by reputed Indian artistes like Pandit Hariprasad Chaurasia and Pandit Jasraj. In the latter part of my stay, when we wanted to up the visa-issuance rate from the normal daily average of about 250, we were able to increase it to about 400 by roping in our families for help! This was only about 40 per cent of the issuance rate in Karachi in the late 1960s but a whopping twelve-fold increase of what was being done in Islamabad at that time.

The officers in the Military Wing, too, did not disappoint and never missed a trick. They alerted me to the existence of a facility in the immediate vicinity of Islamabad that was assembling Chinese-supplied M11 and M9 missiles. Naval Attaché Rakesh Pandit, who had considerable hands-on expertise in missile systems, was quick to inform me, after having studied the TV clip on the launch of the Ghauri missile in April 1998, that the test had not been successful due to improper fuel burn.

Despite our best endeavours, Pakistan's obduracy and prevarications kept us from building residences for the officers and staff deployed in our High Commission in Islamabad. Accordingly, we were compelled to rent premises for them as indeed had been the case since the time the High Commission had been set up in the mid-1960s. The drawback in so doing was that it increased the opportunities for the ISI to harass and intimidate our officials. Had they all been housed together in premises built by us on one plot of land, as was our endeavour, they would have been much more secure. The situation was much worse than that which prevailed in Karachi when I was serving there, as all our officers and a substantial element of our staff were grouped together in Indian-owned properties. Moreover, harassment was lower at that time, as the Pakistanis were aware that any such action on their part would invite prompt retaliatory moves against their officers and staff in India. Regrettably, my efforts to convince our government to engage in such retaliation, as and when our staff faced harassment, were not successful. I had personally taken this up with Prime Minister Rao, but he was adamant that we could not stoop to any such tit-for-tat retaliation. Consequently, most working in our High Commission, particularly at the lower level, faced considerable harassment, which inevitably led to some demoralization.

We were, however, fortunate in having been able to build our own chancery in the late 1980s. It was a large, well-furnished and functional property that also housed our security guards and chauffeurs. It was, however, not particularly well-designed, as the rooms were relatively small, and too much space was eaten up by corridors. This was in stark contrast to our chancery in Karachi that, though constructed in the late 1950s, was not only more elegant but also had more effective space management. The High Commission chancery at Islamabad, however, had a very pleasing appearance at all times on account of an arrangement with a local contractor for petty repairs and retouching of its paintwork on an on-demand basis. This excellent practice had been instituted by my predecessor, which I readily continued.

I inherited a lovely, well-located residence that had originally been taken on lease by one of my predecessors, Mr K.S. Bajpai. Over the years, the lease was periodically renewed. The residence had a spacious entertainment area, sufficient bedrooms to accommodate both family and guests, and two good-sized patches of lawn. It was equipped with 100 per cent electricity back-up so that we had assured electricity supply 24/7.

◆

When I took up my assignment in Islamabad, relations between India and Pakistan were distinctly frosty. There was no meaningful dialogue between the two, terrorism in Kashmir was at a high and Pakistan was still digesting its failure to successfully move a Kashmir-related resolution against India at UN fora. The Prime Ministers of the two countries—Benazir Bhutto and Narasimha Rao—did not have a very high opinion of each other. Indeed, when, as recommended by my predecessor, I suggested to Mr Rao that one could, perhaps, explore the possibility of a meeting between him and Benazir Bhutto at the 1995 NAM summit, he displayed no interest in the matter. Similarly, many months later, Benazir Bhutto lamented that she was unable to have the same sort of cordial relationship with Mr Rao that she enjoyed with Rajiv Gandhi. She put this to Mr Rao's objecting to US arms sales to Pakistan and, in particular, the F16s. I reacted by explaining to her that Mr Rao's objections were only natural and that the Rajiv Gandhi government had also the same objections, as reflected in its answers to Parliament Questions which, in fact, had been drafted by me. The failure of Benazir Bhutto to relate to Narasimha Rao was, in my view, at least in some measure, due to an issue of lineage. As a Bhutto with a feudal mindset, she equated herself to the Nehru–Gandhi family and found it more difficult to relate to Mr Rao who, in her eyes, was a mere commoner.

The trust deficit in India–Pakistan ties was on open display when I presented my credentials to President Farooq Leghari in the presence of Pakistan Foreign Secretary Najmuddin Shaikh. After the usual exchange of pleasantries, the President probed me about fast-tracking the Iran–Pakistan–India oil and gas pipeline that was under consideration at the time. I suggested that we could explore this as an undersea project. This suggestion was based on the logic that an undersea project as compared to an overland project would be much less prone to disruption by Pakistan. The President was, however, insistent that this only be considered as an overland project. Noting my lack of enthusiasm for the same, he smilingly commented that India need not be too worried, as conflicts between the two countries were not long-lasting and, accordingly, supply disruptions by Pakistan in the event of war would be for no more than a couple of weeks! It goes without saying that I sent a message to the Ministry of External Affairs highlighting these comments of the Pakistani President and underlining that we should never get into such strategic projects with Pakistan, which could, at a moment's notice, strangulate our critical supplies. Regrettably, my views did not carry much weight, as we have never ceased to contemplate similar linkages involving Pakistan such as the Turkmenistan–Afghanistan–Pakistan–India (TAPI) pipeline.

◆

Within a few days of my arrival in Islamabad, and even before I had presented credentials, I received a phone call from Minocher Bhandara, popularly known as Minoo Bhandara, whom I had met a couple of nights earlier at a dinner hosted by a colleague, inviting me for lunch the following day at his house in Rawalpindi. Bhandara was a former MP and Home Minister in one of Zia's governments, but more importantly, a typically outspoken Parsi. He also happened to be the owner of Murree Breweries, renowned for its beer, which I was familiar with from my earlier Karachi posting. I readily accepted his invitation, and at the lunch met an even more outspoken, acerbic and irreverent Parsi based in Karachi by way of Ardeshir Cowasji, who had been a shipping magate till his business was nationalized by Bhutto in the 1970s. Both Bhandara and Cowasji became good friends of mine and a wonderful source of information and insights into Pakistan. Also present at the lunch was Mr Agha Shahi, one of Pakistan's most formidable diplomats and a former Foreign Secretary and Foreign Minister. A few days later, Bhandara told me that, following our lunch, Shahi and Cowasji, who left together, were tailed and later interrogated by the ISI! The message that I carried from this was that meeting the Indian High Commissioner, even for former dignitaries, was not cost free! Such episodes were a constant occurrence.

◆

The behaviour of Pakistanis towards Indians if not outrightly hostile is at best schizophrenic in nature. The average Pakistani, particularly the Punjabi, is by nature extremely hospitable, social and consumed by curiosity about India. Thus, on meeting visiting Indians, his natural inclination is to display great warmth and friendship. However, beneath this veneer there lurks a deep-seated hostility towards India, which is the result of decades of brainwashing promoted by the Establishment through the media, the religious parties and the educational system. Indian visitors, ranging from housewives to officials—serving or retired, civil or military—and from businessmen to hard-bitten journalists, while interacting with Pakistanis, are usually taken in by the lavish hospitality bestowed on them and find it hard to believe that they have an inherent anti-Indian mindset. In these circumstances, I took to advising all Indian visitors to Pakistan that before drawing any conclusion about how 'good' Pakistanis are, they should consider talking about India–Pakistan relations with their local interlocutors and that the responses thereto would show the latter in their true colours!

Infinitely more disquieting than the phenomenon of Indians failing to detect the inherent hostility of Pakistanis towards India was that some did not take kindly to efforts to alert them to this and went so far as to openly criticize India in the presence of Pakistanis. For instance, at a briefing specially organized by me for a group of Indian visitors, including some senior retired military officials, they were unhappy that we had excluded their Pakistani hosts from the same and took umbrage at our suggesting that we should not take their hosts' expressions of friendship at face value. Worse still, on another occasion, a former IFS officer, at a dinner hosted by me in his honour, unabashedly asserted in the presence of our Pakistani guests that the IFS was more responsible than its Pakistani counterpart for the sorry state of affairs between the two countries! Similarly, whilst I was in Dhaka, an Indian MP, while addressing a public gathering, made out that the Farakka Agreement was unfair to Bangladesh and should be appropriately amended. Such instances where Indians, particularly those in high places, run down the country whilst abroad not only reflect poorly on them but also reveal that even a basic sense of nationalism is foreign to some of us.

◆

In September–October 1995, Pakistan was shaken by a coup bid undertaken by fundamentalist army elements aimed not merely against the Benazir Bhutto government but also against the top layers of the Armed Forces, including Army Chief General Abdul Waheed Kakar. One of the main architects was none other than Major General Abbasi, who while a Brigadier and Pakistan's Defence Attaché in Delhi in the 1980s had been declared persona non grata after having been caught red-handed engaging in spying activities in India. Based on the intelligence provided by Lieutenant General Ali Kuli Khan Khattak, Director General, Military Intelligence, about the coup bid, the same was put down by Lieutenant General Karamat, who was then the Chief of General Staff and later became Army Chief. Over 30 Army officers were arrested for involvement in this coup bid, revealing that the fundamentalism so assiduously promoted by General Zia had taken deep root in the Pakistan Armed Forces.

The fact that terror and violence is always in the air in Pakistan was vividly brought home to me a few weeks after I had presented credentials, when, at around 9.30 a.m., a vehicle laden with over 1,000 kilograms of explosive material was detonated at the gate of the Egyptian Embassy, located about 500 yards from our High Commission. An estimated 15 people were killed and around 80 were injured in this incident. The Egyptian Embassy itself took massive damage and was reduced to a crumbling hulk. The intensity of the blast was such that some papers on my desk flew off onto the floor, a few glass panes developed cracks and a metal shard, vaulting our 10-foot-high perimeter wall, damaged the rear window of one of our cars. The Japanese and Indonesian Embassies, which were closer to the Egyptian Embassy, took much heavier damage. The attack directed against the Egyptian State was undertaken by the Egyptian terrorist outfit Al Jihad, and some of the perpetrators were caught in the succeeding weeks. Many of these elements had fought in the war against Afghanistan and had the free run of Pakistan. I was decidedly lucky, as just a day earlier, my wife and I were in the Egyptian Embassy compound on a courtesy call on the Egyptian Ambassador and his wife.

◆

In early 1996, General Karamat took over as Chief of Army Staff. Having known him slightly from his participation in the Siachen talks in the late 1980s when he was Director General Military Operations, I promptly sought an appointment with him through the Ministry of Foreign Affairs, as was the norm. Predictably, the appointment did not come through for weeks. I, however, happened to run into him on the occasion of the wedding of President Leghari's son and, congratulating him, stated that I had wished to do so in person at his office but that privilege had been denied me, as the Foreign Ministry had not cleared my requested appointment. The General was most warm and effusive and mentioned that we would meet the very next day. I duly received a call from his office next morning alerting me to an appointment with him in a couple of hours in Rawalpindi. During our meeting, after a lengthy exchange of pleasantries, in which he fondly recalled his visits to Delhi and enquired after some of the Indian officials with whom he had interacted, I sought to draw him out on the possibility of his visit to India. General Karamat was scrupulously correct and averred that he could not comment on this and that all such issues would have to be decided by Prime Minister Benazir Bhutto. He was also disinclined to get drawn into any political exchanges. However, at the personal level, he oozed warmth and ever the gentleman, he handed me a telephone number as I left, mentioning I should not hesitate to use if I was ever in any 'trouble'.

General Karamat's resignation in the second-half of 1998 was a completely unexpected event and a highly unusual one in a country in which the civilian leadership invariably deferred to the military. The resignation was triggered by General Karamat's advocacy for the creation of a National Security Council for the purpose of a better and more institutionalized interface between the civilian and military leadership in the country. Nawaz Sharif, seeing it as a move for increased military involvement in Pakistan's governance, was incensed and demanded General Karamat's resignation. The latter surprisingly agreed to do so. Most other Pakistani Generals would not have acceded to Nawaz Sharif's demands, and Karamat's resignation was highly unpopular in the Pakistan military, which felt that it had been humiliated by the civilian leadership. Indeed, Lieutenant General Khattak, who resigned following Musharraf's appointment as Army Chief, as he had been superseded, was vituperative in his criticism of Karamat's meek submission to Nawaz Sharif and unequivocally told me that had Karamat resisted, he would have had the full backing of the military.

General Karamat stood out in stark contrast to his successor, General Pervez Musharraf, who took over from him as Army Chief. Suffice it to say that my assessment of the latter is based on a half-hour tête-à-tête I had with him at a farewell dinner hosted in my honour just prior to my leaving Islamabad in late December 1998 by former Army Chief General Mirza Aslam Baig. During our interaction, I posed to General Musharraf the identical question that I had put to General Karamat as to whether he would go to India on the basis of our long-pending invite for the Pakistan Army Chief. The response, without a moment's thought, was in the affirmative. I then proceeded to quiz him on his approach to Karamat's suggestion for the creation of a National Security Council, knowing its popularity in the military, and pointing out that India, too, was in the process of setting it up. Without batting an eyelid, Musharraf stated that it was not really necessary. From our brief discussion, I carried the clear impression that Musharraf was an ambitious and scheming individual, a hardliner on India, and a crafty political animal who could turn out to be another Zia and topple the civilian government if the circumstances provided him with an opportunity to do so.

As things turned out, my assessment was on the mark as, following the Kargil Conflict, Musharraf fell out with Prime Minister Nawaz Sharif, and soon thereafter, masterminded a coup against him. His moves vis-à-vis India were also distinctly inimical, as he was the author of Kargil and sought to pull wool over our eyes time and again.

◆

Notwithstanding the strained India–Pakistan ties, many Pakistanis long to visit India either to meet relatives or to visit shrines, or to partake in seminars, conferences or cultural events, or simply to indulge in shopping! The grant of a visa is, thus, always a point of leverage with the Indian High Commission. It is due to this leverage that I developed an equation with the Pakistan Interior Minister, Major General Naseerullah Babar. He had, on an occasion, approached me for the urgent grant of a visa to one of his acquaintances. My prompt compliance with his request marked the beginning of a friendly association with him and assured me of access at short notice. During one of our meetings, I sought his help to trace an Indian lady who had reportedly been abducted by a Pakistani to Quetta. He promised all help and, a couple of days later, indicated that she had, in all probability, been taken to Afghanistan, but there would be no problem in tracing her, as the Taliban were 'Pakistan's children'. On noting my smile, he tried to retrieve the situation, stating that it was only on minor issues that they listened to Pakistan. At another interaction, General Babar sought my intervention on the release of an alleged Pakistani journalist who was in prison in Kashmir. In providing details of this individual, General Babar used a pseudonym. It turned out this individual was none other than the notorious terrorist Masood Azhar, who was one of the hostages released consequent to the hijacking of Indian Airlines Flight 814 and who went on to form the Jaish-e-Mohammed.

◆

The situation faced by Indian diplomats in Pakistan was radically different from that faced by their counterparts in India. Thus, while Indians, including even those in officialdom, were relatively relaxed about attending functions organized by Pakistani diplomats and the Pakistan High Commission, Indian diplomats in Pakistan faced an uphill task in this regard, and my invitations even to senior Pakistani officials and dignitaries were usually spurned unless sent in connection with the visit of an officially approved delegation or event. Indeed, chastened by my experience in Pakistan, I, on return to India as Secretary National Security Council Secretariat (NSCS), made it point to never accept any invitation by the Pakistan High Commissioner, even though one of the incumbents, Aziz Khan, was well known to me and whom I had, in the not-too-distant past, regarded as a friend. When he chided me for never accepting his invitations, I had no hesitation in frankly telling him that I had little option but to do so, as when I was High Commissioner in Pakistan and had sought to establish contact with him, he had avoided me like the plague!

A useful mechanism for overcoming the problem of meeting Pakistani dignitaries was the Commonwealth High Commissioners' Group, which held monthly luncheon meetings at which a Pakistani dignitary was invited as the chief guest for an exchange of views. These interactions sometimes provided fascinating insights into Pakistani thought processes on a variety of issues that otherwise did not get the attention they deserved. For instance, at a luncheon hosted by me for the Group, the Bangladesh High Commissioner casually cited the vastly improved performance of his country in the area of human development indicators. In response, the Pakistani chief guest bluntly asserted that this could not be correct, as the figures cited were much better than those of Pakistan. It was only after much argument and after I informed our guest that Bangladesh's performance was indeed very good and in fact better than that of India on some parameters that he quietened down. My takeaway from the exchange was that Pakistan had not lost any of its arrogance vis-à-vis Bangladesh, and it could simply not accept that the latter's performance in many areas was now far ahead than that of Pakistan. On another occasion, at a luncheon hosted by the Canadian High Commissioner, when the chief guest was asked about the precarious economic situation in the country, he responded that Pakistan had no worry on this account, as the West would always bail it out.

◆

An unusually outspoken and fearless dignitary who I became acquainted with in Pakistan and one who did not carry the customary bias against India was Miangul Aurangzeb, son of the last Wali of Swat. He had been educated in the Doon School, Dehradun, and in St. Stephen's College, New Delhi. He had been a member of the Pakistan National Assembly on many occasions and, in 1997, was appointed Governor of Balochistan. Interaction with him was a delight, as he never hesitated in calling a spade a spade and, if critical of India, he was even more so of Pakistan. Moreover, unlike most others, he was not scared of visiting my residence. Thus, he would often come home for a game of bridge and for dinner even if invited at short notice.

In view of my special equation with Miangul Aurangzeb, whom I held in high esteem, I decided to visit Quetta soon after his appointment as Governor of Balochistan. On arrival at Quetta airport, Beneeta and I were received by Miangul's Protocol Officer and were whisked away to his residence for a meeting over tea. He met us warmly and, when we were alone, told me that he had deliberately sent his Protocol to receive me and had us brought to his house because he wanted the message to go across to the ISI that we were on extremely good terms.

◆

Whilst in Quetta, I met with some of the local tribal chiefs representing the Mengals, the Marris and the Bugtis. While all were kind enough to interact with me, the most impressive was Nawab Akbar Khan Bugti, who insisted on inviting Beneeta and me home to dinner. As we left the hotel, about halfway to his home, we noticed that the ubiquitous ISI vehicle following us had been replaced by a vehicle filled with a dozen fierce-looking tribals with AK-47s. My chauffeur informed me that this change had taken place as we were now in Bugti territory and the Pakistani ISI tended to steer clear of it. On arriving at the Nawab's abode, I was asked to disembark and was taken to him, while Beneeta was taken to another section of the home to interact with his wife and other ladies of the household. She joined me later sans the ladies of the household just before dinner was served. She was given to understand that while the ladies of the household travelled abroad from time to time, whilst in Quetta, they never left the zenana. Visiting the market for shopping was prohibited and should they want anything, it was brought home to them.

Nawab Bugti was an impressive personality, radiating both physical well-being and intellectual acumen. Indeed, there were reports of him having killed people with his bare hands. He himself narrated that in his youth, he used to consume an entire chicken, and it was only of late that he had given up eating meat and focussed on vegetarian food and fish. Tall, lean and very fit, he was remarkably well-read and completely au fait with developments local, regional and international. As a youngster, he had spent some time in Shimla and cherished fond memories of India. His magnetic personality held all his guests, some of whom were local dignitaries and numbered around 30, spellbound. Indeed, such was the awe inspired by him that none dared to speak or eat till given the nod to do so. This was, of course, in part because as the tribal chief, he had the power of life and death over his clansmen.

During my interaction with the Hindu community in Quetta, I received further corroboration of the extent of power exercised by the Nawab in Balochistan. Most of them had migrated from places like Multan to escape the persecution faced by them there, and in the areas controlled by the Nawab, they were fully protected and allowed to freely practise their faith. They indicated, however, that while earlier the Nawab had actively dissuaded those who wanted to leave for India, assuring them that he would not let any harm come to them, of late, he had made known that those who wished to leave may do so. In this, the Nawab was, no doubt, prescient, as a few years later, Musharraf had him eliminated.

I remained in touch with the Nawab throughout the remaining part of my stay in Islamabad and had the opportunity of hosting a dinner in his honour. The wife of one of the invitees for the dinner fortunately alerted us to the fact that it was customary for the Nawab's host to also provide dinner for the dozen or so bodyguards who invariably accompanied him. Accordingly, the requisite arrangements were duly made, and I was saved from any embarrassment on this account.

Noting the Nawab's political importance, I suggested that he visit India. While not evincing any interest in this, he indicated that one of his sons would like to visit Kashmir if this was possible, as he was interested in Shahtoosh shawls. I sounded out Farooq Abdullah about this, and the latter was most supportive, indicating that though there were restrictions on the sale of such shawls, these could be waived off for the Bugti family. Regrettably, the Ministry of External Affairs showed no interest in my proposition, and the visit never materialized. Indeed, through my stint in Islamabad, there was little inclination on the part of the Ministry to reach out to alternate power brokers in the country. We, in fact, seemed to specialize in both losing old friends and not making new ones.

India's dealings with the Khudai Khidmatgars, led since their inception in 1929 by Khan Abdul Ghaffar Khan, popularly known as the Frontier Gandhi, and their successors in the National Awami Party and later the Awami National Party (ANP), are a classic example of betraying old friends in Pakistan. As is well known, in pre-Partition India, the North-West Frontier Province (NWFP) was under a Congress Government, which had been elected to power in 1946 supported by the Khudai Khidmatgars, with the Frontier Gandhi's elder brother, Dr Khan Sahib, being the Chief Minister. Nehru's Congress, however, accepted the holding of a referendum in the NWFP as proposed by the British in order to determine whether it should accede to India or Pakistan. This was a gross departure from the norm, whereunder decisions on such matters were taken by the elected provincial assemblies. What is worse is that this was done without consulting the Khudai Khidmatgars, which led Khan Abdul Ghaffar Khan to tell Gandhi that his people had been thrown to the wolves. With the NWFP acceding to Pakistan in a doctored referendum boycotted by the Khudai Khidmatgars, the latter were a potentially strong lobby for India. While initially, some ties were maintained with them, over the years, these withered away and there was little effort on India's part to sustain a meaningful relationship with them.

During my call, accompanied by Beneeta, on the Frontier Gandhi's son, Khan Abdul Wali Khan and his family, including his wife Naseem Wali Khan and son Asfandyar Wali Khan, at their Charsadda home, we were received with great warmth. However, their bitterness was evident at India having agreed to a plebiscite in the NWFP on the issue of its accession to Pakistan rather than having insisted that this be decided by the existing duly elected provincial legislature. It was clear that they felt abandoned by India and harboured a sense of being let down. This was unfortunate, as the ANP under their leadership was committed to democratic and secular principles, had a considerable standing in the NWFP, was an important source of information and looked up to India. In these circumstances, I made a conscious effort at maintaining contacts with the ANP leaders, both through visits to Peshawar and providing them ready access to the High Commission. Indeed, Peshawar was the city where I felt most at ease in Pakistan because of the sincere and unconditional friendship bestowed upon me by the ANP. It is, however, unfortunate that the Ministry did not see the need to cultivate this Party—arguably the only important pro-India lobby in Pakistan. I was particularly put out when the Ministry did not deem fit to ensure that the External Affairs Minister send a letter of condolence to Wali Khan on the occasion of his elder brother's demise. Despite the Ministry's disinclination to maintain links with the ANP, I made it a point to do so and in the process gained invaluable insights into Pakistan's polity. As a result of my visits to Peshawar, I developed a taste for Frontier cuisine and had the opportunity of playing golf at the city's century-old golf course, which was a delight because of its lush fairways and splendid layout.

◆

As High Commissioner, I visited Karachi more than any other city in Pakistan. This was only natural, as the High Commission owned several properties there, as it was the country's financial and commercial hub, as it was much more 'open' than Islamabad and, thus, a good source for fresher insights into Pakistan, and as it was the point of arrival for some of our dignitaries whom I had to receive.

Having served in Karachi earlier, my visits there brought back nostalgic memories. My very first visit to the city as High Commissioner was traumatic, as the elegance, order and quietude which had characterized it in the 1960s had given way to a disquieting coarseness, disorder and raucousness. Even the Sind Club, which had been the epitome of class and elegance, was dusty and in disrepair and had clearly fallen on evil days. Our properties in Karachi were in very poor shape. While this was, to an extent, to be expected, as they had not been occupied since end 1994, on account of the closure of our Consulate General, what I was unprepared for was the extent to which they had been vandalized.

Particularly distressing was the case of India Lodge, which was a gracious and well-appointed property right next to Zulfiquar Ali

Bhutto's house in Clifton. It originally served as the residence of our High Commissioner and later of the Assistant High Commissioner and Consul General. The property was not only run down, but drug addicts had been allowed by the local authorities to strip it of all metal parts, like door handles, latches, fans, faucets, etc. Even metal conduit pipes had been dug out of the walls and floors. Clearly, the vandals had a free run of the premises, and the police deployed to protect the property had at best done nothing to prevent it and at worst connived in the exercise. In these circumstances, I made a strong pitch to the Ministry that we should lease our properties in Karachi to other Embassies that had shown interest in the matter. Regrettably, my suggestion did not elicit a positive response, with the Ministry making out that it could not let a foreign flag fly on our properties. This, I felt, was a much better outcome than allowing our properties to be vandalized, but wiser minds in Delhi prevailed!

Visits to Karachi were also an opportunity to engage with the commercial and business community. Some amongst them were keen to interact with India and felt that their government should enhance commercial linkages. Indeed, in an open interaction with the local Chamber of Commerce, a Pakistani businessman was bold enough to assert that rather than constantly espousing the Kashmiri cause, Pakistan would be better off thinking about its own people, who had much to gain from closer commercial ties with India.

My visits to Karachi were also an occasion to interact with the Dawoodi Bohra community, whose coreligionists were, inter alia, located in even larger numbers in Maharashtra and Gujarat. They were a peaceable Shia community mainly interested in business and with close links in India. They were a great help to us in the absence of a regular Indian presence in Karachi in the management of our properties there. We, in turn, provided all possible help to them to visit India for purposes of meeting their kith and kin.

◆

Two of my trips to Karachi were necessitated by the visits there first of Chief Justice A.M. Ahmadi and later of Chief Justice J.S. Verma at the invitation of their Pakistani counterparts. These were professionally useful occasions enabling me to meet extensively with elements of the Pakistani Judiciary. My main takeaway from these interactions was the clear impression that the Pakistani Judiciary held its Indian counterpart in the highest esteem and was envious of the freedom it enjoyed from Executive interference.

My exchanges with Chief Justice Ahmadi and Chief Justice Verma also brought home to me the striking difference between the two. While the former came out as haughty, reticent and distant, the latter was down to earth, open and friendly. While the former did not see fit to seek my inputs into his interactions with his local interlocutors, the latter made it a point to apprise me of the issues likely to be raised and to solicit my views thereon. Chief Justice Verma also readily shared with me the essence of his exchanges with his Pakistani interlocutors, which was an invaluable input for me.

Whilst in Pakistan, I made it a point to visit my ancestral properties in Lahore and Multan. I was fortunate enough to be able to do so accompanied by my eldest sister who, along with her husband and my niece, visited us in Islamabad. As I was only five years old when we left Lahore for India in June 1947, I myself had no meaningful recollections of these properties.

Lahore, my birthplace, is, to this day, a wonderful city. With a canal running through it, beautiful parks, gracious bungalows set in manicured gardens, exquisite cuisine, a lively cultural scene, excellent educational institutions and a panoply of historical monuments, Lahore is more than a match for Delhi. Indeed, in 1947, it was, without doubt, the premier city of Northern India. Such was the lure of Lahore at the time that when my father was offered land at a throwaway price in Connaught Place in New Delhi, he rejected it out of hand, as he was clear that he would settle in Lahore, where he had a house in the plush Model Town area as well as several plots of land on the canal bank.

During my earlier visits to Lahore, my efforts at locating my father's house in Model Town had not proved successful. However, my sister, who was 10 years my senior, had a clear memory of this house, and was able to locate it easily. I had been unable to do so on earlier visits to the area as, in a part of the property facing the road, several small apartments had been constructed that obstructed a clear view of it. My sister was able to conclusively identify the house by the colour of the flooring. Though born while my parents were living in the house, I had no sentimental attachment to it, as I had no memories of it. My sister, however, who had been a teenager at the time, had vivid memories of it and spent several minutes walking through the premises and reliving moments of the past.

Model Town was a residential cooperative society on the outskirts of Lahore set up in an area of about 2,000 acres. Each plot was around 1,800 square yards, and in between each block, there were huge parks and gardens equal in size to at least a football field. In 1947, 1,100 of the 1,300 residents in Model Town migrated to India, and the plots vacated were declared evacuee property, which were taken over by the Pakistani authorities. When my father came to Delhi, he felt that it would be good idea if like-minded friends got together to establish a residential cooperative society on the lines of Model Town. The result was the establishment of Friends Colony in New Delhi, of which he was one of the several founder members. Apart from my father, the founder members included many notables like Rai Bahadur Nathu Ram, who did all the spade work to set it up, Mr R.N. Bannerji, ICS, who went on to become Chairman of the UPSC, Mr Mehr Chand Mahajan, who was later the Chief Justice of India, Mr Achhru Ram, who was a very prominent lawyer, Mr S.R. Chaudhuri, IP, Delhi's first Inspector General of Police, etc.

Apart from Model Town, we also took time out to visit Aitchison College, earlier known as Punjab Chief's College, where my elder brother had his early schooling. The school, inter alia, catered to the children of India's princely rulers and those of the elite. Thus, its ambience, inclusive of its grounds and facilities, was far superior to that of some of our premier schools such as the Doon School.

Another must-see was the Government Officers Residential area, where my father had stayed in houses at Club Road and Aikman Road. These homes were very similar to those for senior civil servants in Lutyens' Delhi. Here again, while I had only very faint memories, my sister instantly related to them and recalled the very happy times that she had experienced there.

◆

Visiting Multan was naturally on my must-do list, as my parents hailed from this area. While my mother belonged to Multan city proper, my father came from a land-owning family from Sikandrabad, a village 26 kimometres south of Multan city. My grandfather had a huge house in the village resembling a fort. My sister instantly recognized it because of its size and intricately carved wooden entrance doors. The size of the house can be gauged from the fact that it was occupied not by one but by several families. Ironically, most were refugees from Gurgaon! Here again, I felt no attachment to the property, but my sister obviously did and instantly related to some of the rooms, as she had lived in this house. However, I must confess that something tugged at me when I saw my father's name on the merit list of the village school.

Whilst in Multan, I met some of the local notables and, inter alia, took the opportunity to address the local Chamber of Commerce. I had intended to make my address in English but switched to Saraiki on popular request. In so doing, I struck an instant rapport with those present, much to the discomfort of my ISI minders, who had difficulty in following our exchanges. The affection showered on me by the locals was touching, as they went out of their way to please us. My sister's requests for esoteric and rather special Multani delicacies were readily complied with, and we were plied with delicious food. In a way, this was not surprising, as I don't think Multan had ever hosted a Saraiki-speaking foreign envoy!

◆

If while posted to Karachi one had a recreational cottage on the beach at Hawke's Bay, while posted to Islamabad, there was one at Murree in the mountains, barely 30 kilometres away. Visits to both these places, however, required prior clearance from the Foreign Office. Located at an altitude of 7,000 feet, Murree was a quaint little town, but its chief attraction was that it gave us the opportunity to escape the heat in Islamabad. Much wilder, more attractive and far less frequented was, however, Nathiagalli, at an altitude of around 9,000 feet and about another 30 kilometres beyond Murree. I was invited there by Minoo

Bhandara for lunch at his cottage. The most memorable part of the trip was walking the last 4 kilometres to Nathiagalli on a small cart road along the thickly forested mountainside. The solitude, the cool, clean, crisp air, the heavily wooded mountainsides, and the sound of the breeze as it rustled through the trees were sheer bliss. Bhandara gave me to understand that Nehru had travelled on this very cart road in the 1930s on a tonga!

Another pleasant getaway near Islamabad was Taxila, a mere 35 kilometres away. Purportedly founded by Bharata and a centre of learning in ancient India, it is a UNESCO heritage site. It has considerable archaeological remains and a small but quaint museum with many specimens of Gandhara art. On my first visit to Taxila, Professor Ahmad Hasan Dani, a leading archaeologist and historian, gave me a conducted tour of the museum. He was given to projecting the view that Pakistanis were closer to the people of Central Asia than to the rest of India. This idea found fuller vent in Aitzaz Ahsan's *Indus Saga and the Making of Pakistan*, in which he floated the idea that the people of Pakistan were quite distinct from the people of India and that their civilization was shaped by the Indus and the geographical construct in which they are located. This line of thinking reveals the extent to which Pakistanis suffer from a lack of sense of identity and their desperation to define themselves as somehow different from Indians.

◆

One of the most important issues that occupied me in Islamabad was the effort to get an India–Pakistan dialogue process underway. It may be recalled that from the mid-1980s till early 1994, India–Pakistan Foreign Secretary-level talks were a fairly routine affair and took place annually or every other year. The sixth round of these talks, notably between Mr Shahryar Khan and Mr Dixit, took place in August 1992. The next round of these talks between them was in early January 1994 and was largely devoted to Kashmir. Thereafter, there was a long hiatus in the Foreign Secretary-level talks, as Pakistan was not keen on them because it wished to project a breakdown in the dialogue process so as to strengthen its case for third-party involvement in Kashmir and an internationalization of the issue. This induced India in 1996 to try and revive talks between the two countries under the composite dialogue process. There were four or five months of behind-the-scenes talks about talks between the two sides; basically, only four people were involved, notably, Indian Foreign Secretary Salman Haider, Pakistan Foreign Secretary Najmuddin Shaikh, my Pakistani counterpart Riaz Khokhar and myself. The four of us first met at Hyderabad House over lunch away from the glare of publicity to discuss as to how we could get a dialogue underway. The Pakistanis were not particularly keen on its resumption and insisted on the following preconditions: a written agenda, a visibly higher profile for the Kashmir issue in the dialogue process and no forward movement on any issue unless there was some progress on Kashmir.

In examining the Pakistani preconditions, we felt that there was no problem in discussing Kashmir, as we were, in any case, committed to so doing under the Shimla Agreement. Pakistan's insistence on a written agenda for the dialogue process was not to our liking, as it did away with the flexibility of past practice when agendas were drawn up separately for each Foreign Secretary-level meeting as per requirements after informal consultations. We were, however, prepared to live with a predetermined written agenda as demanded by Pakistan in order to get the dialogue going. Provision of a higher profile to Kashmir was a bigger problem, but we felt that this could be addressed tactically. The sticking point was Pakistan's demand of linking forward movement on any issue to that on Kashmir. We were, naturally, averse to this and could not agree to it directly. During the June 1997 Foreign Secretary-level talks in Islamabad, the basic framework for the composite dialogue to be handled by the Foreign Secretaries was hammered out, in which an agenda comprising the following eight items was agreed upon:

1. Peace and Security, including Confidence-Building Measures (CBMs)
2. Jammu and Kashmir;
3. Siachen;
4. Wullar Barrage Project/Tulbul Navigation Project;
5. Sir Creek;

6. Terrorism and Drug Trafficking;
7. Economic and commercial cooperation; and
8. Promotion of friendly exchanges in various fields.

Towards this end, it was agreed that a 'mechanism' would be set up, including working groups, to address these issues in 'an integrated manner'. While the first two issues would be dealt with directly by the Foreign Secretaries, they would also coordinate and monitor the work of all the working groups.

Over time, there was some fine-tuning on the mechanics of the dialogue. Ab initio, we had held out that the first two issues, notably Peace and Security, and Kashmir, which were to be dealt with by the Foreign Secretaries, would be handled together in one session, but on Pakistan's insistence, we agreed under the National Democratic Alliance (NDA) government that they would be handled in separate sessions, even though this gave a higher profiling to Kashmir. The thorny issue of linking progress on any issue to that on Kashmir was finessed by providing that the dialogue process would be monitored and coordinated by Foreign Secretaries. This essentially meant that should Pakistan not want progress on any item, they could block it at the Foreign Secretary level.

The question that arose from our point of view was what should be the burden of our talk on Kashmir with Pakistan. Here, we were guided by the February 1994 Parliament resolution on Kashmir. Accordingly, the Indian brief for the dialogue with Pakistan in regard to Kashmir was that it should be focussed on Pakistan's vacation of aggression from the areas of Kashmir held by it and on an end to its export of terrorism. It was not to be a dialogue on the disposition of the part of J&K in India's possession as has been misconstrued to be the case by some. This approach was finalized during Mr I.K. Gujral's premiership. He was extremely sagacious, particularly on Pakistan. While many referred to him as a peacenik on Pakistan, I disagree. He was very clear-headed on Pakistan and understood, more than most Indians, of the extent of its animosity towards India. Hence, the very first point in the Gujral doctrine calling for India to accommodate its neighbours like Bangladesh, Bhutan, the Maldives, Nepal and Sri Lanka, to the extent possible without insistence on reciprocity, does not include Pakistan.[12] On a couple of occasions, he asked me whether he should visit Pakistan. I responded in the negative, and he concurred. It is to his credit that, though he had no blinkers on Pakistan, he was able to sustain a very warm and cordial relationship with his fellow Punjabi and Pakistani counterpart, Prime Minister Nawaz Sharif.

In view of the limited support enjoyed by the Gujral government in the Lok Sabha, he ensured that any major move on his part on Pakistan must have the support of the Bharatiya Janata Party (BJP) and the Congress. Accordingly, Mr Brajesh Mishra was kept in the loop about our talks about talks. I was also deputed to sell the idea of the composite dialogue process, which we were quietly exploring with Pakistan, to Mr Vajpayee and to Mr Mishra. They were not averse, in principle, to dialogue with Pakistan but were initially reticent about the inclusion of Kashmir in the agenda for dialogue. This, however, rapidly melted away once I explained to them that under the Shimla Agreement, we were committed to talk to Pakistan on Kashmir and, in any case, our dialogue on it would be squarely in terms of our Parliament Resolution. I also explained to them that I had no great expectations of any radical improvement in India–Pakistan ties as a result of the dialogue process but that it would certainly ease international pressure being faced by us as a result of the complete absence of any bilateral talks. Their reservations were not so much on the dialogue process per se but more on the profiling of Kashmir, and accordingly, they argued that Peace and Security, and Kashmir, be handled together in one session, preferably at the end of the dialogue process, after the remaining six issues had been dealt with. This held back progress on the agreement on the dialogue process for some time, but, ironically, once the NDA government assumed power, it accepted an even higher level of profiling of Kashmir than that contemplated by the Gujral Government. As a result of this more relaxed approach, we agreed that the issues of Peace and Security, and Kashmir, be handled by the Foreign Secretaries in distinct sessions rather than together and

[12]Text of 'Aspects of India's Foreign Policy,' a speech by I.K. Gujral at the Bandaranaike Center for International Studies in Colombo, Sri Lanka on January 20, 1997.

that these issues would be addressed at the beginning of each round of the dialogue process rather than at the very end.

◆

In our interaction with the Congress, Foreign Secretary Salman Haider, Joint Secretary Vivek Katju and I called on Mr Narasimha Rao and Mr Pranab Mukherjee separately. The former was not enthusiastic about the talks, but that is not to say that he was against them; he, however, predicted—which echoed my sentiments as well—that they would not yield anything. Mr Narasimha Rao, perhaps one of our most cerebral Prime Ministers, understood Pakistan perfectly. He argued that there could be no understanding with the Pakistani leaders until they came to terms with the realities of the situation in the subcontinent, notably that India was the bigger power and Pakistan the smaller power. Once they did, all problems would be resolved, and until then, none would be satisfactorily addressed. Notwithstanding this, if the government still wished to talk to Pakistan, the Congress would not oppose it. Mr Mukherjee was, however, far more enthusiastic about the initiative to explore the possibility of a resumption of dialogue with Pakistan.

Thus, it was through a process of pre-consultations that Mr Gujral got both the BJP and the Congress to agree to the composite dialogue process. This also explains the longevity of the composite dialogue process, which lasted till the assumption of power by the Modi Government. With the benefit of hindsight, it is clear that the composite dialogue process achieved little apart from a temporary improvement of the international ratings of the two countries and some enhancement in people-to-people ties. There was no reduction in the trust deficit between the two countries nor a resolution of any of the big-ticket items between them.

◆

If the efforts to get a dialogue process underway met with success, albeit with no lasting benefits to India–Pakistan relations, the endeavours to persuade Indian Airlines Corporation (IAC) to undertake flights on the Delhi–Lahore sector were an abject failure.

As per a bilateral intergovernmental agreement, Pakistan International Airlines (PIA) and IAC were each permitted two flights per week on the Delhi–Lahore sector. Regrettably, instead of availing of this opportunity while continuing to maintain an office in Lahore, the IAC ceded its rights to PIA, which accordingly, flew into Delhi four times each week instead of merely twice. Such an approach is illustrative of how India has, on more than one occasion, shot itself in the foot in its dealings with Pakistan, as it enabled the latter to score over us politically, psychologically and commercially. In my interventions with the Ministry of Civil Aviation, it contended that IAC's reluctance to ply on the Delhi–Lahore sector arose from the feeling that it was commercially not viable, as a very high load factors alone would make it so. There was, however, no comeback to my riposte that I could guarantee a 75–80 per cent plus load factor for each flight by ensuring that the High Commission would only issue visas to those who could show confirmed IAC tickets. Clearly, the commercial non-viability argument was just a ploy to hide the real reason for IAC's unwillingness to fly to Lahore, which possibly was that there were other more attractive destinations. In any case, the entire episode revealed that India was unable to use a whole-of-government approach to its advantage in its dealings with neighbours like Pakistan. If the Civil Aviation Ministry was reluctant to make IAC act in a manner advantageous to India, the Ministry of External Affairs should have taken a more proactive position and prevailed upon it to do so.

◆

With the advent of the Vajpayee government in March 1998, relations between India and Pakistan experienced a precipitous dip due to the nuclear tests by both countries in May 1998. I was aware about the inevitability of our going nuclear in the event of Mr Vajpayee's assumption of power, as Mr Brajesh Mishra had alerted me to this during a dinner meeting at the Delhi Golf Club in 1995–96. However, I received advance information of our testing a couple of days before we did so quite by accident. On the Friday prior to our testing, I happened to call on Mr Mishra, in his capacity as Principal Secretary to Prime Minister, as I was in Delhi on consultations. During our meeting, he ordered me to cut short my visit and return forthwith to Islamabad. While he did not outright tell me that we would be undertaking our nuclear tests, I guessed that this was on the cards. In the event, I returned to Pakistan on the very eve of our nuclear tests.

The news of our tests provoked outrage in Pakistan, and the government came under great pressure locally to respond in kind. At the same time, it was also offered all manner of inducements by the US to desist from so doing. Had Pakistan not tested for a year or two, it would have received enormous assistance from the West, both military and economic, and its treatment would have been clearly preferential as compared to that meted out to India. However, it was my considered view that Pakistan would not act in its best interests and that local pressures from the anti-Indian lobbies, most notably the military, would impel it to resort to tit-for-tat testing. This was duly conveyed to the Ministry. The accuracy of our assessment was borne out, with Pakistan testing a fortnight or so after our tests.

On the eve of Pakistan's nuclear tests, I was woken up by a phone call from the office of the Pakistan Foreign Secretary, Shamshad Ahmad, at around 11.00 p.m., summoning me immediately for an urgent meeting. I spoke to him, asking if the matter could not wait for the next morning. On his insisting that the issue could not wait and that I must come over immediately, I responded that it would take me at least an hour to do so, as I would have to get my car from the High Commission premises and get one of my senior colleagues to accompany me. My thought process was that if the Pakistanis were going to spoil my sleep, I would do likewise! In the event, I reached Shamshad Ahmad's office accompanied by Deputy High Commissioner Sharad Sabharwal at around 1.00 a.m.

Shamshad Ahmad, contrary to normal practice when he was assisted by one colleague, on this occasion, had with him three or four other colleagues. He told me that I had been summoned at this late hour as Pakistan had credible information that India was about to attack its nuclear facilities using F16 aircraft currently based at Chennai. He went on to add that he had been directed to ask me to inform the Indian government that if such an attack was launched, it should expect 'massive retaliation with devastating consequences'.

This language was clear shorthand for nuclear retaliation. Expressing my surprise at this démarche, I pointed out that no such attack was being envisaged. Besides, India did not possess any F16s and, indeed, if any attack on Pakistan were to take place, the Chennai airfield was an unlikely launch pad. Shamshad Ahmad responded that the F16s referred to by him were Israeli aircraft. To my query about whether the nuclear facilities referred to by him were those included in the lists handed over by Pakistan to India as a part of the annual exchange of lists of nuclear facilities, Shamshad Ahmad mentioned that it was these and 'other' facilities. The meeting wound up in a matter of minutes. I had little doubt that Pakistan's accusations were something of a charade and that it had no genuine apprehensions of an Indian attack, as the atmosphere at the meeting was relatively relaxed and there was no air of tension, which would have been palpable if Pakistan was genuinely apprehensive of an imminent Indian attack.

In any case, following the meeting, I went straight to the High Commission to report on our midnight tryst in the Pakistan Foreign Office in detail along with analysis to concerned officials in our Foreign Ministry, both through a secure telephone connect and through cipher cable. In so doing, while underlining that Pakistan had held out a nuclear threat to us, I pointed out that the whole exercise was for publicity purposes and to justify their impending tests, which were on the cards anytime. I was through with reporting by around 5.00 a.m. and with a view to de-stressing instead of returning home I headed to the golf course!

◆

My Islamabad posting straddled almost equally the premierships of Benazir Bhutto and Nawaz Sharif. Though I cannot claim to have been close to either, my equation with the latter was far better than with the former. There was also a greater effort by the latter to reach out to India, which perhaps explains his warmer and more frequent interactions with me as compared to his predecessor. This was also due to the fact that at a personal level, he had a much closer relationship both with Mr Gujral and Mr Vajpayee than that enjoyed by Benazir Bhutto with Indian Prime Ministers in her second term in office. At a more trivial level, having a Punjabi Prime Minister in Pakistan resulted in a distinct uptick in the quality of cuisine served at state functions! This was all the more so as Nawaz Sharif himself was something of a gourmet.

Apart from his culinary interests, Nawaz Sharif was also a movie buff, with a particular fondness for Indian cinema and its leading actors. Indeed, he went so far as to invite Dilip Kumar and Saira Bano to Pakistan as his personal guests and to bestow upon the former Pakistan's highest civilian award, the Nishan-i-Imtiaz. Dilip Kumar and Saira Bano were treated as state guests. They were put up at Sind House and were richly wined and dined by Nawaz Sharif. Apart from the large formal functions organized in honour of Dilip Kumar, Prime Minister Sharif also organized several smaller events for him, to some of which I, too, was invited.

The Peshawar-born Dilip Kumar, originally known as Yusuf Khan, took Pakistan by storm and, apart from visiting Islamabad, also visited Peshawar and Karachi.

Beneeta and I had the privilege of hosting our biggest ever reception for him and his wife at our residence. The residence could at most comfortably accommodate about 150–175 guests, but such was the demand for invitations that there were about 250 people for the reception in his honour.

Dilip Kumar and Saira Bano were excellent ambassadors for India. They were deft at putting across the message of peace and goodwill, and skilfully avoided any faux pas on the innumerable tricky queries posed to them. I could not but be impressed with Dilip Kumar's intelligence, humility and sense of pride in India. He anticipated problems and unhesitatingly sought and went by advice given to him on how to deal with them.

Nawaz Sharif's outreach to India was fully reciprocated by Mr Vajpayee. In fact, a back channel was operating between them. This, on our side, comprised Mr R.K. Mishra and Admiral K.K. Nayyar, and on the Pakistan side involved Mr Niaz Naik, former Pakistan High Commissioner to India and Foreign Secretary. The effort on the Indian side was to play on Nawaz Sharif's business instincts and to project that India–Pakistan cooperation would help get the Pakistani economy, which was in poor shape, out of the woods. Indeed, a very senior executive of one of our leading business houses, who had just completed a tour of Pakistan, told me that his company was seriously thinking of investing huge sums in that country to set up production units. I did my best to pour cold water on his grandiose ideas, pointing out that while it was fine to trade with Pakistan, setting up local production units was best avoided, as bilateral relations were rocky, more often than not, and as Indians in the country would even at the best of times be subject to harassment. Happily, all such airy-fairy ideas did not fructify.

Nawaz Sharif himself exuded considerable positivity on the India–Pakistan bilateral relations. Indeed, in one of his meetings with me, he made a strong pitch for a total abolition of visas between the two countries. I argued at length with him that this was not a practical proposition and the most that we could aim for was a more relaxed visa regime. The Pakistan Foreign Office officials present were astonished at the line taken by their Prime Minister and delighted to note that I tried to restrain him on this issue.

Given Nawaz Sharif's approach to ties with India and the bonhomie he exuded, it was natural that he struck up an excellent personal rapport with Prime Minister Vajpayee, who, in turn, was keen on repairing bilateral ties. Indeed, I noted that Nawaz Sharif had charmed him to such an extent that, following a tête-à-tête between them during the SAARC Summit in Colombo in 1998, when we requested Mr Vajpayee to give us a blow-by-blow account of their exchanges, he riposted that there were some things said that he would not reveal!

My farewell call on Nawaz Sharif, which took place on virtually my last day in Islamabad at the end of December 1998, lasted nearly an hour. It was a very friendly meeting, in which he was at pains to repeatedly underline the high esteem in which he held Mr Vajpayee. He also made out that he was genuinely interested in improving the bilateral relationship and taking the dialogue process forward. On a personal note, he expressed unhappiness that I was being transferred and made out that he would have liked me to stay on.

My move to Delhi had been under consideration for two to three months on completion of my three-year tenure in Islamabad in August

1998. Foreign Secretary Raghunath had asked me whether I would like to stay and if not, where I would like to go. I told him that I was not interested in continuing in Pakistan and would either like to go to New York as PR or as Ambassador to Brussels. He told me that both posts were already earmarked, but there were alternatives like Australia and Switzerland. However, if these did not interest me, he would be delighted if I came to the Ministry as one of the Secretaries. On my responding in the affirmative, he told me that I should expect to move towards the end of the year. Accordingly, I was taken totally by surprise when I received a phone call from Naresh Dayal, Secretary in the Ministry of External Affairs, indicating that he had been asked by Mr Brajesh Mishra to inform me to come to Delhi immediately as the head of the about-to-be-set-up National Security Council Secretariat (NSCS).

◆

As someone who belongs to what is now Pakistan and who has invested so much of himself in working for improved India–Pakistan ties, I cannot but be saddened by the fact that despite their shared heritage and innumerable commonalities, India–Pakistan relations have been troubled since inception. After much reflection and my dealings with Pakistan over the decades, I am of the view that this is in the main due to Pakistan's visceral antipathy towards India, which regrettably animates all its actions.

Pakistan's antipathy towards India is rooted in its failure at having established a sense of identity for itself and in using anti-Indianism as a glue to hold the country together. This has, over the years, metamorphosed into Pakistan's search for parity with India. The fact that this is impossible because of India's vastly greater comprehensive national power has added to Pakistan's frustrations and animus against the former.

Pakistan has, of course, over time, sought to make up for its power differential with India by entering into opportunistic linkages with foreign players, by adopting a focussed policy of militarization and by creating an infrastructure of terror for use against India. These policies, instead of helping Pakistan, have hurt its evolution as a stable, economically prosperous and progressive nation. Opportunistic alliances have undermined its independence of action, militarization has come at the cost of democracy and development, and the use of terror has had a horrific blowback impact, making the country a hotbed of fundamentalism and extremist violence.

As detailed by me in a monograph:

> The situation has been exacerbated by the fact that for much of its history Pakistan has been has been [sic] governed by a military junta—either directly or by remote. Genuine democracy has been unable to strike root in such an hostile environment. In order to keep themselves in power and democracy at bay, successive military regimes in Pakistan have also had a vested interest in vigorously promoting the idea of an Indian bogey. It is no surprise, therefore, that an adversarial mindset vis a vis India is inbuilt into the Pakistani establishment and has become a part of the national psyche.[13]

It has been further underlined in the monograph that the Kashmir issue is merely an excuse for the troubled relationship. Were it to be somehow resolved, other issues would be found to keep the two countries apart.

Pakistan's inimical mindset towards India finds expression in a multiplicity of activities designed to enervate the latter and, if possible, to promote its disintegration. These, inter alia, include the export of terrorism, attempts at exacerbating communal tensions, pumping in fake currency and drugs, and establishing a nexus with criminal elements for destabilizing the country. Clearly, it is this mindset that is at the root of the rocky India–Pakistan relationship and not the differences per se between the two countries.

As stated by me while addressing Pakistan National Defence College in 1996, Pakistan's negative mindset, which has been the stumbling block to the normalization of India–Pakistan relations, is

---

[13]Chandra, Satish, 'India's Relations with Its SAARC Neighbours,' Vivekananda International Foundation, New Delhi, July 2019, https://bit.ly/3Tdg0NV. Accessed on 7 November 2022, p. 75–76.

reflected in and feeds off the cultivation and propagation of a number of ridiculous myths about India. The most notable of these are that India has never reconciled itself to the creation of Pakistan; that it has hegemonic designs on Pakistan; that it is averse to good neighbourly ties with Pakistan; and that India is a Hindu state and, therefore, inimically disposed to Pakistan.

The contention that India has never been reconciled to Pakistan's creation is totally ill-founded. In this context, we need only recall that Prime Minister Nehru, while speaking at the convocation ceremony at Aligarh Muslim University as early as 24 January 1948, categorically asserted:

> We have been charged with desiring to strangle and crush Pakistan, and to force it into a reunion with India. That charge, as many others, is based on fear and a complete misunderstanding of our attitude.... Compulsion there can never be and an attempt to disrupt Pakistan will recoil to India's disadvantage.... There is no going back in history. As a matter of fact, it is to India's advantage that Pakistan should be a secure and prosperous state with which we can develop close and friendly relations. If today, by any chance, I was offered a reunion of India and Pakistan, I would decline it for obvious reasons. I do not want to carry the burden of Pakistan's great problems. I have enough of my own.[14]

More recently, Indian leaders like Mr Vajpayee and Dr Manmohan Singh echoed Mr Nehru's view whilst asserting that they would like to see a stable and prosperous Pakistan.[15]

Similarly, there is also no basis to the suggestion that India has hegemonic designs on Pakistan. This is evident from the fact that though much stronger, it has never usurped Pakistani territory but, on the contrary, even returned to Pakistan the very substantial territorial gains made by it during the 1971 conflict. Indeed, as pointed out by

[14]Gopal, S. (ed.), *Selected Works of Jawaharlal Nehru*, Jawaharlal Nehru Memorial Fund, New Delhi, 1987, pp. 24–26.

[15]Chandra, Satish, 'Indian Foreign Policy vis-à-vis Pakistan: Dialogue and Prospects', *CLAWS Journal*, New Delhi, Summer 2011.

Air Marshal Asghar Khan in the late 1980s, all the India–Pakistan wars were started by Pakistan. India did not initiate them.[16] In fact, while India has been a status quo state, Pakistan has stopped at nothing to change the status quo against India.

The projection of India as a Hindu state is obviously incorrect, and the subsequent deduction that it is, therefore, ill-disposed to Pakistan is prima facie unwarranted. Even if India were a Hindu state, to regard it as inimical purely on grounds of religion would be a gross misreading of Hinduism, since it is not an aggressive proselytizing faith and not only tolerates all religions but celebrates them.

Finally, the assertion that India is averse to good neighbourly ties with Pakistan flies in the face of facts. On the contrary, India has throughout tried to improve ties with Pakistan and made enormous concessions and gestures over the decades. Some of these may be listed as follows:

1. Payment of ₹75 crore to Pakistan on account of division of assets of undivided India even while troops of the two countries were battling it out in Kashmir. While making the aforesaid payment, India did not seriously pursue its claims vis-à-vis Pakistan for non-payment of the latter's partition debt of ₹300 crore.[17]
2. Despite being an upper riparian and holding all the cards in the matter, India concluded an overly generous Indus Waters Treaty with Pakistan in 1960, whereunder it settled for a mere 20 per cent of the flows of the Indus basin rivers even though it had 40 per cent of the catchment area. Furthermore, India paid Pakistan over £62 million for building irrigation canals, etc., as per Article V of the Indus Waters Treaty.
3. Similar misplaced generosity quite unparalleled in international affairs was shown by India in 1972 by concluding the Shimla Agreement with Pakistan for across-the-board normalization of relations, whereunder India returned the 5,386 square miles

---

[16]Ibid.

[17]'Economic Survey 2021–22', Statistical Appendix, Table 2.5 titled 'Outstanding Liabilities of the Central Government', p. 61, https://bit.ly/3E7lxRz. Accessed on 7 November 2022.

of Pakistani territory captured by it in Sind (5,000 square miles) and Punjab (386 square miles) without exacting a quid pro quo.[18] Unlike the Allies who, after World War First, imposed very onerous terms on Germany under the Versailles Settlement, including massive reparations, India, though the victor in the 1971 conflict, not only returned most of the territories captured by it but also failed to clinch a final settlement of the Kashmir issue even on an eminently reasonable as is where is basis. This would have required the conversion of the Line of Control (LoC) into a de jure border between India and Pakistan, which it did not insist upon and preferred to trust Bhutto's reported assurances that this would be done later.

4. It is often forgotten that around 93,000 Pakistani PoWs taken captive in December 1971 owe their lives to India. Had India left them in Bangladesh, it is probable that many would have been lynched by the Bangladeshis on account of the genocide perpetrated by them against the local population. It is also significant that India went on to obtain 'the concurrence of Bangladesh'[19] for the return of the Pakistani PoWs held in India under the India–Bangladesh Joint Command without asking for or getting anything in return from Pakistan. India, furthermore, brought to bear its considerable influence with Bangladesh to give up on the idea of trying 195 of these PoWs for war crimes.
5. India facilitated Pakistan's entry into NAM in 1979 and its re-induction into the Commonwealth in 1989.
6. India unilaterally accorded Most Favoured Nation treatment to Pakistan in 1996, which has not been reciprocated to date. This concession was withdrawn in 2019 following the Pulwama terrorist attack engineered by Pakistan.
7. In 2011, under the Manmohan Singh government, India withdrew its objections to the application of zero duty by the European Union on Pakistan's textile exports, thereby facilitating these at

[18]Dhar, P.N., *Indira Gandhi, the 'Emergency,' and Indian Democracy*, Oxford University Press, New Delhi, 2000, p. 184.

[19]Raza, Rafi (ed.), *Pakistan in Perspective 1947–1997,* Oxford University Press, Karachi, p. 112.

> the cost of its own textile exports. It is estimated that the annual benefit to Pakistan from this move was of the order of $1 billion, much of it at the cost of the Indian textile industry.[20]

Clearly, the jettisoning of such myths that demonize India is essential for changing Pakistan's inimical mindset in regard to the former. This, together with Pakistan's giving up on its export of terror to India, are a prerequisite to any genuine improvement in ties between the two. Despite Pakistan's unrelenting hostility, India has more often than not sought normalization of relations through dialogue. Even today, India is ready to do so, provided Pakistan stops its involvement in terrorist activities directed against it.

Until this happens, dialogue with Pakistan would be futile. India would, therefore, be ill advised to respond positively to the Pakistan Prime Minister's recent call for a dialogue which, as a Times of India editorial of 17 January 2023 titled 'What Talks, Mr Sharif?' aptly termed it, is 'half desperation and half humbug'.[21] Desperation, because Pakistan's polity, economy and situation on its western borders are in dire straits, and humbug because, as in the past, it only wishes to talk about Kashmir and shows no inclination of ending its inimical policies towards India, such as its involvement in terrorist activities directed against the latter.

As pointed out in my monograph mentioned above, Pakistan's India policy and India's Pakistan policy have been remarkably consistent. While the former has been characterized by unmitigated hostility and an unwavering effort to undermine India by all possible means, the latter has generally fluctuated between engagement or neglect and shown little inclination, barring in 1971, and as evidenced in the surgical and Balakot strikes, to impose costs on Pakistan. It is also an unfortunate fact that engagement has led more often than not to India making concessions, with Pakistan firmly sticking to its maximalist position.

---

[20] Chandra, Satish, 'PM Bails Out Pakistan', *The Pioneer*, 24 August 2011.

[21] 'What talks? Mr Sharif: Pak economy is a basket case, its people are suffering. Its PM should stop obsessing over Kashmir', *The Times of India*, 17 January 2023, https://bit.ly/3WBoeRv. Accessed on 24 January 2023.

India's pusillanimity has emboldened Pakistan. Its default policy of engagement with Pakistan, spiced on occasion with outright appeasement, has not mitigated the latter's hostility to India. Accordingly, a more proactive and sustained approach designed to impose costs on Pakistan for its use of terrorism as an instrument of foreign policy against us would be more appropriate in deterring it from so doing.

This is all the more so, as nothing good can emerge from a nation created by the UK out of its angst against India, nurtured and promoted by the US at least partially to balance India, and cultivated with massive military, economic and diplomatic assistance by China in pursuance of its anti-India agenda.

Unfortunately, many Indians, including those within my own fraternity, feel that we should continue to 'manage' relations with Pakistan as we have been doing for decades and desist from policies designed to impose costs on it. The arguments trotted out in support of such an approach are specious and may be listed out as follows:

- Harsher policies towards Pakistan could trigger a nuclear war.
- Since Pakistan is a neighbour, we have no option but to mend fences with it.
- Dialogue with Pakistan will strengthen democratic elements within it and redound to our benefit, particularly as civilian elements are now beginning to question the Army's role and realizing that a modus vivendi with India is in Pakistan's interest.
- A break-up of Pakistan is not India's interest, as it could lead to a massive refugee influx, and a rump Pakistan comprising a nuclear-armed Punjab would be difficult to manage.

The contention that policies designed to impose costs on Pakistan would lead to a nuclear conflict is unfounded, as India, too, is a nuclear-armed state and its possession of nuclear weapons is an effective deterrent to a nuclear attack. Moreover, our policies to deter Pakistan from its use of terror against us must naturally be carefully calibrated and not entail the use of excessive force so that it is not induced to contemplate the use of nuclear weapons against us.

The argument that we have no option but to accommodate Pakistan just because it is a neighbour is untenable, as it fails to recognize that the latter, regarding India as an existential enemy, wants it destroyed and is not interested in any modus vivendi. In these circumstances, an outreach to Pakistan is doomed to fail and serves no purpose other than encouraging its revanchist agenda.

The suggestion that dialogue will redound to India's benefit falls flat, as it is based on two fundamental misconceptions, notably that genuine democracy is round the corner in Pakistan and that its civil society is better disposed towards India than the Army. The reality, however, is that it is the Army that in effect rules Pakistan and the democratic trappings are merely a façade. Whether or not genuine democracy will ever be established in Pakistan is a question mark. Furthermore, it is fallacy to suggest that civil society in Pakistan is very different from the Army in so far as sentiments towards India are concerned, as decades of conditioning have resulted in its populace largely mirroring the Army's mindset in this regard. In this context, it is relevant to recall that Kargil as well as the Mumbai attacks of 1993 and 2008 took place under the watch of Pakistani civilian governments. The suggestion that Pakistani civil society is becoming more discerning and has a genuine interest in a modus vivendi with India is not new. Even when I was in the NSCS from 1999 to 2005, I had heard of this from within the system. We have a propensity to allow ourselves to be duped, and we should only accept this idea as a reality if there is tangible proof of it by way of Pakistan's abandoning its export of terror to India.

Finally, it is specious to suggest that Pakistan's break-up is not in India's interests on the grounds that it could trigger a huge refugee influx into India and that it would be difficult to manage its nuclearized rump. A large Pakistani refugee migration to India is highly unlikely since most Pakistanis see India as an enemy and are aware that crossing the border is a very risky proposition, as it is militarized. As to managing a rump-nuclearized Pakistan, this would be far easier than managing a Pakistan as it exists today because the power differential between what remains of Pakistan will have shifted decisively in India's favour. In fact, it could more appropriately be argued that Pakistan's implosion would be a great boon for India, as it would weaken an implacable foe that has since its inception sought to hurt India in every possible way.

The nature of Pakistan, in particular its mindset based on an inveterate hostility towards India, coupled with the abject failure of the latter's conciliatory policy towards it, convinces me that such a policy must now make way for a more muscular approach. I am impelled to this viewpoint, since as long as Pakistan exists as we know it today, it will spare no effort to undermine India. In these circumstances, India must adopt a punitive policy towards Pakistan designed to deter it from its use of terror against India and to promote its disintegration.

Some of the elements of such a policy were spelt out in my monograph and are detailed below with appropriate elaborations:

1. A vigorous diplomatic campaign to project Pakistan as a terrorist state accompanied by a call for imposition of international sanctions against it, including suspension of military and economic assistance. Such campaigns have been carried out in the past but have not produced the desired results, as they have not been pursued in a sustained manner and been stymied by our adoption, from time to time, of peace initiatives. Our campaign projecting Pakistan as a terrorist state can only succeed if it is pursued vigorously and in a sustained fashion till such time as its export of terror to India is definitively stopped. The credibility of our case on this account would be immeasurably strengthened if we develop a quantified tabulation of the damages suffered by us due to Pakistan's relentless use of terror against us and a demand be registered for its compensating us on this account. In order to carry conviction with the international community, our campaign against Pakistan should be accompanied by an act of Parliament declaring it as a terrorist state, downgrading our representation therein to Chargé d'Affaires level, abandoning any high-level exchanges with it, and eschewing any CBMs with it. Pakistani institutions like the ISI should be branded as terrorist outfits, and its members and their relatives should be banned from getting Indian visas. The holding of multilateral

military exercises or discussions on sensitive security-related issues with Pakistan, albeit within the ambit of entities like the SCO, should be scrupulously avoided in order to buttress the point that we regard Pakistan as a pariah.

2. India should exercise full rights over the Indus waters as permitted under the Indus Waters Treaty. We have, so far, not done so and have not only not built all the storages permitted to us on the Western Rivers but have also allowed some of the waters of the Eastern Rivers to flow into Pakistan. This must be stopped forthwith by minimizing the release of the Indus waters to Pakistan and by maximizing their use in India as permitted under the Indus Waters Treaty. Some moves in this direction have been initiated by the Modi government. But progress has been slow. It needs to be greatly accelerated. Additionally, a notice should be served to Pakistan for a renegotiation of the Treaty, whereby India gets a fairer share of the Indus waters. While India has given a notice to Pakistan in end January 2023 for the modification of the Indus Waters Treaty, it is insufficient as it does not appear to be directed at securing a fairer allocation of the Indus waters but only at the functioning of the Treaty, including, inter alia, rectifying its material breach by Pakistan's contravention of the graded dispute mechanism provided therein. India should, simultaneously, explore the possibility of walking away from the Treaty, as international law does envisage such a possibility in case of a fundamental change of circumstances. Pakistan's use of terrorism against us in default mode, leading to a virtual state of war between the two countries, is arguably such a fundamental change of circumstances that could justify India's walking out of the Indus Waters Treaty. In order to strengthen our position in the matter, we must, as mentioned earlier, quantify the damage suffered by India over the decades as a result of Pakistan's use of terror against it. Such data would lend credence to our argument of the fundamental change of circumstances impelling us to abandon the Indus Waters Treaty, which had been concluded to promote peace and

goodwill between India and Pakistan. Pending our walking out of the Indus Waters Treaty, we should, as suggested by Professor Brahma Chellaney, condition further consultations and information-related exchanges pertaining to the Indus Waters with Pakistan on its abandoning its linkages with terrorist outfits created by it for targeting India.[22]

3. Since Pakistan has consistently exploited India's fault lines, our hesitation in so doing vis-à-vis it needs to be abandoned and an appropriate strategy in this regard based upon deniability needs to be seriously considered. At the very least, we should not shy away from widely publicizing, including at all international fora, its human rights violations in Balochistan, Khyber Pakhtunkhwa, Sindh and PoK, as well as against the minorities. We should also provide asylum to such disaffected elements from Pakistan within the ambit of a broader asylum policy to be framed by us.
4. Covert action, and if need be focussed strikes, should be undertaken on the lines of the Balakot strikes to take out terrorist elements and their supporters in Pakistan. Contingency plans for such actions should always be readily available and duly updated so that, following any Pakistan-sponsored terrorist action against us, as in Mumbai or more recently in Gurdaspur, Udhampur, Pathankot and Pulwama, these can be activated within a matter of hours rather than days.
5. The already-crumbling Pakistan economy, rather than being the object of Indian assistance as in the past, should, henceforth, be targeted for damage with actions such as undercutting its rice and textile exports, withdrawing from the TAPI pipeline and ensuring that the European Union desists from continuing to allow duty-free ingress of Pakistani textile exports.
6. India needs to cultivate good working relationships with both Afghanistan and Iran in order to enhance Pakistan's

[22]Chellaney, Brahma, 'India Can Leverage Water Treaty to Pressure Pak on Terrorism', *The Times of India*, 27 February 2022, https://bit.ly/3WHfTNA. Accessed on 7 November 2022.

> uncertainty on its western borders. This is eminently doable notwithstanding the nature of the regimes in place in those two countries, as we have traditionally had good ties with them. While the Taliban factor is, no doubt, a serious issue with us, if we play our cards right and if Pakistan, as is its wont, remains hegemonistic, a modus vivendi with Afghanistan is a distinct possibility, as its national interests will impel it to mend fences with India. This is all the more so as, apart from the considerable economic assistance that could flow to Afghanistan from India, we have an additional major leverage as we can, at any time, announce that we do not recognize the Durand Line. No nationalistic Afghan and much less a Pashtun can avoid being enormously swayed in India's favour should we adopt such a stance, as Afghanistan does not recognize it and, indeed, even the earlier Taliban government despite enormous Pakistani pressure refused to do so. Similarly, while we have, over the years, enjoyed a fruitful relationship with Iran, the latter's ties with Pakistan have had their share of tension whether over Sunni–Shia issues or over Afghanistan. Unfortunately, India–Iran ties have, in recent times, been a casualty of US pressures, which need to be resisted to ensure that the relationship achieves its full potential.

To be successful, the aforesaid approach must be pursued in a sustained manner on a long-term basis. This will not be easy because our tendency to be overly indulgent and sentimental vis-à-vis neighbours comes in the way of the adoption of a muscular approach and as we are often distracted in the pursuit of our objectives.

The existing geopolitical situation affords some favourable and some unfavourable factors for the proposed get-tough policy designed to deal with Pakistan. Amongst the former are India's vastly greater comprehensive national power and the fact that Pakistan today is, perhaps, more divided at home than ever before with its innumerable fault lines—regional, political, religious, ethnic, political, etc.—clearly exposed and its economy in a shambles. Amongst the latter is the fact that the gap in military capabilities between Pakistan and India has narrowed considerably over the decades and that Pakistan today is not friendless. Though it is known to be in the business of exporting terror, it has a few all-weather friends like China, Turkey and Malaysia, and has been able to woo many in the OIC as well as important players like Russia. The US and the UK, too, appear to continue to have a soft spot for Pakistan. In these circumstances, our moves at isolating Pakistan may not succeed fully in the near term, but the effort would, over time, serve our cause well by keeping Pakistan constantly on the radar internationally for its deplorable human rights record and for its being the fount of terror. Our successes in deterring Pakistan from the use of terror against us would come primarily through moves geared to playing on its fault lines, to punitive military actions and to hurting it economically. In this exercise, our biggest supporter is Pakistan itself, whose gaping fault lines and economic underperformance are largely self-inflicted and the result of its own short-sighted policies and misgovernance.

13

A TRYST WITH NATIONAL SECURITY: NEW DELHI

Somewhat on the lines of my journey back to India on transfer from Dhaka in June 1984, my journey on transfer from Islamabad to India in end December 1998 was undertaken by car. The only difference was that the journey from Dhaka to Delhi was partly by car and partly by air, whereas that from Islamabad to Delhi was entirely by car. The only reason I travelled by car was because air travel would have made it more difficult to bring our Pakistani dog, Pasha, with us. When I tentatively suggested to my family that we consider leaving Pasha behind, they responded that they would rather leave me behind but not their beloved dog!

My first task on arrival in Delhi was to brief the Prime Minister on my farewell meeting with Nawaz Sharif. Noting his happiness on my recounting Sharif's lavish words of praise for him, I cautioned that these be taken with a pinch of salt, as such flattery was second nature to most Pakistani leaders. Given the warm relationship between the two, my cautionary advice had no impact.

Barely a fortnight later, a senior officer in the Prime Minister's Office (PMO), casually sought my opinion, as a former High Commissioner of India to Pakistan, about the desirability of the Prime Minister's visit to that country in February. I advised against it as I felt, on the basis of my earlier involvement in such visits, that not enough planning had gone into it, that it appeared to be decided upon on the spur of the moment, and even more importantly, that there did not seem to be a complete clarity of the outcome.

◆

On Friday, 1 January 1999, I took charge as Chairman of the Joint Intelligence Committee (JIC). My immediate predecessor was holding this office for a year and a half concurrent to his assignment as Secretary (R&AW). The JIC was the apex intelligence assessment body in the country and reported to the Cabinet Secretary. As stated in an article contributed by me to India's National Security Annual Review 2005, the JIC 'lacked clout within the system and was marginalized, with its product rarely receiving the attention it deserved. It had no political support and was not nurtured to play its required role. Not surprisingly, the intelligence collection agencies tended to bypass the JIC in their keenness to be seen as the first to provide important information at the highest level, which resulted not only in an information overload but also in the submission of unprocessed and unassessed intelligence at decision-making levels.'[23] All this was now set to change as the JIC, while continuing to exist, would be subsumed within the NSCS, which would be the engine room of the National Security Council (NSC) system.

The aforesaid nature of change, which I was tasked to oversee, was explained to me by Mr Brajesh Mishra, Principal Secretary to the Prime Minister, who as the National Security Advisor (NSA) Designate was to be my boss. He told me that my immediate task was to formalize the setting up of the NSC system comprising the NSC, the Strategic Policy Group (SPG), the National Security Advisory Group (NSAB), the NSA, and the NSCS. The latter would be headed by me and would be required to service all the institutions within the NSC system. While promising the fullest support, Mr Mishra frankly admitted that the NSC system was an experiment, and for it to take root, successor governments would have to carry the matter forward.

As a token of his assurance of full support, Mr Mishra readily acceded to my request for two officers of my choice from the Ministry of External Affairs. I accordingly made a pitch for two colleagues who had worked with me earlier, notably Dr Arvind Gupta and Mr Dinkar Srivastava. In the event, Mr Mishra, a few weeks later, told me that

---

[23]*India's National Security Annual Review 2005*, Satish Kumar, Vikas Publishing House, Kalpana Shukla, Knowledge World, New Delhi, 2005, pp. 204–205.

he had been able to prevail upon the Ministry for the release of only one officer for deputation to the NSCS, notably, Dr Arvind Gupta. The latter, accordingly, joined the NSCS as Joint Secretary and proved to be an invaluable acquisition.

While my new assignment was daunting and a journey into the unknown, particularly as my knowledge of our security system was patchy, not for a moment did one feel lost, as I enjoyed excellent support from my superiors, colleagues and those working with me in the NSCS. Above all, the assignment was an unparalleled learning opportunity, as it gave me a vantage view of India's security structures, which few are privileged to enjoy. This, together with the fact that I could make meaningful contributions in fashioning and reforming our security system in diverse areas, made this assignment one of my more satisfying ones. Though not a security specialist in the narrow sense of the term, my Foreign Service experience derived from my dealings with Pakistan, Bangladesh, and Disarmament and UN-related issues, provided me with insights that greatly facilitated my work at the NSCS.

◆

It goes without saying that the first few weeks in my new assignment aroused mixed feelings, whether at home or in the office. On both counts, I had little choice and was willy-nilly required to move into pre-determined lodgings. My residence, which I motored into from Pakistan, was located at 52 Lodi Estate, and the office on the third floor of Sardar Patel Bhavan on Parliament Street—the operating headquarters of the JIC. Both were rather run-down premises and a far cry from the neat and clean environment that I had grown accustomed to in Geneva and, indeed, even in Islamabad.

My residence at 52 Lodi Estate was a three-bedroom corner house with a huge garden and several servant quarters. Typical of most government houses in Lutyens' Delhi, built in the 1930s, it was rather decrepit for want of regular upgrading and even repair. This was, of course, compensated by its excellent location in the heart of Delhi, right next to the India International Centre, Khan Market, the Delhi Golf Club and the Lodi Gardens. Houses in Lodi Estate were occupied by senior civil servants and military officials as well as by a handful of MPs and persona like Priyanka Gandhi, whose servant quarters were right opposite my residence. As I moved into 52 Lodi Estate, I could not but recall that during the British Raj, houses in this area had been occupied by section officers, while more senior officials like Joint Secretaries and Secretaries were lodged in far grander premises located, for instance, on Akbar Road, Hastings Road and Aurangzeb Road. Over time, as the political class proliferated and became more dominant, and the bureaucracy more devalued, the latter had to make way for the former and was compelled to occupy the meaner premises at Lodi Estate or the newly built apartments on much smaller plots at Moti Bagh, Pandara Road, etc.

The unkempt appearance of the residence was matched by that of the JIC office at Sardar Patel Bhavan. This was epitomized by grimy windows and stinking loos symptomatic of an officialdom so accustomed to working in a dirty environment that it is oblivious to it. Shortly after assuming charge, I insisted on the regular cleaning of the office premises as well as on punctuality. In a matter of a few months, this began to produce results and a more business-like approach was readily discernable within the Organization. The premises, too, were spruced up and ultimately refurbished. In time, the NSCS became one of the neater sarkari premises in the national capital that could boast of clean toilets.

◆

While learning the ropes at my new assignment and grappling with giving shape to the NSC system, I was simultaneously snowed under with the work connected with the Kargil conflict in May 1999 and, soon thereafter, by that pertaining to the Kargil Review Committee (KRC) and the Group of Ministers (GoM) established to go into reform of the national security system in its entirety. The KRC was set up on 29 July 1999 and submitted its report in December 1999. The GoM was set up on 17 April 2000 and submitted its report in February 2001. My workload in respect of both the KRC and the GoM was heavy, as the NSCS served as the Secretariat for them. I welcomed this, as it not only provided me with an opportunity to speedily come to grips with a wide variety of security-related issues but also to make contributions to the security reform process initiated by these two entities. Following the acceptance of the GoM's recommendations on security reform by the Cabinet Committee on Security (CCS) in May 2001, the NSCS was entrusted with monitoring their implementation. This was not easy, not only because the number of recommendations, in the region of about 340, was large but also because some of the institutions which were to implement them were half-hearted in their response and tried to stall matters.

Kargil Conflict and Kargil Review Committee

My appreciation of the Kargil Conflict was informed by the Intelligence inputs that came my way in my capacity as Chairman, JIC, my interactions with those dealing with it at the highest level through my participation in CCS meetings, and the data collected by the KRC, of which I was Member Secretary.

The mandate of the KRC was to review the events leading up to the Conflict and to make recommendations to safeguard national security against such armed intrusions. The actual handling of the conflict post 26 May 1999 was excluded from its remit.

My appointment as Member Secretary of the KRC was driven by the fact that I was Secretary, NSCS, and as such not only had security-related responsibilities but also had the requisite staff and resources to effectively service its requirements. Had the KRC been left to fend for itself for office and staff resources, it would not have been able to complete its work as expeditiously and efficiently as it did with NSCS support. In fact, this model of utilizing the NSCS for security-related work became a trendsetter. The NSCS was, thus, also utilized as the Secretariat for the GoM set up for reviewing the national security system in its entirety and, over the years, took the lead in many cross-cutting security-related issues on which there was diffidence of one or another institution to take the lead.

The KRC functioned with exemplary openness and transparency. It not only engaged in debate within itself but also with those in the strategic community, including also NSCS officials, some of whom were helping out in its work. This was in large measure due to the personalities of its other constituents, notably its Chairman, the late Mr K. Subrahmanyam, and doyen of India's strategic fraternity; the meticulous Lieutenant General K.K. Hazari, former Vice Chief of Army Staff; and the late Mr B.G. Verghese, one of our most-respected and versatile journalists. I would be remiss in not also mentioning the role of the NSA, namely Mr Brajesh Mishra, in enormously easing the task of the KRC. As a result of his wholehearted support, the entire national establishment opened itself to freely interacting with the KRC and responding constructively to its innumerable queries. He also had the courage and vision to allow the KRC the complete freedom in developing its report without any interference or effort at influencing it. For instance, though I had alerted him in advance that the KRC had decided to recommend that the office of the NSA and the Principal Secretary to Prime Minister (both of which were occupied by him) should not be vested in one person,[24] he made no effort to effect any change in the recommendation.

◆

The KRC consciously desisted from wasting time and energy in fixing responsibility for the undetected Pakistani intrusions on individuals, choosing instead to work in a cooperative mode with all concerned to tease out the lessons that could be learnt from the Kargil experience. In the process, it had in-depth interactions with scores of political leaders, including the highest in the land, military personnel at all levels, Intelligence officials, relevant civil servants, journalists, etc. It also made a number of field visits to J&K, including the area of operations. On the basis of this arduous and extensive exercise, the KRC published its report on 15 December 2015—less than five months after having been constituted.[25]

Credit must be given to the government for having made this

---

[24]Government of India, National Security Council Secretariat, *From Surprise to Reckoning: The Kargil Review Committee Report,* Sage Publications, New Delhi, 2000, p. 253.

[25]Ibid.

report public not only because this was not the norm but also because there were some things in it that did not sit well with the government. The report was also tabled in Parliament.

The main elements of the report, apart from its recommendations, included, inter alia, the nature of the Pakistani action, its authors, its motivations, our response, our so-called Intelligence failure and speculation on whether or not the Kargil War could have been avoided.

The Kargil War was fought from May till 26 July 1999 across an Himalayan front of about 150 kilometres at heights of over 15,000 feet in what was the most inhospitable and unlikely battleground in history. The relatively rapid expulsion of the Pakistani forces from these areas, which had been occupied by them through deception and stealth in early 1999, constituted a major military success for India. The credit for this goes largely to our soldiers, both officers and men.

This victory did not come cheap. As recorded in the KRC Report, the Indian military casualty toll was 474 killed and 1,109 wounded.[26] It also noted that Pakistan suffered 'heavier casualties than those suffered by India'.[27] BBC, on its part, has stated that the estimates of Pakistani casualties range from 400 to 4,000.[28]

Stealth, secrecy and deception were the hallmarks of the Pakistani intrusions in Kargil. The exercise was undertaken with virtually no movement of additional formations from outside the sector and with no extraordinary dumping of stores and ammunition. It involved only around 2,000 men across a front of about 150 kilometres in shallow depths of 5–9 kilometres. Movement of these personnel was undertaken in deep winter, viz. from January to April 1999, when patrolling by our forces was virtually impossible and when some posts were traditionally vacated. Finally, the Pakistani forces came into India masquerading as militants to create the fiction that the

---

[26]Ibid. 23.

[27]Ibid. 250.

[28]Khan, M. Ilyas, 'Kargil: The Forgotten Victims of the World's Highest War', BBC, Islamabad, 26 July 2019, https://www.bbc.com/news/world-asia-49101016. Accessed on 10 November 2022.

action was being undertaken by freedom fighters and not by the Pakistani Army.

The Kargil intrusions were part of a plan formulated in the 1980s but never executed. The author of this exercise was General Musharraf, who had been made Chief of Army Staff by Nawaz Sharif in October 1998 over the heads of two other Generals. Even within Pakistan, knowledge of the operation was confined to a small coterie of Generals around Musharraf on a need-to-know basis. Neither the Air Force nor the Navy were kept in the loop. It is uncertain as to how much Nawaz Sharif knew, though the KRC took the stand that 'the balance of possibility suggests that he was fully in the picture'.[29] It further asserted that he was at least aware of the broad thrust of the plan when he welcomed Mr Vajpayee in Lahore in February 1999.

Clearly, the Pakistani intrusion completely surprised India. This was due to the manner in which it was planned and executed. By end April, the Pakistani forces had occupied several high points across a 150-kilometre front without detection. Furthermore, even after detection in the second week of May, we believed that what we confronted were militants and not the Pakistan Army. It was not till a few weeks later, after active engagement, that we realized that what we were up against were not militants but the Pakistan Army. It is true that there were some militants amongst the Pakistani infiltrators, but these were in the nature of support elements. It was estimated that the bulk of the intruders were regular soldiers, and the militants were no more than perhaps 30 per cent of the total force.

♦

As recorded in the Kargil Review Committee Report[30] as Chairman JIC, I came to know that something was afoot in the Kargil sector only in the second week of May 1998, when officials from some Intelligence

[29]Government of India, National Security Council Secretariat, *From Surprise to Reckoning: The Kargil Review Committee Report,* Sage Publications, New Delhi, 2000, p. 226.

[30]*From Surprise to Reckoning: The Kargil Review Committee Report,* Sage Publications, New Delhi, 2000 p. 135

agencies claimed in a meeting taken by me that they had reports about Pakistani intruders' ingress into India. This contention was vehemently opposed by some other Intelligence agencies. While these agencies were in the process of reconciling their differences and arriving at a consensus, the matter became public. In retrospect, we know that the Army had some information of the intrusions in the first of week of May itself, though it assessed the same as a militant and not a Pakistan Army intrusion.

Pakistan's Kargil adventure was motivated by several factors, notably the desire to internationalize the Kashmir issue as a nuclear flashpoint and encourage third-party intervention, to alter the LoC, and use the areas captured as a possible trade-off against Indian positions on Siachen, to interdict the Srinagar Leh road and to provide a fillip to insurgency in Kashmir.

The main assumptions on which Pakistan's move was predicated may be listed as follows:

1. Early third-party intervention would take place in Pakistan's favour, thereby enabling it to retain possession of the areas captured by it and bargain from a position of strength.
2. Its nuclear capability would deter any larger Indian riposte across the International Border (IB) or even the use of air power.
3. India would not be able to mount a swift and resolute response.

These assumptions were not validated by developments and proved to be off the mark on all counts, barring India not countering with cross-IB retaliation.

If Pakistan took India by surprise in terms of its occupation of the Kargil heights by stealth, India equally took Pakistan by surprise with its swift and effective retaliation, compelling it to vacate aggression. Indeed, if one looks back, this is not the first time that Pakistan underestimated the firmness of the Indian response. This happened in 1947, it happened in 1965 when we crossed the IB, it happened during the 2016 surgical strikes and it happened at Balakot. Miscalculations by Pakistan about the Indian reaction occur, in part, because its military is fairly contemptuous about 'Hindu' India's ability to respond firmly, and, in part, because India has usually reacted with caution and restraint even to the most heinous provocations, such as the 1993 or the 2008 Mumbai terrorist attacks.

After the initial detection of the intrusions in the second week of May, the Indian response was prompt and effective. A comprehensive set of actions was initiated to establish contact with the intruders, to fix the extent of the incursion and to contain it. Adequate troops and firepower were moved in. It was, however, only after some encounters that we realized that the bulk of the intruders were regulars. By the last week of May, it was decided to also deploy the Indian Air Force, though it was restricted from crossing the LoC and, thus, made to operate in a straitjacket. Appropriate covering moves were also undertaken by the Army along the IB, and the Western Fleet was augmented by elements from the Eastern Fleet, not only to keep Pakistan from further mischief but also placing it on notice that India was intent on ensuring that it pulled back. Pakistan's efforts at negotiating were rebuffed and the message given was that it must first vacate aggression. India's firm and unequivocal moves were well understood and respected by the international community and, in the event, secured Pakistan's total retreat from the positions occupied by it on Indian soil by 26 July 1999.

♦

Through the course of the Kargil conflict, the NSCS as well as an NSAB subgroup were tasked to separately provide inputs to government on the actions we needed to take. There was considerable anxiety that dislodging the Pakistan Army from the Kargil heights through frontal action would not only be time-consuming but also costly in terms of the casualties we would take. Accordingly, the NSCS and NSAB subgroup suggested different but more aggressive moves. Neither of these suggestions gained traction, and we engaged in a conventional slugfest with Pakistan in the Kargil sector, taking heavy casualties. However, we got them out much sooner than anticipated due to the valour of our Armed Forces and good leadership. The diplomatic factor was, no doubt, at the back of the minds of our leadership, which, perhaps rightly, felt that the diplomatic support that India enjoyed would diminish if we retaliated by crossing the IB or even the LoC or by engaging in heavy cross-LoC air attacks.

Through the Kargil conflict and its aftermath, much was made of India's so-called Intelligence failure,[31] both in terms of the long-delayed detection of the intrusion and in terms of the composition of the intruders. It is, of course, a fact that India was caught unawares, and to that extent, there was technically a failure of Intelligence. But due consideration should be given to the fact that detection of such an intrusion was extremely difficult in the absence of high-quality surveillance equipment, whether by way of requisite helicopters or by way of satellite imagery, and inability to mount effective patrols due to extreme weather conditions.

Furthermore, the intrusion was virtually impossible to foresee, as it defied logic, being a high-risk low-reward exercise which carried within it the seeds of its own defeat and which prudence militated against. It was high-risk because, having been launched in the height of winter, it was prone to heavy weather-related casualties, which, in fact, occurred as evident from the diaries of captured Pakistani soldiers.[32] Furthermore, early detection of the intruders and their consequent elimination was always a possibility, which, luckily for Pakistan, did not happen. It was low-reward because the intrusion could not possibly have been sustained for meaningful follow-up action, as it was carried out by a relatively small number of troops essentially from within the sector in order to avoid detection. Any meaningful induction of more troops including from formations from outside the sector would have entailed detection, but not doing so resulted in the intrusions having a limited shelf-life. Finally, the sustainability of such an intrusion required an enormous logistic effort, which Pakistan could not deploy in stealth. Accordingly, Lieutenant General (Retd) Ali Kuli Khan Khattak, one of Pakistan's most professional Generals, dubbed the Kargil war as the 'worst debacle' in Pakistan's history and

[31] *From Surprise to Reckoning: The Kargil Review Committee Report,* Sage Publications, New Delhi, 2000, p. 233–38.

[32] Ibid. 20, 228.

asserted that 'its conception and planning at the highest level had been poor—in fact, so poor that the only word which can adequately describe it is unprofessional. We all know that the main duty of the high command is to ensure that with their meticulous planning they create conditions whereby their junior combatants can fight easily. This was certainly not done at Kargil. It is also fairly obvious that the Kargil Operation was not conceived in its totality...'[33] and brought ignominy to Pakistan.

The KRC, however, felt that there 'was a significant gap in information' arising out of the R&AW's inability to 'accurately monitor and report changes' in Pakistan's troop levels in the region during 1998-1999 and to a 'lesser extent' of Military Intelligence 'to notice the additional forward deployment of troops in the vicinity of the LoC'. This finding was based on the KRC's assessment that there had been a 'net increase of two battalions' in the region over and above R&AW's projections as well as 'a forward deployment of two battalions within the sector'.[34]

In this context, while in the process of report writing, the Chairman of the Committee suggested that some of the Intelligence failure must also be attributed to the JIC. He argued that in 1962, the JIC had failed to connect the dots and predict the Chinese attack, and he was convinced that the same, too, had happened in 1999, and hence its failure to foresee the Pakistani attack. I, ab initio, challenged this line of thought, pointing out that before drawing any such conclusion, we must examine all the available Intelligence data and ascertain as to whether or not it had been shared with the JIC. Accordingly, it was decided to tabulate all the intelligence inputs generated that could have led to the projection of the Pakistani intrusion and determine the entities to which these had been sent. On completion of this exercise, it was found that, in all, there were a total of about 45 Kargil-related

[33]'Zehra, Nasim, *From Kargil to the Coup*, Afzaal Ahmad Sang-e-Meel Publications, Lahore, 2018, p. 356.

[34]*From Surprise to Reckoning: The Kargil Review Committee Report*, Sage Publications, New Delhi, 2000, p. 235–36.>

Intelligence inputs,[35] of which barely 25 per cent had been sent to the JIC, which, naturally, made it impossible for it to predict the Pakistani action. Accordingly, the effort to pin the responsibility of an Intelligence failure on the JIC was given up! The fact that just about 25 per cent of the Intelligence inputs generated by the agencies made their way to the JIC speaks volumes about its lack of clout and its actual standing in India's Intelligence community.

During the aforesaid debate between the Chairman and myself, the former also gave vent to the view that the Ministry of External Affairs, which has often been something of a whipping boy in the Indian bureaucracy, had been found wanting by not drawing attention to Musharraf's duplicitous nature and adventurist proclivities, as this could have alerted India to the possibility of Pakistan's intrusions. I riposted that this had, in fact, been done by me in my capacity as High Commissioner to Pakistan in a top-secret telegram following a meeting with Musharraf in December 1998, which had been shared with the JIC. In the telegram, I had characterized Musharraf as ambitious and scheming, a hardliner on India whose elevation to Chief of Army Staff may not bode well for bilateral ties, and who may well topple the civilian regime as done by Zia.[36]

On reading the above-mentioned telegram, the Chairman promptly gave up his critical line of thought about the Ministry of External Affairs and insisted on including its relevant extracts in the KRC report after appropriate declassification.

◆

The KRC pointed out that the Kargil War could have been prevented had the Indian Army plugged all loopholes across the LoC and guarded every square inch of territory, but this was, naturally, not done, as it was neither politically nor militarily cost-effective. It went on to underline that the Army must never be used as a border-guarding force

---

[35]*From Surprise to Reckoning: The Kargil Review Committee Report*, Sage Publications, New Delhi, 2000, p. 152

[36]*From Surprise to Reckoning: The Kargil Review Committee Report*, Sage Publications, New Delhi, 2000, pp. 140–141

and that it should only be used for war fighting. Using it in a border-guarding role would adversely affect its war-fighting capability.

The KRC made around two dozen recommendations of which the most important one was the need to undertake a thorough review of the national security system in its entirety by an independent body of credible experts. This recommendation was promptly accepted and a GoM chaired by the Home Minister was constituted in April 2000 to undertake the proposed review.

Following the aforesaid GoM report, some of the KRC's recommendations came to be implemented and some were not.

Some of the recommendations that were implemented include the setting up of an exclusive techint organization modelled on the US National Security Agency, which took the form of the National Technical Research Organisation (NTRO), the establishment of a Defence Intelligence Agency (DIA), acceptance of a two-stream approach—civil and military—for downloading and analysing imagery, the acquisition and development of high-quality UAVs and satellites, integration of the Armed Forces Headquarters with the Ministry of Defence, and the establishment of an institutional mechanism, which took the form of the Intelligence Coordination Group (ICG) chaired by the NSA for purposes of coordinating the work of the intelligence agencies as well as tasking them and evaluating their functioning.[37]

Notable amongst the recommendations not implemented was the call for reduction of colour service from 17 to 7–10 years and diversion of the released manpower to the paramilitary formations, enhanced defence outlays, publication of a white paper on India's nuclear weapon programme, publication of authentic accounts of the 1965 and 1971 Wars as well as of the Kargil Conflict, review of information policy to develop structures and processes to keep the public informed of vital national issues, the undertaking of credible measures in J&K to win back alienated sections of the population, and the adoption of a declaratory policy that violation of the LoC's sanctity would meet with

[37]Public Lecture by Sri Satish Chandra at the Institute of Defence Studies and Analysis, New Delhi, on the 20th Anniversary of the Kargil conflict on the topic, "Kargil War: Recollections", 6 August 2019.

retaliation in a manner, time and place of India's choosing.[38]

It is to the credit of the current national security establishment that the important recommendation regarding reduction of colour service that had been pending for decades was implemented through the Agnipath Scheme announced by the Government. This will go a long way in keeping a young, operationally and technically updated profile of the human resources manning our Armed Forces. It will also address the current imbalances in the skewed ratios of capital budget versus the revenue budget, an issue that few commentators are talking about. Additionally, the manpower turnover every four years will open up fresh employment opportunities for the youth and create a much needed reservoir of young, well-trained and disciplined personnel for absorption in diverse areas in the civilian sector.

GoM Report on Reforming the National Security System

The GoM, constituted on 17 April 2000 to review the national security system in its entirety, was chaired by the Home Minister Mr L.K. Advani, and included the Defence Minister, Mr George Fernandes, the External Affairs Minister, Mr Jaswant Singh, and the Finance Minister, Mr Yashwant Sinha.

While the remit of the KRC was limited to reviewing the events leading up to Pakistan's aggression in Kargil and making recommendations to prevent such armed intrusions, that of the GoM was much wider. It was required to review the national security system in its entirety and, in particular, to consider the recommendations of the KRC and formulate specific proposals for implementation.

Since the GoM was serviced by the NSCS, much of the burden of its work fell directly on me. It is a matter of satisfaction that the GoM was able to submit its report barely eight months after being set up in February 2001. The GoM had a total of 27 meetings. The minutes of each of these were personally recorded by me immediately and following the Home Minister's approval, were circulated within a couple of days to the other principals. This practice ensured the

---

[38]Ibid.

expeditious and efficacious completion of the GoM's work.

At the GoM's very first meeting held on 27 April 2000, I flagged the necessity of taking a more precise view on the extent of its mandate as the one accorded to it in its widest sense would, apart from traditional security issues, also include non-traditional ones like food security, energy security, economic security, water security, etc. The GoM decided to occupy itself only with national security as more traditionally conceived and exclude non-traditional security issues.

The GoM further set up four task forces, with one each to make recommendations in the areas related to Internal Security, Border Management, Higher Defence Management and Intelligence, to help it in its work. Each of these task forces had around half-a-dozen experts selected by a Chairman nominated by the GoM. The Chairmen selected by it were Mr N.N. Vohra for Internal Security, Dr M. Godbole for Border Management, Mr Arun Singh for Higher Management of Defence and Mr Girish Saxena for Intelligence. All had impeccable credentials, particularly on security related issues with Mr Vohra and Dr Godbole being former Home Secretaries, Mr Saxena being a former R&AW Chief and Mr Arun Singh being an Advisor Security in the Ministry of External Affairs and a former Minister of State for Defence. The NSCS attached one of its officers to each of these task forces. Two of the task forces were serviced by the NSCS and two by the Home Ministry.

I was asked to contact each of the individuals nominated as Chairperson for each task force to secure their concurrence. While three readily accepted, the one originally selected for Border Management, notably Mr C.G. Somiah, whom I had worked with many years earlier in his capacity as Home Secretary, refused on the grounds that having been Comptroller and Auditor General, it would be inappropriate for him to do so. My effort at trying to persuade him by suggesting that in taking up this assignment it would be he who would be doing the government a favour rather than the other way around was not successful. He was adamant, thereby demonstrating the very high ethical standards observed by him, which some of his successors have not. While I had the highest regard for Mr Somiah on the basis of my numerous interactions with him when he was Home

Secretary in the mid and late 1980s, the position taken by him on this occasion further increased my respect for him.

When I apprised Mr Advani of Mr Somiah's refusal to accept the offer of chairing the task force on Internal Security, he asked me to suggest an alternative. My suggestion of Dr Godbole's name, who had formerly been Home Secretary and with whom I had worked in the DEA in 1972, found ready acceptance. On my conveying the same to Dr Godbole, the latter expressed surprise, as he had opposed the action taken by the BJP leading to the destruction of the Babri Masjid whilst he was Home Secretary and had gone so far as to resign from the Narasimha Rao Government on its inept handling of the issue. It was only on my informing him that Mr Advani had personally approved of his appointment that he accepted the offer. It is to Mr Advani's credit that he selected Dr Godbole purely on merit and did not let what had happened in the past colour his decision. In the event, the appointment of Dr Godbole was amply vindicated, as his task force submitted a very high-quality report and that too a month earlier than the other three.

◆

Following submission of the task force reports, these were first presented to the GoM by their respective Chairmen and then examined and commented upon by the concerned administrative ministries. The comments of the ministries were thereafter processed in inter-ministerial meetings chaired by the Cabinet Secretary for the benefit of the GoM. The latter, thereafter, had a series of meetings with all concerned to fine-tune the recommendations that it intended to make. All these discussions had to be closely monitored by me in order to enable me to prepare the GoM report.

One of the most hotly debated and contentious recommendations made by the GoM was that pertaining to the creation of the Chief of Defence Staff (CDS). This recommendation emanated from the task force on Higher Management of Defence chaired by Mr Arun Singh. It was his brainchild and had been the subject of much heated debate in his task force but had found acceptance within it through the sheer force of his personality. In the GoM, the recommendation was vehemently resisted by the Air Chief. He had a counter to every argument in favour of the recommendation, but at the end of the day, graciously mentioned that if, notwithstanding his objections, the recommendation found favour, the Air Force would accept it. Given the overwhelming body of opinion favouring the creation of the CDS, the GoM decided to recommend it.

A couple of days prior to the last meeting of the GoM for the finalization of its report which was scheduled for the coming Monday, the EAM phoned me, expressing his extreme displeasure that his objections and suggestions had not been taken on board and that he would complain against me. I responded that while he may do as he pleased, his charges were unwarranted as, invariably after each GoM meeting, I had circulated the minutes containing the agreed recommendations to all concerned and that if, therefore, he had any disagreements, he should have aired them at that time. In any case, if he felt so strongly in the matter, he should send me a detailed note indicating that changes he wanted made in the draft report. Later that evening I received the requested note from the EAM which, along with his complaint, was also copied to the other members of the GoM. I had, meanwhile, alerted Mr Advani as well as Mr Fernandes to this development, and both agreed that the complaints were unwarranted.

Early on Monday morning, I called on Mr Advani to discuss the strategy for the GoM meeting scheduled for the afternoon. I was hoping that he would resolve the matter directly with the EAM but instead he sought my suggestions. I told him that on the issues raised by EAM, there were a few on which there could be no compromise, some on which we could give in and others on which we would need to negotiate language. I further mentioned that I believed that the proposed changes actually emanated from Mr Arun Singh, Advisor Security in the Ministry of External Affairs, and, if he so desired, I could attempt to sort out the matter with the latter, but in order to do so, I must be given a negotiating carte blanche. Mr Advani readily agreed. Accordingly, I had a one hour meeting with Mr Arun Singh and was able to appropriately sort out all the issues flagged by EAM to our mutual satisfaction. I also received an assurance from Mr Arun Singh that during the GoM meeting, EAM would not raise any of these issues. In these circumstances, the final GoM meeting passed off amicably and no contentious issue was raised.

In early May 2001, the GoM presented its report to the Prime Minister, and I briefed him on the details of the major recommendations. He appeared to be fully satisfied and in agreement with all the recommendations. However, the following day, just before the CCS meeting at which the report was to receive formal approval, he indicated that all the recommendations would be approved barring those pertaining to the CDS, which would have to wait till there was a political consensus thereon. This came as something of a surprise, as only the previous day, he had shown absolutely no reservation on this account. This was unfortunate, as the creation of the CDS was essential for effective Higher Defence Management. It was only some 19 years later, in 2020, that it came to be created under the Modi government. This is a very bold and forward-looking initiative. In fact, the government has gone further and also set up a Department of Military Affairs under the CDS. These initiatives will bring about much-needed synergy in joint operational planning, optimization of resources and greater jointness among the Armed Forces for future wars.

Monitoring Reform Implementation

Following the acceptance of the GoM report an important element of the NSCS's work was monitoring the implementation of its roughly 340 recommendations.[39] Initially, the progress was quite good, but over time, bureaucratic inertia took over, and in the next three to four years, no more than 50–60 per cent of the recommendations were implemented.

While some organizations made full use of the recommendations to upgrade their capabilities, others were strangely unwilling to do so and adopted a blatantly non-cooperative approach. One of those in the former category benefitted enormously in, inter alia, getting many additional posts, but another one in the latter category lost

[39]*India's National Security Annual Review 2005*, Satish Kumar, Vikas Publishing House, Kalpana Shukla, Knowledge World, New Delhi, 2005, p. 217

an invaluable opportunity for the same. Indeed, when the NSCS sought information from an organization in the latter category about the progress in implementation of the recommendations made by the GoM, it responded that there was no progress in respect of one of them as, in its view, the recommendation should not be implemented. I, of course, took the concerned organization to task for such a cavalier approach to a decision of the CCS, but the short point is that some in the system took even such high-level decisions somewhat casually, and there was no passion in ensuring the early and efficacious implementation of much-needed security reform.[40] Indeed, there was also an occasion when one nodal entity made out that a particular reform stood implemented, but subsequently, I learnt purely by accident that this, in fact, was incorrect.

But leave aside the bureaucracy, even at the political level, there were occasions when there appeared to be little commitment to security reform and national interest. For instance, the Minister for HRD, Science and Technology and Ocean Development stymied the move of the Ministry of Defence for setting up a Maritime Commission as the apex body for institutionalized linkages between the multiplicity of entities involved on ocean-related issues which had been made in pursuance of a GoM recommendation. The Ministry of Defence had prepared a detailed note in the matter after due consultation with all concerned, including the Department of Ocean Development but just before it could be sent to the Cabinet, the Minister convened a meeting questioning the need for creating a Maritime Commission. The fact that his own Secretary had been consulted in the matter that it was in pursuance of a GoM decision, and that it had even approval of the PM cut no ice with him. Even the suggestion that the proposed Maritime Commission be chaired by him was effectively turned down by his indicating that he would do so only if security issues were removed from its purview. Clearly, this was an instance of issues of turf trumping those of national interest and security. Indeed, issues of turf also made it difficult for the successor Manmohan Singh Government to create a Maritime Commission.

[40]Ibid. p. 223–4.

I understand that such a coordinating entity by way of Vice Admiral (Retd) Ashok Kumar designated as the National Maritime Security Coordinator (NMSC) was finally created by the Modi government in mid-February 2022. He is located in the NSCS and reports to the NSA. His prime objective is 'ensuring synergistic coordination among the various authorities, which ranges from central ministries and departments (external affairs, defence, home, shipping, fisheries, etc.) and state governments to the Navy, Coast Guard, customs, intelligence agencies, and port authorities'.[41] This decision of the Modi Government like the appointment of a CDS, the creation of a Department of Military Affairs and reduction in colour service is in tune with the spirit of the many path-breaking recommendations made over two decades ago by the KRC and the GoM on security reform.

◆

Apart from the foregoing, I saw several other critical recommendations languishing, such as the creation of a specialized security cadre, the inculcation of patriotism particularly amongst the youth, the instilling of greater probity in the political class and in civil servants, creation of a specialized marine police, introduction of a multipurpose national identity card along with compulsory registration of nationals and non-nationals in the country, etc.[42] Unhappy with this state of affairs, I approached Cabinet Secretary Kamal Pande, who was overseeing the implementation of the GoM recommendations, around March 2004, and told him that I would have to report the dilatory implementation of security reform to the NSA. He promised urgent action, but in order

---

[41]'India Appoints "First National Maritime Security Coordinator" for Marine Security', NewsOnAir, 17 February 2022, https://bit.ly/3hlugqs. Accessed on 8 November 2022.

[42]Chandra, Satish, 'India's Security Apparatus Far From Satisfactory', *The Tribune*, 15 January 2015, https://www.tribuneindia.com/news/archive/comment/india%E2%80%99s-security-apparatus-far-from-satisfactory-30037; Vohra, N.N., 'Management of National Security: Some Concerns', *USI Journal*, July-September 2014, https://usiofindia.org/publication/usi-journal/management-of-national-security/; Satish Chandra, 'National Security System and Reform', *India's National Security Annual Review 2005*, Satish Kumar, Vikas Publishing House, Kalpana Shukla, Knowledge World, New Delhi, 2005.

to do so, requested that he be specifically empowered to bulldoze the pending reforms. I, accordingly, obtained the NSA's approval for the same. However, just as Kamal Pande was about to start the process of expeditious security reform implementation, the Vajpayee Government fell, and he, along with the Home and Defence Secretaries, were replaced overnight by the Manmohan Singh Government. This severely compromised the effective implementation of security reform.

It is a pity that the recommendations of the GoM were only partially implemented, as many of the security-related shortcomings we experience to this day are a result of it. Certainly, the Mumbai attack could have been foiled had these recommendations been fully implemented.

◆

One of the areas where security reform was undertaken but the results were less than optimal was that pertaining to the establishment of an apex technical intelligence organization. The idea for creating such an entity emanated from the KRC based on its recognition of the deficiencies in techint, which had come to light during the Kargil conflict and on its perception that in the coming years, new and emerging technologies would increasingly need to be harnessed in the cause of Intelligence. Accordingly, it argued for the setting up of an apex techint organization modelled on the US National Security Agency. This apex organization would not only take charge of all the existing communication and electronic Intelligence capabilities in the country, barring some redundancies for the defence services, but would also invest in futuristic technological capabilities relevant for Intelligence gathering. Taken to its logical conclusion, this would, inter alia, have required the stripping of such capabilities already available in some of the civilian Intelligence outfits and placing them in the newly established apex techint organization.

This, unfortunately, never happened, largely due to considerations of turf and the unwillingness of those at the helm of affairs to read the riot act to the affected civilian Intelligence agencies. The required clarity in this matter was evaded by the Task Force on Intelligence set up by the GoM as well as by the GoM themselves. To make matters worse, successive Principal Scientific Advisors to Government charged, inter alia, with finding a solution to this issue were unable to do so satisfactorily. In these circumstances, the newly created apex intelligence organization initially termed as the National Technical Facilities Organisation (NTFO) and later renamed the National Technical Research Organisation (NTRO) had a rocky start characterized by fractious turf wars. The successful emergence of the NTRO from these critical teething problems and its evolution into a viable techint agency was due, in large measure, to the considerable intellectual capacity, perseverance and finesse of its first Chairman, Major R.S. Bedi. Without his able guidance, the NTRO would have floundered and have been a shadow of what it is today. Since the NSCS was deeply involved in the creation of the NTRO, Major Bedi and I fought many a battle together, and in the process, developed a lasting friendship.

National Security Council System

The creation of the NSC system arose from the long-standing unhappiness with the prevailing security set-up and an awareness that the holistic nature of national security required more responsive structures for its oversight and direction. Such structures were created in India in 1999 by way of the NSC system comprising the NSC, and other adjuncts by way of the NSA, the NSCS, the NSAB and the SPG.

The dissatisfaction with the existing apex-level political and bureaucratic decision-making bodies on security such as the CCS and the Core Group of Secretaries, respectively, arose from the fact that they tended to focus only on matters of immediate concern. Neither of these bodies had the time or inclination to study, debate, analyse and develop medium- and long-term policy options and strategies. None of them were also geared to view security holistically. Their horizon usually extended only to hard security issues such as defence, foreign policy, terrorism, law and order, insurgencies, etc. The security aspects of issues such as governance, health, environment, technology, water and energy were rarely the focus of discussion in these bodies.

Accordingly, since the 1980s, some experimentation had been

underway to put in place new systems and structures to better address security-related issues. Indeed, in August 1990, the V.P. Singh Government announced the establishment of a NSC along with supporting structures. This exercise was, however, as short-lived as the Singh government.

With a view to reviving the NSC, the BJP government, in April 1998, set up a task force under Mr K.C. Pant to work out the constitution, role and functions of a new NSC. Influenced in part by the recommendations of this task force and in part by the system briefly set up in 1990, the BJP government established a new-look NSC with the objective of ensuring a more proactive, coordinated and holistic approach to security management. This was done through the Cabinet Secretariat Resolution of 16 April 1999, which put in place the NSC system underlining that national security needed to be viewed 'not only in military terms, but also in terms of internal security, economic security, technological strength and foreign policy' and that national security management required 'integrated thinking and co-ordinated application of the political, military, diplomatic, scientific and technological resources of the State to protect and promote national security goals and objectives'.[43]

As pointed out in my article titled 'National Security System and Reform' published in *India's National Security Annual Review 2005*[44], the NSC system was not meant to supplant existing apex-level institutions, like the CCS or the Committee of Secretaries, but to provide additional support to them and to cover the gaps left unaddressed by them. These gaps arose from the fact that the existing mechanisms were essentially geared only to handling crisis situations in areas traditionally associated with security and unable to bring to bear coordinated action across the entire spectrum of national life designed to promote national security. The decision to introduce the NSC system was a clear reflection of the realization

[43] *The Gazette of India*, 19 April 1999, https://bit.ly/3tcF6BH. Accessed on 8 November 2022.

[44] *India's National Security Annual Review 2005*, Satish Kumar, Vikas Publishing House, Kalpana Shukla, Knowledge World, New Delhi, 2005.

that efficient national security management required not merely the effective handling of crisis situations but also their pre-emption. While the former demanded coordinated action by several different departments, agencies and authorities, the latter required undertaking threat assessments—short, medium and long term—identification of contingencies likely to impact the nation, and formulation of alternative strategies to counter such contingencies. The newly created NSC system was required to see all aspects of national life through the prism of national security, constantly analysing threats and opportunities, and providing alternative courses of action and strategies even if these ran counter to existing policies.

Accordingly, the Cabinet Resolution that set up the NSC gave it an extensive remit in order to enable it to address security holistically, specifically calling upon it to deal with the following broad subject areas:

- external security environment and threat scenario;
- security threats involving atomic energy, space and high technology;
- trends in the world economy and economic security threats in the areas of energy, foreign trade, food, finance and ecology;
- internal security, including counter insurgency, counterterrorism and counter-intelligence;
- patterns of alienation emerging in the country, especially those with a social, communal or regional dimension;
- security threats posed by trans-border crimes such as smuggling and traffic in arms, drugs and narcotics; and
- coordination in Intelligence collection and tasking of Intelligence agencies so as to ensure Intelligence is focussed on areas of concern for the nation.[45]

Furthermore, this Resolution required all ministries/departments to 'consult' the NSC Secretariat 'on matters having a bearing on national security.'[46]

[45] *The Gazette of India*, 19 April 1999, https://bit.ly/3tcF6BH. Accessed on 8 November 2022.

[46] Ibid.

It is a common misconception propounded even by some experts that the NSC's remit was limited to medium- and long-term issues. This is incorrect. There was no limitation on the NSC's remit and, accordingly, it was left free to address all security issues, including those of immediate import.

◆

While the NSC as constituted was limited to an advisory role, the conclusions it arrived at were readily implementable, as it included all the members of the CCS—the apex security decision-making body—notably the Prime Minister, the Home Minister, the Defence Minister, the External Affairs Minister, and the Finance Minister—as well as the Deputy Chairman of the Planning Commission.

The NSC's performance was somewhat below par and inferior to its adjuncts. This was partly because its meetings were few and far between and partly because of its inability to engage in freewheeling brainstorming sessions, which are a prerequisite for generating out-of-the-box solutions to current as well as future challenges.

◆

The NSAB has been one of the more active sub-structures of the NSC system. It comprised a Convenor and persons of eminence outside government with expertise in diverse security-related areas. While the first NSAB had as many as 27 members, subsequent NSABs were kept smaller in the interests of greater cohesion and efficacy. It was essentially a mechanism to tap expertise from outside the government, and its role was to provide inputs to the NSC on security-related issues. Its members were nominated by government for a one- or two year term, and its agenda was set by the NSA. The latter made it a point to attend its first and last meetings annually, but on occasion, met it more frequently. The NSAB met in plenary at least once a month and sometimes more often, but its subgroups met more often. The first few NSABs had eminent personalities like K. Subrahmanyam, M.K. Rasgotra, J.N. Dixit, George Verghese, Brahma Chellaney, Air Commodore Jasjit Singh, N.N. Vohra, Professor Roddam Narasimha, etc., as its members. The output of the Board in its first couple of years was high class, and its meetings an intellectual treat. In its initial years, it produced two seminal high-quality papers: one on India's nuclear doctrine and another titled 'Strategic Defence Review'.[47] Much of what was contained in the former became a part of our nuclear doctrine and the latter formed the bedrock of subsequent national security reviews.

The performance of the SPG, which was set up to assist the NSC as the principal mechanism for inter-ministerial coordination and integration of relevant inputs for formulation of national security policies, was patchy. It was a 17-member body chaired by the Cabinet Secretary and, inter alia, comprised the Chiefs of Staff of the Armed Forces, the heads of Intelligence agencies, the Governor of the Reserve Bank of India, the Secretaries of several key ministries and the Secretary of the NSCS as Member Secretary. The SPG was expected to meet once a month to discuss the NSCS monthly Intelligence report and security analyses as well as security-related papers developed by the NSCS or other organizations for action-oriented decisions. Its meetings could also be called by the NSA, but in practice, this was never done, and the SPG remained a creature of the Cabinet Secretary. The frequency of its meetings, thus, depended on the latter's interest in security-related issues. Accordingly, while in some years, the SPG met seven or eight times, in others, it met much less frequently. Quite clearly, therefore, the SPG was not as effective as it should have been.

It is heartening to note, therefore, that in order to address the performance deficit of the SPG, it was brought under the chairmanship of the NSA in 2018 with the Cabinet Secretary being included as a member responsible for coordinating the implementation of its decisions by the concerned Ministries and State Governments. This will add immeasurably to the efficacy and utility of the SPG.

The NSA was clearly the fulcrum of the NSC system, particularly as he was the Prime Minister's pointsman on security-related issues. The NSA worked the NSC system through the NSCS, which was his

[47] *India's National Security Annual Review 2005*, Satish Kumar Vikas Publishing House, Kalpana Shukla, Knowledge World, New Delhi, 2005, p. 219.

secretariat for this purpose and which reported directly to him. He was the prime and sometimes the only recipient of NSCS studies, recommendations and assessments, some of which were specifically commissioned by him. The NSCS kept the NSA informed of all developments pertaining to the NSAB and SPG as well as of its own interactions with government entities and, in particular, Intelligence agencies.

The NSA had a critical role in the selection of the NSAB members, the setting up of its agenda, providing it with guidance and appropriately utilizing its output. He also had a key role in setting up meetings of the NSC and of establishing its agenda.

Under the NSC system, the NSA became the undisputed intelligence tzar in the country.[48] Not only did all the Intelligence agencies provide him with inputs, but he was also the recipient of regular assessments and evaluations thereof from the NSCS. Additionally, his role as the coordinator of Intelligence was formalized with the creation of the Intelligence Coordination Group (ICG) under his chairmanship and of which the NSCS was the secretariat. Through this mechanism, the systematic tasking and evaluation of the agencies was undertaken on a regular basis for the first time in the country. The ICG also became the forum for interface between the consumers and producers of Intelligence as well as for sorting out, inter se, problems between the agencies.

Conscious of the critical importance of informatics, the first NSA also presided over the establishment of the institutions and mechanisms to address it, notably the NTRO and the National Information Board. While the former dealt with the operational aspects of such matters, the latter had more of a policy role. Both functioned under the guidance of the NSA.

Over and above the foregoing, the NSA was deeply involved with the entire range of internal and external issues facing the nation both in terms of day-to-day developments and in regard to policy

[48]'Brajesh Mishra: India's first intelligence tsar', *Rediff.com*, https://www.rediff.com/news/column/brajesh-mishra-indias-first-intelligence-tsar/20121004.htm. Accessed on 8 November 2022.

formulation. Additionally, the first two NSAs played a critical role in the operationalization of our nuclear deterrent and in ensuring its credibility. They were largely responsible for establishing the entire range of structures to handle our nuclear deterrent and put in place the related management principles and doctrines.

Though the various adjuncts of the NSC dreamt, thought and breathed security, it must be acknowledged that the nation's performance in this area can be further improved. Greater security consciousness at both political and executive levels would ensure continuous implementation of security reforms.

Evolution of National Security Council Secretariat

I can look back to the evolution of the NSCS, which was my primary preoccupation, with some satisfaction. When created in April 1999, it had virtually no name recognition, had only around a dozen professionals and functioned out of rather shabby premises. The lack of name recognition was unsurprising, as it was the successor to the JIC, whose output was limited to a monthly Intelligence report and a few commissioned studies. By the time I left in February 2005, the NSCS had been able to carve a respected niche for itself in the Indian security system on account of a vastly enhanced role as compared to the JIC. This enhanced role arose not just from the fact that it served as the secretariat for a host of structures such as the NSC, NSA, NSAB, SPG, the National Information Board, the ICG, etc., but also because it emerged as an effective Intelligence coordinator and evaluator, a think tank producing scores of objective and well-researched studies on a wide range of security-related issues, an impartial monitoring agency and an interlocutor with foreign counterpart entities.

In the area of Intelligence, it not only took over the task of the JIC by producing apex-level monthly Intelligence reports for presentation to the CCS but also strove to make the Intelligence agencies work more cooperatively and cohesively. The NSCS worked proactively to promote a more cooperative culture, including a sharing of information. Equally importantly, it put in place a system for the first time in the country for the annual tasking and evaluation of the agencies.[49] Hitherto, the Intelligence agencies collected whatever they came by and passed the same on to the relevant consumers. Since this, obviously, was a most unproductive utilization of resources, the NSCS introduced a system whereby every consumer was required to indicate in a prioritized manner the Intelligence inputs required by it annually. These were then fed to the agencies, and their output was evaluated on the manner in which they had met the requirements raised against them. There was initially much opposition to this from the agencies, but with the support of the NSAs, notably Mr Mishra and later Mr Dixit, this reform was pushed through.

My close interaction with the Intelligence agencies, while revealing their suboptimal performance, equally brought home to me the thankless nature of their work. Collection of Intelligence and its analysis is a painful and arduous exercise requiring enormous patience, effort and teamwork, and those involved in it are condemned to remaining faceless. Accordingly, while the innumerable successes of the Intelligence agencies go totally unheralded, one failure, real or imagined, brings instant and stinging condemnation!

An upside, on the personal level, of the NSCS's Intelligence-related work was that it enabled me to get to know and form close friendships with counterparts heading some of our Intelligence agencies, notwithstanding differences of opinion on matters official. Some of the more valued of these friendships were with Lieutenant General Ravi Sawhney, who headed Military Intelligence, and with Mr Ajit Doval, who headed the Intelligence Bureau. Having an exceptional understanding of our wider national security challenges and the framework in which they could best be addressed, it is only appropriate that Mr Doval came to be appointed as NSA under the Modi Government. I may mention that prior to joining the Modi Government, Mr Doval set up the Vivekananda International Foundation in 2009, which has since developed into a very well-regarded think tank. It was at his behest that Lt Gen. Sawhney, former

---

[49]*India's National Security Annual Review 2005,* Satish Kumar, Vikas Publishing House, Kalpana Shukla, Knowledge World, New Delhi, 2005. p. 216.

R&AW Chief C.D. Sahay and I joined it at its inception and have since been associated with it.

◆

As a think tank, the NSCS undertook many studies and developed scores of papers on security-related issues: some highly detailed, some brief, some dealing with issues of current import, and some with those requiring treatment over a longer time frame, some addressing 'soft' security issues and some with issues more traditionally regarded as security-related. The NSCS sought to ensure that its papers were well-researched; that inputs from all its senior staff were factored in; and, above all, that the recommendations offered were independently arrived at and not simply a regurgitation of conventional thinking. Indeed, it was repeatedly made clear to all those in the NSCS that our advice must be based on our own thinking and not geared to that prevailing in the system and, accordingly, we must not be afraid of projecting views that were against conventional wisdom. Some of the seminal papers developed by the NSCS pertained to the nuclear doctrine, cyber security, energy security, water security, including issues pertaining to the Indus Waters Treaty, pandemics, climate change, WMD Terrorism, National Security Index, etc.[50] Most of these studies were self-initiated, but some were prepared at the government's request. They were circulated at the highest levels within the system and some were the subject of inter-ministerial discussion in the SPG or other fora, where decisions were taken on implementation of the recommendations contained in them.

The study on cyber security was a very detailed and path-breaking exercise running into some 150 pages and undertaken by Arvind Gupta. It originated from a short paper prepared by me calling for the urgent development of offensive and defensive cyber warfare capabilities in India, which was discussed in the SPG. Following these discussions, the Cabinet Secretary took the view that while offensive cyber warfare capabilities be kept on the back-burner, the NSCS should develop a

[50]*India's National Security Annual Review 2005,* Satish Kumar, Vikas Publishing House, Kalpana Shukla, Knowledge World, New Delhi, 2005. p. 216.

comprehensive study on cyber security. It was in this backdrop that Arvind Gupta took up this exercise. The study produced by him was a meticulous and painstaking effort stretching over six months, entailing discussions with all stakeholders in the matter, ranging from the banking community to the aviation sector and from the Intelligence community to the military. It was rich in recommendations that, inter alia, included the need to set up computer emergency response teams (CERTs), put in place systems to produce thousands of cyber experts, create facilities for the indigenous manufacture of chips, focus attention on upgrading India's encryption and decryption capabilities, ensure the fail-safe security of communications between government agencies and institutions, establish cooperative relations with the US in this area so as to enhance our capabilities, etc. It is heartening to note that many of these recommendations found acceptance and have been implemented if not in toto, at least in part. The work done on cyber security was taken forward in the subsequent years, including the appointment of a National Cyber Security Coodinator in the NSCS and several other initiatives that have been reported upon in detail.

The study on the Indus Waters Treaty was commissioned by the MEA in the backdrop of Pakistan's repeated raising of objections to the projects being undertaken by us on the Western Rivers. The exercise was greatly facilitated by the finding that large amounts of the waters of the Eastern Rivers were flowing into Pakistan, though it was not entitled to any such flows. This input came to us not from the Ministry of Irrigation and Power but from the Army, whose Corps of Engineers noted this during Operation Brasstacks and, at the direction of the Army Chief, brought it to my attention. As a result of this and an in-depth analysis of the matter, the NSCS prepared a detailed paper that underlined the highly iniquitous nature of the Indus Waters Treaty, pointed out that Pakistan's use of terror against us gave us a good opportunity to opt out of it, or at least suspend its operation, as it was totally out of sync with the circumstances under which it had been concluded, and suggested that we maximize the use of the Indus Waters as permitted under it. The latter could be achieved by totally stopping the flows of the waters of the Eastern Rivers to Pakistan and by building appropriate storages on the Western Rivers to the extent permissible under the Treaty. Both Mr Mishra and Mr Dixit agreed to the logic of the suggestion that we maximize our use of the Indus Waters and, under them, some work was initiated to drastically curtail the flows of the Eastern Rivers to Pakistan. Regrettably, work in this regard proceeded at a snail's pace. It has, however, picked up in the last two or three years under the Modi Government, which, I understand, also intends to use the waters of the Western Rivers to the extent possible as per the Treaty.

The study on Pandemics was self-tasked. My interest on this had been aroused by the increasing incidence of bird flu in late 2003 resulting in the deaths of millions of birds and by the fact that the Spanish flu of 1918 had killed around 50 million people. I was afraid that should there be a gene shift making bird flu transmittable between humans, we would have an unparalleled catastrophe, as its mortality rate was 60 per cent as against that of the Spanish flu, which was only 15 per cent. Moreover, both in 1957 and 1968, the world had a million deaths each on account of the Asian flu and the Hong Kong flu, respectively. I had also noted that during an Influenza Pandemic Preparedness meeting in Geneva in March 2004, the head of the WHO had warned, 'We know another pandemic is inevitable. It is coming... we also know that we are unlikely to have enough drugs, vaccines, healthcare workers, and hospital capacity to cope in an ideal way.'[51] In these circumstances, our study underlined that we were facing an impending threat of huge proportions and that it was critical for us in India to have a surveillance system to promptly detect any major flu outbreak in real time, to ensure that we were properly equipped to address it in terms of medical gear, supplies and facilities and, above all, that we must have the capacity for rapid production of vaccines in adequate quantities, as this was the magic bullet to quell it. The NSA, Mr Dixit, appreciated this study, and the same was widely circulated within the system. This theme was also the subject of a talk by me at an international conference in Berlin in May 2004. Like most futuristic warnings and predictions, while it evoked much interest I do not think it had a lasting material impact.

---

[51]'Risk of the Inevitable Influenza Pandemic', *The Age,* 19 March 2004.

◆

The NSCS's emergence as a monitoring body was a natural corollary of the fact that it was perceived as a neutral body with no axe to grind or turf issues. Thus, it was automatically tasked to monitor the implementation of security reform. As an outcome of its studies on the infrastructure along our neighbourhood, it was required to monitor the upgradation of the same. Similarly, resulting from its seminal paper on information security, it became the nodal agency for cyber security issues.

The NSCS also played a path-breaking role in encouraging the creation of greater security consciousness in the country. Towards this end it:

1. Encouraged resource persons to write on security-related issues, inter alia, by commissioning studies and papers on them;
2. Funded the publication of *India's National Security Annual Review* (INSAR) of which, over the years, several editions have appeared containing scores of scholarly articles on national security-related issues;
3. Developed a National Security Index, which was published in 2002; and
4. Helped design mid-career training courses on security conducted by the Lal Bahadur Shastri Academy of National Administration for civil servants and military personnel.

In the same spirit and with a view to creating greater consciousness in the country about matters nuclear and, in particular, about our nuclear doctrine, I delivered a keynote address at the Delhi Policy Group seminar on 'Nuclear Weapons and Security' in August 2004.[52]

By the time I demitted office in early 2005, the NSCS, in keeping with its growing role in the Indian security system, had doubled its officer cadre, tripled and refurbished its office space at Sardar Patel Bhavan, which had become one of the neater offices in Delhi, with

[52]Chandra, Satish, 'Keynote Address Delivered by Satish Chandra, Deputy to the National Security Adviser, at the Delhi Policy Group Seminar on "Nuclear Weapons and Security", 30–31 August 2004, New Delhi.'

computers, conference rooms, library, dining facility, etc. While expanding and retaining the multidisciplinary nature of its officer cadre, the NSCS employed professionals not only from within the government but also from without, including think tanks. Above all, the NSCS tried to consciously promote a work culture that placed a premium on innovative thinking, sharing of information amongst its officers, cutting across hierarchical lines and projection of views irrespective of whether or not they conformed to the commonly held positions within the system. It is to the credit of the first two NSAs, with whom I worked, that they permitted the NSCS to maintain its independence of thinking even if it involved being critical of government's policies or views. In turn, I took a principled policy decision of never going public with its views or indeed even having any interaction with the media.

◆

I would be less than fair if I did not acknowledge the stellar role played by all those who worked with me in transforming the JIC—a relatively small and little-known institution—into the NSCS, which is today a key institution in India's security set-up. These colleagues came from diverse institutions and backgrounds but worked seamlessly as a team to fashion the NSCS which, transcending service or institutional allegiances, was singlemindedly focussed only on the broader national interest.

Brajesh Mishra and J.N. Dixit: Ideal NSAs

Both Brajesh Mishra and J.N. Dixit, though very different personalities, were very effective NSAs, and it was a delight to work with them.

Both were strong personalities, quick decision-makers, always accessible, supremely confident of themselves, ready to delegate powers to those they trusted and willing to listen to contrarian views.

At the time I assumed the office of Secretary, NSCS, in 1999, I had no special equation with Brajesh Mishra and had known him only slightly on account of his visits to Algiers and Geneva, and a little interaction in my capacity as High Commissioner in Pakistan. From day one, he, however, treated me with respect and, as a result, the mandarins in Delhi realized that they had to take what I said seriously. This facilitated my work and benefitted the NSCS enormously. The projection of contrarian views in some of the papers prepared by the NSCS, was taken by Brajesh Mishra in his stride, and he never once criticized me in this regard. Indeed, even in discussions with foreign dignitaries, I was allowed the liberty of expressing myself freely, even if my views were at variance with those of Mr Mishra.

It was reflective of the mutual respect for each other that in February 2004, Mr Mishra had orders passed that my term as Secretary, NSCS, and Deputy National Advisor be extended by a further two years. However, consequent on the BJP's electoral defeat in May 2004 and the advent of the UPA government, I asked Mr Dixit that I be relieved immediately. He would, however, have none of it, arguing that I was a professional and not a politician. Noting that I was still adamant, he requested that as an old friend, I stay on to help him find his feet as the NSA. This was not something that I could refuse and, therefore, agreed to stay on, not for two years as requested but till the end of February 2005.

The advent of Mr J.N. Dixit made little change to my work life, as the latter was as committed to the NSC system as Mr Mishra. During my first briefing to Mr Dixit, his only comment was that he was as committed to the NSC system as his predecessor and that he only wanted to know how things could be further improved. I was also aware that the two were in regular contact. My relationship with Mr Dixit was far closer than with Mr Mishra, as I had known him since 1967 and had worked with him in one capacity or another over the decades. Consequently, my interaction with Mr Dixit was much greater than with Mr Mishra. In fact, nearly every evening after finishing work, I would drop into his office for a chat. He, like Mr Mishra, was highly supportive and was prepared to back me up against all concerned when I took a stand.

Exchanges with US and UK Counterparts

As Secretary, NSCS, I, inevitably, had some exchanges with foreign counterparts, of which the most notable were those with the Head of the UK JIC, John Scarlett, and the US Deputy NSA, Stephen Hadley.

My visit to London sometime in October 2002 was a part of our regular institutional exchanges with the UK JIC. Prior to the visit, the NSA had indicated to me that during the Prime Minister's recent visit to the UK, his British counterpart, Tony Blair, had informed him that they were awaiting my visit to brief me of the conclusive evidence available with them about Iraq's possession of weapons of mass destruction.

While our exchanges with the British JIC were invaluable on matters like the tasking the Intelligence agencies, the evaluation of their output, and the modus operandi of addressing cybercrime, its briefing about the range and sweep of Iraq's chemical, biological and nuclear weapon programmes left me unconvinced about its claims in the matter, which I felt were hugely exaggerated. Indeed, I was constrained to tell my counterpart, John Scarlett, that I regarded the evidence provided in this regard as sketchy and less than conclusive.

My interactions with Stephen Hadley in September and December 2003 were to work out the process of evolving a strategic partnership between India and the US. The exercise had been kick-started by Brajesh Mishra following the normalization of India–US ties resulting from the bilateral discussions in the aftermath of India's nuclear tests. Mr Mishra, while evincing keen interest in closer India–US ties, frankly pointed out to his US interlocutors that this would, to a large extent, depend on whether or not the US stopped treating India as a pariah and was prepared to share sensitive nuclear- and space-related technologies with it. He underlined that this should not be difficult, as India was a responsible power and was far more cautious than most countries on sharing such sensitive technologies with third countries. This line of argumentation struck a chord with the US side, which evinced interest in commencing negotiations with India on how to concretize strategic cooperation between the two.

Mr Mishra was scheduled to lead our delegation for the negotiations in this regard in Washington DC with his counterpart Condoleezza Rice. However, since she was not available at the time, I was, at extremely short notice, asked to proceed to Washington for this purpose for talks with her Deputy, Hadley.

The manner in which I was pitchforked into these negotiations was somewhat bizarre. One September afternoon in 2003, I received a phone call from Joint Secretary PMO, asking me somewhat jocularly as to whether I would like to visit Washington. I reacted that I was not particularly keen, as I had plenty to do in Delhi, but if I had to go, perhaps, I could do so in a week or so. Joint Secretary PMO, becoming more businesslike, responded that I had no option, that I would have to proceed the following evening, that my visa and ticket on a direct JAL flight to Washington had been organized, that the NSA would brief me before I emplaned and that the requisite briefs had been prepared and would be provided to me by the delegation accompanying me on the aircraft!

On emplaning, I used the travel time to absorb my brief and for intensive discussions with the members of my delegation. Accordingly, by the time I landed in Washington, I was ready for the first round of my discussions with Stephen Hadley. These were followed by another round of discussions with him in December just before Christmas. These discussions resulted in an agreement between us for a press release to be issued simultaneously by Prime Minister Vajpayee and President Bush. The Indian version of the press release reads as follows:

> In November 2001, President Bush and I committed our countries to a strategic partnership. Since then, our two countries have strengthened bilateral cooperation significantly in several areas. Today we announce the next steps in implementing our shared vision.
>
> India and the United States of America agree to expand cooperation in three specific areas: civilian nuclear activities, civilian space programmes, and high technology trade. In addition, we agree to expand our dialogue on missile defence. Cooperation in these areas will deepen the ties of commerce and friendship between our two nations, and will increase stability in Asia and beyond.
>
> The proposed cooperation will progress through a series of reciprocal steps that will build on each other. It will include expanded engagement on nuclear regulatory and safety issues

> and missile defence, ways to enhance cooperation in peaceful uses of space technology, and steps to create the appropriate environment for successful high technology commerce. In order to combat the proliferation of weapons of mass destruction, relevant laws, regulations and procedures will be strengthened, and measures to increase bilateral and international cooperation in this area will be employed. These cooperative efforts will be undertaken in accordance with our respective national laws and international obligations.
>
> The expanded cooperation launched today is an important milestone in transforming the relationship between India and the United States of America. That relationship is based increasingly on common values and common interests. We are working together to promote global peace and prosperity. We are partners in the war on terrorism and we are partners in controlling the proliferation of weapons of mass destruction and the means to deliver them.
>
> The vision of India-US strategic partnership that President Bush and I share is now becoming a reality. [53]

The understanding encapsulated in the aforesaid press release of 13 January 2004 constitutes an inflection point in India-US relations as it committed the two to cooperate on civilian nuclear activities, civilian space programmes, and high technology trade as also expand their dialogue on missile defence. Such cooperation had hitherto been an anathema to the US and crossing this hurdle was, as had been pointed out by Mr Brajesh Mishra, a sine qua non for a meaningful improvement of India-US ties. It is no surprise, therefore, that this understanding paved the way for the India-US nuclear deal and the subsequent efflorescence of bilateral ties between the two.

---

[53]Statement by Prime Minister on Next Steps in Strategic Partnership with USA, PMO Archives, 13 January 2004, https://bit.ly/3EteGkv. Accessed on 22 November 2022. The American version can be found here: Statement on Next Steps on Strategic Partnership with India issued on 12 January 2004, https://bit.ly/3WDlvIB. Accessed on 8 November 2022.

Saying No to the Prime Minister

Following Mr Dixit's sudden demise in early January 2005, the Prime Minister made it known that he would like me to continue to stay on in the NSCS. I, however, made it plain that I had no desire to continue and, in this context, told him that I had, in fact, wanted to leave when the NDA had demitted office and had stayed on only at the request of Mr Dixit and that too till end February 2005. The Prime Minister admitted that he had seen the file that I had moved in this regard in September 2004 for the selection of my successor and remarked that I was exceptional in the sense that while most were desperate to hold on to their chairs, I had no such inclination and actually wanted to leave. Noting that I was adamant, he queried as to why I wished to demit office. I responded that I felt that bureaucrats should normally leave office at the appointed age of retirement and an extended stay was only justified if there was something critical for which they were needed. In my case, I had an absorbing interest in overseeing the implementation of security reform, but I felt that this would never happen because neither those of his ilk, notably the politicians, nor those of mine, namely the bureaucrats, would allow it. In these circumstances, my further stay in the system was pointless. Despite a few more efforts to get me to change my view, I remained adamant and demitted office as scheduled on 28 February 2005.

My stint in the NSCS incarnation was one of the happier periods of my career. I not only learnt a great deal about security-related matters but also was able to make some contribution in creating a security structure unique to the nation. It is a matter of some satisfaction that the NSCS, when I left it, was a close-knit, tightly run outfit, wherein fresh thinking was encouraged and which was informed by a culture of information sharing. It would not be out of place to mention that the NSCS has grown exponentially from its modest origins, not only in terms of resources and multi-disciplinary manpower, but also in terms of mandate and stature. The credit for this exercise must go equally to the vision of the political dispensation and to the dynamism of Mr Ajit Doval—our longest-serving NSA. I have no doubt that the NSCS system, inclusive of its sub-structures, is today well-placed to play a role commensurate with national requirements. It is to be hoped that within the NSC system, as originally envisioned, its sub-structures are encouraged to provide objective assessments, even if they go against conventional wisdom and instituting systems to avoid stove piping. Such assessments could be encouraged if our political class opts to abandon thinking merely in five-year political cycles in favour of an approach with a much longer time frame. In purely structural terms, the NSCS would benefit enormously with the addition of a legal wing and by adding to its expertise in the area of economic security.

EPILOGUE

I look back at my 40 years in the IFS with a great sense of happiness and fulfilment. This stems from the fact that it provided me with a highly variegated work experience in differing environments not merely in the realm of diplomacy, both bilateral and multilateral, but also in many other areas, including those related to the entire spectrum of national security issues, both conventional and non-conventional. Accordingly, throughout my career, I had the good fortune to be on a learning curve, which enabled me to expand my horizons and to grow. Attempting to master the issues involved, upgrading my skills and delivering my best in whatever I did, irrespective of the result, had its own rewards and was a deeply satisfying process.

As in any other profession, I had my highs and lows, but I was blessed, as my career had hardly any dull moments and innumerable fun moments. There were, of course, also spells of much tension, which is, I imagine, par for the course, but there was compensation, as these were spiced on occasion with high-octane excitement.

While my associates and I often put in long hours of work together, this was not done mechanically as a chore but as an exercise expected of us in the national interest and undertaken usually with a sense of humour and a spirit of comradery. Work was, therefore, never a drudgery but a source of satisfaction and even enjoyment. It is no surprise, therefore, that many of those that I worked with are today close friends. Even though we may have had differences of opinion, these were taken in a constructive spirit and rarely adversely affected relationships. If anything, they bred greater mutual respect.

One of my most important takeaways from my career was that optimal outcomes are directly correlated to the extent to which those involved in any endeavour enjoy a harmonious relationship. The latter is best promoted by encouraging a free exchange of ideas, an across-the-board sharing of information and a resolution of differences with openness and transparency. Accordingly, as I went up the seniority ladder, I sought to apply the aforesaid principles and made it a point to run a democratic ship, vigorously discouraging stove-piping and absorbing inputs from all concerned so that even the junior-most had a sense of involvement. Such an approach paid rich dividends, not only in achieving the desired outcomes but also enabling me to forge friendships with my associates both within and outside the IFS.

Finally, I would be remiss in not acknowledging that while in the IFS, as I had anticipated before joining it, I was able to be my own man and speak my mind. There was barely an occasion or two when I felt muzzled or unable to project my viewpoint. It is a tribute to my superiors in the Service that, by and large, they allowed me to do so without harming me in any way, even though their thinking was at variance with mine.

INDEX